How to Study an **Organisation**

How to Study an Organisation

(For the Students of Sociology and Management)

Prof. GIUSEPPE BONAZZI

S. CHAND & COMPANY LTD.

(AN ISO 9001 : 2000 COMPANY)

Ram Nagar, New Delhi-110 055

S. CHAND & COMPANY LTD.
(An ISO 9001 : 2000 Company)
Head Office : 7361, RAM NAGAR, NEW DELHI - 110 055
Phones : 23672080-81-82; Fax : 91-11-23677446
Shop at: **schandgroup.com**
E-mail: **schand@vsnl.com**

Branches :

- 1st Floor, Heritage, Near Gujarat Vidhyapeeth, Ashram Road, **Ahmedabad**-380 014. Ph. 27541965, 27542369
- No. 6, Ahuja Chambers, 1st Cross, Kumara Krupa Road, **Bangalore**-560 001. Ph : 22268048, 22354008
- 152, Anna Salai, **Chennai**-600 002. Ph : 28460026
- S.C.O. 6, 7 & 8, Sector 9D, **Chandigarh**-160017, Ph-2749376, 2749377
- 1st Floor, Bhartia Tower, Badambadi, **Cuttack**-753 009, Ph-2332580; 2332581
- 1st Floor, 52-A, Rajpur Road, **Dehradun**-248 001. Ph : 2740889, 2740861
- Pan Bazar, **Guwahati**-781 001. Ph : 2522155
- Sultan Bazar, **Hyderabad**-500 195. Ph : 24651135, 24744815
- Mai Hiran Gate, **Jalandhar** - 144008 . Ph. 2401630
- 613-7, M.G. Road, Ernakulam, **Kochi**-682 035. Ph : 2381740
- 285/J, Bipin Bihari Ganguli Street, **Kolkata**-700 012. Ph : 22367459, 22373914
- Mahabeer Market, 25 Gwynne Road, Aminabad, **Lucknow**-226 018. Ph : 2626801, 2284815
- Blackie House, 103/5, Walchand Hirachand Marg , Opp. G.P.O., **Mumbai**-400 001. Ph : 22690881, 22610885
- 3, Gandhi Sagar East, **Nagpur**-440 002. Ph : 2723901
- 104, Citicentre Ashok, Govind Mitra Road, **Patna**-800 004. Ph : 2300489, 2302100

Marketing Offices :

- 238-A M.P. Nagar, Zone 1, **Bhopal** - 462 011. Ph : 5274723.
- A-14 Janta Store Shopping Complex, University Marg, Bapu Nagar, **Jaipur** - 302 015, Phone : 2709153

© *2006, Giuseppe Bonazzi*

All rights reserved. No part of this publication may be reproduced, stored in a retrieval system or transmitted, in any form or by any means, electronic, mechanical, photocopying, recording or otherwise, without the prior permission of the Publisher.

Published by **S. Chand & Company Ltd.,** New Delhi in arrangement with Ms. ILMULINO SPA, Bologna, Italy.

First Edition 2006

ISBN : 81-219-2636-X

PRINTED IN INDIA

By Rajendra Ravindra Printers (Pvt.) Ltd., 7361, Ram Nagar, New Delhi-110 055 and published by S. Chand & Company Ltd. 7361, Ram Nagar, New Delhi-110 055

PREFACE

The novel feature of this book with respect to previous ones on the same subject, including my own, is the manner in which it is organized. Long years of reflection and classroom teaching have enabled me to arrive at a conceptual simplification of the matters addressed. The book does not reconstruct the history of organizational thought by presenting a series of authors in chronological sequence. Rather, it singles out five thematic areas, or broad strands of thought, or ways to discuss organizations, which form a succinct but acceptably complete framework for examination of the theories put forward by of scholars in the area. Each of these strands of thought begins with one or more authors who proposed an original and influential approach to organizations. The approach is then taken up, discussed, criticised, elaborated upon, and modified by other authors in different social contexts to form an integral body of thought. Each strand adds something new to the one before it: a different perspective, new factors to consider, or hitherto unconsidered problems.

Corresponding to these five strands of thought are the five chapters set out in the table of contents of the book. The chapters are preceded by an introduction and followed by the conclusions. The introduction uses the expedient of describing a student's typical day in order to explain how the book construes the notion of 'organization'. It suggests that we should discard the conventional idea that organizations are formal structures, as opposed to informal ones, and it stresses instead the importance of the processes of *organizing*, and thus takes up the notion of 'structuration' proposed by Giddens. Although this idea underpins the book in its entirety, it is developed gradually as the five chapters unfold, and it is only fully explained in the conclusions.

The conclusions also outline what recent studies indicate as the type of organization that will typify the twenty-first century. At micro level, minimal firms will proliferate as a result of people's actions and the meanings that they attach to them. At macro level, increasing globalization will call traditional organizational practices into question, and with them the categories employed to analyse them.

This brief outline should suffice to show that the book, although intended for university-level study, is not a handbook in the conventional sense of the term. Nor is it a monograph written to put forward a specific point of view. Instead, it seeks to steer a middle course between a purely informative handbook and a critical essay on a particular topic. The aim of this book is to furnish information on the main currents of thought in organizational studies while also encouraging discussion, interpretation, and comparison. Above all, it seeks to show that the ideas expounded in the various chapters are not merely a set of notions to be remembered passively; rather that they can also be used actively as 'tools' for research. Indeed, the discussion sections which conclude each chapter suggest areas of inquiry in which the sociological notions just learnt can be put into practice.

A final warning: *How To Study Organization* is not intended to take the place of already-existing textbooks but to supplement them, in the belief that the availability of several sources aids learning – just as any object observed from several points of view acquires depths and details invisible from a single apodictic standpoint.

— GIUSEPPE BONAZZI

CONTENTS

Chapter 1

INTRODUCTION— WHAT ARE ORGANISATIONS ?

Organizations are explained by following Laura, a university student, through a typical day of study and work. It is discovered that there are numerous kinds of organizations, large and small, formal and informal, and that our daily behaviour helps structure them. Finally presented is the general plan of the book, divided into five chapters plus conclusions.

What is an organization? If someone asks us this question, we will probably think of a few large organizations of we have had direct experience or of which we have heard. We might answer that an organization is the company for which we work, or for which one of our relatives does; that a hospital is also an organization, as are banks, the army, the Jesuits, and the United Nations with all of its agencies and branches worldwide, and so forth. On closer consideration, we see there is something of the bureaucratic in all of the organizations mentioned. Bureaucracy and hierarchy (that is, where someone gives orders and others obey) seem to be common to all of these organizations. But is this always so? We shall see that an organization is not always synonymous with bureaucracy and hierarchy alone. The concept is much broader, for it includes situations that have very little to do with bureaucracy. If we are to understand this point thoroughly, we must take a different approach.

1. LAURA'S DAY

A more unusual way to answer the question "what is an organization?" is to review the everyday events in our lives. Let us imagine that Laura is a girl who lives in a city, where she attends university and does odd jobs to supplement the monthly allowance sent by her family. Laura shares an apartment with three other girls. Each has her own room, and they share a kitchen and a living room. The four girls have established clear rules about when each of them does the housework and about how much money each must contribute to household expenses. They have also decided that they can only entertain male friends in the parts of the apartment that they share, not in the bedrooms.

Laura goes out around eight and buys the paper and a ticket for the bus at the newsstand. While waiting for the bus, she exchanges a few words with the newsagent: "The bus service has gone worse recently", he says. "We should complain to the Bus Company, but they probably wouldn't listen to us anyway!" "They might listen to us", retorts Laura, "but it's not easy to organize a protest. May-be we should form a committee…"

Finally Laura's bus for the University arrives. She attends two hours of classes and then goes to the library to photocopy an article to prepare for an examination. While she is making the photocopies, she talks Marilyn and John about some of the courses. As they are talking about one of the lecturers she says: "Green explains things very clearly, but he expects a lot and you really must attend his classes. But what's White like?" John tells her that he is boring and that it does not matter whether you go to class or not, but that the module taught by his assistant Black is interesting and well organized. "Too bad that it's at the same time as Green's class. I really have to go to it because I'm counting on doing my dissertation with him..." Laura sighs. "It's absurd the way the registrar's office has organized the schedule this year. You're on the academic committee", she says to Marilyn. "Why don't you raise the issue and talk about next year's schedules again?"

Around noon Laura goes to her medical centre to pick up an x-ray taken a few days earlier, and on the way she stops at the supermarket to buy a few items. Then she returns to the University and goes to the cafeteria, where she has an appointment with some of her classmates. They need to talk about a group research project they are preparing for a seminar. It is a long discussion because they must decide what each of them is going to do. In the end, Andrew, who acts as some sort of natural leader of the group, decides for everyone. "But", Laura asks him, "What about Peter? He never comes. Should we keep him in the group or tell him to leave?" Andrew says he will call Peter that evening, and then they will all decide whether to keep him or tell him not to come anymore.

In the afternoon Laura works for three hours at a dental surgery, where she goes two days a week to update the patients' database. It is routine work, but Laura enjoys doing with some creativity. When the work is finished, she will have to teach a girl newly hired by the surgery how to use the file, which will nearly halve the time required to manage the medical records. The secretary tells her that the work must be finished in two months time, which means that Laura will have to work on Saturdays as well. Laura agrees, but she asks for a pay increase. The secretary hesitates and Laura tells her: "I'd like to speak to the doctor in person!" But then she remembers that she cannot work that Saturday because she must return to her home town for her cousin's wedding.

After work, Laura goes home to read the article she photocopied that morning. At eight she watches the news on television. But then during dinner her housemates start arguing. Irene accuses Sylvia of having let strangers into the apartment without telling the rest of them. Sylvia retorts: "And what about you? Whenever we're away at the weekend you take advantage and let your boyfriend sleep here." Irene: "What's that got to do with it? Mike is my boyfriend and you all know him, but *you* let perfect strangers in." Susan, the fourth girl, tries to calm everyone down. Laura warily stays out of it, but realizes they either have to agree on this rather vague rule or they will not be able to live together for much longer. The argument reminds her that a couple of days earlier she opened the door to a young man asking for Sylvia. She let him in and then went back to her room without thinking any more about it. Now she wonders whether she did the right thing. May-be when the man left she should have put it nicely to Sylvia that the visit seemed to have broken a rule they had established. May-be they could have cleared the air more peacefully.

Just before nine, Laura goes out for the weekly meeting of a voluntary association for the disabled, of which she is an active member. At the meeting she takes the floor to say that they must organize themselves better. The volunteers' shifts are so badly organized that urgent calls take too long to answer. The members agree with her and decide to set up a committee, and ask Laura to sit on it. While she is happy about this, she is also rather worried about the extra work that it will involve. "Now I'll have to give up some sleep", she thinks to herself as she accepts. She gets home around eleven, but before going to bed she spends an hour or so at the computer in a chat room. She has met some entertaining people there that she can relax with, writing a bit of nonsense before going to bed.

2. WHAT DOES LAURA'S DAY TELL US?

Laura's day was a typical one of study, work, social engagements, amusement and domestic relations. But her day tells us a great deal. First of all, it tells us that it is wrong to believe that organizations are only big business concerns or the large bureaucracies mentioned at the outset, such as factories, banks, hospitals or the army. Laura's entire day was spent in organizations of all shapes and sizes, some bureaucratic, others certainly not. The familiar group of girls with whom she shares the apartment is a small, informal organization. A multinational communications company publishes the newspaper that she bought in the morning, and although the newsstand where she bought it is privately owned, it is part of an organized sales network. The bus she took belongs to the Bus Company, a regional public service organization. The University is a large state organization divided into faculties, library, cafeteria and many other services which can be considered its internal sub-organizations. Even the classes Laura attends are organized, complete with classrooms, schedules, deadlines, and explicit as well as implicit rules about what to study and how much time to devote to an examination. The supermarket Laura went to that morning is a medium-sized commercial organization. The medical centre where she picked her x-ray is a large public health organization, while the dental surgery where she works twice a week is a small one. The national television network whose news broadcast Laura watched is a big public organization, while the voluntary association whose meeting she attended after dinner is a small cooperative linked with sister cooperatives to form a network organization, with branches throughout the country. And the network of the people to whom Laura talks on the chat line before going to bed can be viewed as a virtual organization. Laura's entire social life takes place within organizations. It is no exaggeration to say that not only would Laura be unable to have a social life, but she would not even be able to survive if she did not use organized services, and if she did not continually interact with the organizations that in various ways cover her entire day. In this regard, Peter Drucker, the noted author of organization studies, has aptly commented as follows: "Young people today must learn to move from one organization to another, just as their ancestors learned to cultivate fields and raise livestock".

We have also seen that Laura performed very different roles in the organizations that she encountered during her day: as a consumer, an employee, and an active member with a 'voice'. These roles, however, do not adequately describe Laura's behaviour. She is an altogether marginal, anonymous, ephemeral consumer in her relationships with the Bus Company, the newspaper, the supermarket and the national television network,. She is also an anonymous consumer at the clinic where she picked up her x-ray. But if by some misfortune the doctor were to find that she had an illness, then her relationship with the health facilities would become a good deal more personalized and long-lasting. On the other hand, at the University, where she pays tuition fees, Laura has a more active role: she makes her own photocopies in the library, asks for and gives information about courses, and participates in a study group where she helps set the rules that make it work. Laura has an even more important role in the voluntary association, and perhaps also within the network of virtual friends that she meets on-line. Within the apartment where she lives, however, Laura must perform the role of intermediary among the girls; a role necessary for the group's very survival. Everything depends on what she chooses to say, for it will have a powerful effect in determining whether they continue to live together, perhaps with new rules.

Finally, we have seen that Laura cares enough about her job at the dental surgery to accept work on Saturdays, as long as she earns a little more, and she realizes she will have to speak to her boss in person to get the raise. But then she remembers that on the first Saturday she must go to her cousin's wedding, which is even more important than her job.

The wedding is an institution, not an organization, although its success depends on being well organized. Getting married requires recourse to other official institutions and their bureaucratic organizations, such as the city government, the parish, and private businesses like the photographer, the restaurant and the florist. Moreover, the interest taken by the couple and their families in the ceremony is important for its outcome: the cooperation of the various family members is a temporary organization as well. Each member of this organization is independent of the others, but they work together as a coordinated group whenever a wedding or some other event requires it.

3. WHAT CAN WE LEARN FROM LAURA'S DAY?

The discussion thus far yields numerous ideas for further development. For example, when Laura thinks about having to sacrifice a few hours of sleep to reorganize the shifts at the voluntary association, she teaches us two things. First, *the inadequacy of a purely instrumental view of organizations*. It is not enough to say that an organization's importance, size or efficiency is relative, we must add that there are organizations that we find more congenial, and to which we are willing to devote more time and energy. Our willingness to contribute to an organization, be it a workplace or any other kind, does not depend solely on material incentives like a good salary, a secure career, or a comfortable environment. It may also spring from purely moral, idealistic or symbolic incentives. Because people are altruistic to different degrees, the manner in which they relate to a particular organization varies widely according to their motivations. Money, ambition or ideals influence people to greater or lesser extents, and this diversity influences their relationships with organizations just as it does their relationships with people. On the one hand there may be extreme cases in which a person identifies so closely with an organization that he or she is willing to do anything for it, just as there are other extreme cases where an organization seems to be a dreadful Moloch from which the only desire is to escape.

The second lesson to be learned is the *inadequacy of a purely objectivistic approach to organizations*. As the term suggests, by 'objectivistic' is meant an approach to what are imagined to be the 'objective' aspects of an external reality which studies them in the most neutral, ascetic and scientific manner possible, using numerical data expressed in graphs, tables, trend indicators and so on. Such data, however, furnish only a partial account of the reality. For example, a medical diagnosis tells us that a patient has a certain weight, height and anatomical features, as well as certain levels of triglycerides and hemoglobin in his blood. This information is necessary for treatment of the patient, but it says nothing about his personality, tastes, beliefs or culture, or about important episodes in his life. Knowing more about these requires talking to the patient, interviewing him and, if possible, observing him for a certain period of time in his everyday environment, and perhaps finding out what those who know the patient think about him.

Similar considerations apply to organizations. A report on a company's budget, investments and market shares is of help in deciding whether or not to buy its stock, but the report says nothing about the company's culture, spirit or atmosphere, or what working for it means to employees. In all organizations there exist not only 'hard' material aspects but also immaterial and intangible ones. If we wish to explore the latter, we cannot neglect the feelings and the images that an organization evokes internally and externally, what makes it likeable and friendly or instead unpleasant. Laura is willing to devote her evenings to the voluntary association because she believes in what it does, and she likes the people that work for it. If circumstances at the association deteriorated, however, she would probably withdraw from it and perhaps look for a different one. In order to determine these various aspects, we would have to talk to Laura, and perhaps to her colleagues in order to discover their perception and estimation of her.

But Laura's day affords us numerous other insights. One of the most important is that *people have differing abilities to alter the organizations that they encounter*. This is apparent from Laura's different discourses during the day: the conversation with the newsagent about the Bus Company, the information exchange with her friends on courses and lecturers, the discussion with her flat mates about household affairs. The Bus Company strikes Laura as a distant and foreign entity, and she does not believe that a private citizen is able to improve the service that it provides. At the university, on the other hand, information exchange can increase or decrease the number of students attending a class, it can determine whether or not a seminar appears on the programme. And it should not be forgotten that Laura asks Roberta to raise the question of the course schedule at the next meeting of academic committee, thus directly influencing the way in which classes are organized. A University is a large organization, but it is organized in such a way that students (as well as teaching staff) are able to change the way in which it operates. Words carry even more weight in the way that Laura and the other girls organize their household.

It was said earlier that it is wrong to believe that there exist only formal and official organizations, such as businesses and public bureaucracies. We may add that it is also wrong to believe that it is impossible to change organizations and that they lie beyond our influence, or that it is they that condition us and make us feel small and helpless. Although this is the case of large and impersonal organizations, it is not so of the small ones within reach, so to speak. Laura is unable to change the bus schedule and routes, the services supplied by the medical centre, the television network's programs, or the university's fees or degree courses. She can, however, influence her study group, intervene in the organization of her household and have its rules to change, and negotiate with the secretary at the dental surgery on her pay, work schedule and results. She can act to reorganize the work shifts for the volunteers, and she can even organize a real meeting with the friends that she has made on the Internet.

Huge, formal and powerful organizations, impossible to change from the outside, therefore represent only one particular instance of 'organization', for the concept can be applied just as well to the smaller settings that we encounter every day. The greengrocers on the corner is just as organized as General Motors. Obviously, their complexity, technology, division of labour, knowledge and struggle for power cannot be compared. A greengrocer is able to change his supplier or reorganize the display of his products in a morning, whereas a business merger or an organizational change at General Motors takes a long time; such organizations require complex and difficult decisions, as well as mediation among the various parties concerned.

We know that General Motors uses the most prestigious and well paid experts; that it draws upon all the knowledge accumulated in the field of management; and that it organizes seminars and round tables. And finally we know that the decisions taken by General Motors will become the subject of research and teaching at business schools. Yet, whilst the complexity and importance of the decisions made by businesses have given rise to management science as an academic subject, with its own community, literature and rules, there is no reason in principle why, sociologically, the organization of small units like shops, households, dental surgeries, libraries, voluntary associations, or even convents, cannot be studied in the same way as large companies. Each of these units can be viewed as an organization. What changes is the nature and weight of the variables considered.

At this point it might be objected: are the family And a group of friends who get together purely because they enjoy each others' company are these not subjects of study for the sociology of organizations? And if they are, what is the point of sociology of the family and of small groups? The answer is that those sociologies study aspects and problems specific to those situations, and there is no danger that one discipline will be annexed by another. But it must nevertheless be recognized that the family and small groups can also be studied in regard to their organizational aspects: for example, who takes the decisions, in what areas and how, who handles the money, and so on.

The same applies to other, broader social phenomena studied by other types of sociology, such as urban or economic sociology, or sociology of religion, and many others besides. Study can be made of the organizational aspects of a city, of production systems, of the church, and more generally of all those segments or portions of a society in which diverse actors are interconnected on a relatively stable basis. Actors may be individuals (people) or groups (associations, businesses), and their interconnections may be sanctioned by formal agreements or exist only *de facto*: for example, the linkages that exist within a given geographical area among businesses, the vocational schools where their workers are trained, the industrial associations, and the trade unions. These actors will have shared as well as conflicting interests, but if their interactions produce a socially significant outcome, then together they form a relatively stable and well-defined network whose organizational aspects can be studied. Indeed, the network is nothing but an *organization of organizations*. The sociology of organizations is, therefore, a discipline which is not restricted to a specific sector of society but can study all social areas that are in some way organized.

The phenomena discussed raise numerous issues of interest to sociological research: who formed the organizations and how; in what way do the organizations work and according to what rules; what goals do they pursue and what results do they achieve; do they have a common culture; what form of leadership has developed within them; what power struggles have taken place; what meanings do their members give to participation; and so on. Which of these aspects is studied depends on the researchers' interests and working hypotheses, their conceptual tools, and their methods of analysis.

4. A CONCLUSION AND A CAVEAT

We may now sum up the discussion thus far. The starting point is the terrain on which the sociology of organizations operates. We have seen that this terrain comprises not only organizations formally recognized as such, but any organized phenomenon, provided that the researcher believes that it can yield significant information on some aspect of social reality. These phenomena can be observed at both the microsocial level (interactions and relationships within a small group) and the macrosocial one (large national and international institutions).

Saying that any organized phenomenon may be subjected to analysis has important consequences for research. It signifies that both the *structures* as well as the *processes* of organization can be studied. The structures are stable entities 'out there': for example an office with a hierarchy, rules, procedures, rituals, and a communication system. The processes, on the other hand, are ongoing entities which pass through various phases and constantly change. The commonsense view is that organizations are structures rather than processes. Yet the discussion thus far has sought to highlight the importance of organizational processes. Such processes are more easily observed in small and accessible organizations: Laura interacts with people at the university, the dental surgery, the cooperative, and in her apartment. She thus activates processes which will bring about change in the existing order of things. Obviously, there are processes that give rise to changes in large organizations as well, but ordinary people like Laura cannot observe their dynamics; they can only see their most visible outcomes: for example, deterioration in the bus service.

Thus, structure and process should be understood as two different aspects of the same phenomenon: structure is the static aspect of an organization, whilst process is the dynamic one. This ambivalence can also be expressed by the noun *organization* (structure) and the verb *to organize* (process). The conventional idea that organizations are pre-existing entities independent of people must be abandoned, for it gives the impression that organizations are like houses in which different people can live without moving the walls, doors and windows. The metaphor can be extended by saying that the arrangement of the furniture, the colours of the walls, and the behaviour of the inhabitants of the house are integral parts of the organization.

Metaphors aside, if we encounter an organization previously unknown to us, we soon realize that it is not a static structure. On closer examination, the organization seems to be swarming with people, each with some kind of role, and whose work follows rather predictable routines. However, we also observe that different members of the organization perform their roles with varying degrees of dedication, ability, creativity, ambitiousness, propensity to work in a group, or on their own. It is often a matter of how ambiguous the rules are. It may also be seen that these people act as if they are following a script which leaves margins of freedom in its interpretation. The performance thus seems to follow a routine repeated from day to day, and yet each performance differs slightly from the one before it because of adaptations, improvisations and new knowledge. Moreover, the organization's members, just like actors, are able to enact different scripts according to the situation.

It should also be pointed out that we often have only very vague and limited knowledge of what the consequences of our actions will be. Moreover, we often explain our actions in retrospect, in the light of what happened after them. Yet even retrospective explanations contribute to the changes in the pre-existing order. The result is that every member of the organization, to varying extents, knowingly or otherwise, contributes to creating its culture and climate, to interpreting its regulations, to establishing who wields power and who does not, to setting the levels of efficiency and expectations, and to forming the organization's image in the surrounding environment.

We must, then, familiarize ourselves with the idea that day by day, people, whatever their role, help form the organizations to which they belong. On the one hand, given that organizations are structures, they condition the behaviour of their members with regulations and technical, economic and cultural constraints; on the other, their members reproduce (and modify) organizations by the manner in which they interpret and modify those constraints. This ongoing process of construction is called *structuration* (a concept first employed by the English sociologist, Giddens).

Finally, a word of caution. The reader may ask whether the ideas presented here reflect a position shared by all schools of thought on organization, or whether they represent a specific tendency. S/he may want to know for how long these ideas have been current. The answer is that even if the discussion thus far seems straightforward and commonsensical, it is radically innovative with respect to traditional ways of describing and studying organizations. The main thesis put forward – that it is equally important, in principle, to study both the formal organizations and the micro-organizations of everyday life, or rather organizations as structures and processes – is relatively recent, and it pertains to a school of thought which, though influential, is not necessarily endorsed by all those who study organizations.

In other words, presenting Laura's day as the basis for discussion of organizations is a device inspired by one, but not the only, achievement of much study of organizations. Some decades ago it would have been impossible to imagine beginning a discussion of organizations with a day in the life of an ordinary person, for the way in which organizations were considered was quite different from the notion of them today. Research interests, theoretical models, methods of analysis, and the concept of organizations itself have changed. And the change is not only mental. The object of analysis too has changed, in that organizations and the way in which they are designed and managed have changed. This change has forced researched to reconsider the foundations of the theory of organizations, and in its turn, the new way of conceiving them has a backwash effect on the way they are constructed in practice.

At this point a question may arise: if today organizations are conceived so differently from the past, what has happened to earlier authors and their ideas?

Should they be discarded? Should they be studied for the sake of erudition, or are they in some way still valid? It is not difficult to answer the question. They certainly are important and they certainly need to be studied, for they represent an immense and irreplaceable heritage of knowledge, reflection and insight. It is impossible to understand how we have reached our position today without understanding those authors – or at least the principal of them – and the debates that they initiated.

On the other hand, what can be done to prevent the reader of an introductory course such as this from being submerged in a survey of numerous debates of little interest to him or her? The book overcomes the problem by using a method which can be conveyed by the metaphor of playing music. Consider certain great composers like Vivaldi, Mozart Beethoven, Brahms, Wagner, Schönberg, and imagine that a concert is to be devoted to each of them. What musical instruments should be used? What type of message, aesthetic emotion, vision of the world can be obtained by playing Vivaldi – and only Vivaldi – for the entire evening? What variations and interpretations can be drawn from his pieces? The, other evenings will be dedicated to Mozart, Beethoven, and so on.

It is likewise possible to identify in organizational thought a number of authors who initiated a particular way of conceiving organizations and analysing them. We can then 'play' these authors, in the sense that, after outlining the main features of their thought, we can extend the discussion to other authors who have drawn more or less directly on their theories, discussed them, enriched them, and modified them. It thus becomes possible to highlight the knowledge-generating potential of a given approach. 'Playing' an author also means abandoning criteria of truth or falsehood in evaluating his or her thought. No author has a monopoly on the truth; all authors offer only tools which are more suitable for analysis of some problems and less suitable for analysis of others.

Using this method, five chapters and the conclusions suffice to illustrate the main stages through which the development of organizational thought has moved. Each chapter adds a perspective of analysis to the one preceding it. The first chapter begins with the ideal model of bureaucracy propounded by Weber and asks: if we now consider these ideal features as variables, what type of analysis can be conducted? There emerges an extremely rich range of variations on the theme of bureaucratic organization up until most recent post-bureaucratic models of the workings of organizations. Chapter Two begins with Barnard's analysis of organizations as cooperative systems. It then examines the problems that become amenable to analysis when the focus is on the relationship between organizations and their members, and finishes with discussion of a number of variations on, and integrations to, Barnard's model. Chapter Three is entirely devoted to the relationship between organizations and external institutions. It begins by discussing a celebrated study carried out by Selznick in the 1940s and then turns to the body of thought known as new institutionalism, which has profoundly altered the interpretation given to that relationship by Selznick half a century before. Chapter Four describes two other ways of viewing organizations. The first is transaction costs theory, which raises the problem of the boundaries of organizations and shows that the latter may be not only bureaucracies but also networks, markets, or more generally any relatively stable connection between two or more elements (which relates to the new manner of viewing organizations illustrated when Laura's day was discussed). The fourth chapter also discusses the 'ecological approach' which takes entire organizational populations as its object of analysis and furnishes instruments with which to examine the great changes engendered not only by the adaptation of organizations to newness but also by their birth and death. Chapter Five addresses the theme of so-called 'soft' approaches to organizations. It shows that besides those scholars who choose to study organizational cultures, there are others who adopt a cognitivist approach which maintains that organizations are constantly created by the meaning that people give to their experience. Finally, the Conclusions outline the prospects for the twenty-first century, depicting a scenario of minimal and flexible organizations at the service of actors able to modify them at will, but also the growing divide between the symbolic and material aspects of production which accompanies the globalization of the economy.

A final caveat. This book does not take up a position for or against any of the theories that are described. Its sole purpose is to furnish material for reflection so that the reader can form his or her own opinion – but without ever forgetting the intrinsic ambiguity of the phenomena discussed.

DISCUSSION

Many other organizational aspects not yet examined reside in the details of Laura's typical day. Re-read the description and try find everything that may be of relevance to an organizational analysis. Repeat the exercise. This time think about your own typical day. What types of organizations do you encounter? Are there organizations that you have altered in the past or which you can alter? Have you ever taken part in the creation of an organization, formal, bound by a legal contract, or informal?

Chapter 2

BUREAUCRACY AS A RATIONAL ORGANISATION AND ITS HISTORICAL VARIANTS

The chapter describes Max Weber's ideal model of bureaucracy, by which term he meant the administrative machine typical of legal power. The ten main characteristics of the model are presented, followed by discussion of how they have changed from Weber's day until the present.

1. UNDERSTANDING INSTITUTIONS. THE CONCEPT OF THE IDEAL MODEL

The first great name that we encounter is Max Weber (1864-1920), one of the founding fathers of sociology and the author of works of fundamental importance in nearly every field of sociological inquiry: religions, forms of state, political power, economic action, professions, the role of the intellectual. Although Weber's interests extend far beyond organizational analysis, it is not possible to understand the importance of his contribution to that discipline without outlining the fundamentals of his theoretical thought.

The Weberian method of analysis can be defined as *comprehensive* and *institutional*. It is *comprehensive* because the object of sociological study is meaningful action. Weber defines this as "the human attitude to which the acting subject gives his own subjective meaning by taking into the account the attitude of other subjects". The purpose of sociological research is to provide a "comprehensive explanation" of the action of one or more individuals. To *explain* means finding the causes that are thought to have given rise to a certain way of acting. And to *comprehend* means making clear the meaning that the subject attaches to his/her action in relations to those causes. For example the use of force, the legal system, a family bond, a popular tradition, a religious belief, or a financial opportunity may be indicated by the researcher as the causes which have induced one or more individuals to act in a given way; and the meaning that individuals give to their action resides in their fear, respect for authority, affection, habits, faith or self-interest; that is, in their personal motivations. The researcher may also identify causes for their action of which the subjects examined were not even aware.

Moreover, Weberian analysis is *institutional* because it is concerned with the study of the conditions and restraints that certain social institutions impose on both human action and the meaning that people give to their action. Throughout history, human beings have constructed innumerable types of social institutions relating to all areas of human action. There are state institutions (e.g. absolute or constitutional monarchies, presidential or parliamentary republics, unitary or federal states), political institutions (e.g. democracies, dictatorships, party systems), legal institutions (e.g. judiciaries more or less independent of political power), economic institutions (e.g. large landed estates, competitive capitalism, monopoly) religious institutions (churches, sects, monasteries), and many others besides. Many complex institutions do not pertain to a single area of human action but to many, which are regulated by a set of largely consistent rules. Feudalism with its social polarization between the landed aristocracy and serfs was a form of both political *and* economic domination. The same applies to nineteenth-century capitalism, with its polarization between an entrepreneurial bourgeoisie and the proletariat, or to the attempts to build a communist state dominated by party functionaries who also managed economic resources.

Unlike Marx, who gave priority to the economic relations of production, or Freud who privileged the libido, Weber does not point to any one factor as being especially able to explain human action or the social structures within which human beings live. Weber does not seek to give general explanations of history; even less does he claim that human history develops according to 'laws' or predetermined tendencies, as the positivists and Marxists instead contend.

Weber focuses instead on the infinite forms of institutions that have arisen throughout history. He analyses the material, social, economic, cultural and religious conditions that have led to their establishment, the regulatory obligations deriving from them, and the affinities that may exist among institutions apparently very different from each other. A classic example of this inquiry is Weber's study on the relationship between the spirit of capitalism and the Protestant ethic, where he argues that Calvinist ethical and religious convictions (moral rectitude, an active and orderly lifestyle, the propensity to save) were important factors in legitimizing early capitalism. Others of his studies examine the relationships between religious beliefs and the social institutions associated with them, and forms of economic action in various Asiatic countries.

The basic technique used by Weber is the construction of *ideal types*, i.e. models that do not exist in reality but only in the mind of the researcher. In order to construct an ideal type, the researcher observes and selects what appear to be the most significant elements in a given situation, ignoring those that seem irrelevant or incidental. S/he connects the selected elements together, emphasises them, and coordinates them into a representation which must be internally consistent and non-contradictory.

Constructed thus, an ideal type is always an extreme concept, a pure form not to be found in concrete reality, but which serves as a template for study of that reality. The researcher observes a specific situation and evaluates how close it comes to an ideal type. It thus becomes possible to compare and contrast different situations, to establish which situation most closely resembles a given ideal type, and which is furthest away from it. The more in-depth research becomes, the greater the need to construct variants or subspecies of an ideal type so that the differences that appear in the phenomenon being studied can be conceptualized and defined. For example, once the ideal type of capitalism in its most general form has been established, the problem arises of identifying the great variety of forms that capitalism has assumed in various historical periods and geographical areas: from mercantile capitalism to industrial capitalism, from competitive capitalism to monopolistic capitalism, from pure *laissez-faire* capitalism to capitalism regulated by government policies, and so on. It is important to emphasize that an ideal type:

(*a*) does not derive from statistical averages but is a qualitative concept constructed by selecting and accentuating specific aspects of the phenomenon observed. From this it follows that the heuristic (from the ancient Greek *eurisko* = research) capacity of an ideal type depends entirely on the ability of the researcher.

(*b*) is not a model of moral conduct and does not indicate something that can be desired. The ideal model, useful in research, must not be confused with an ethical ideal. Weber writes: "An ideal type has nothing to do with perfection that is not purely logical. There are ideal types of brothels just as there are ideal types of religions" (*Method*, 1958).

There is an ideal type of the Mafia as well as of a Benedictine convent, an ideal type of a *coup d'état* as well as of a financial speculation on the stock market.

2. PURE FORMS OF POWER, LEGITIMIZATION AND BUREAUCRACY

Weber also constructs ideal types in order to study power, which he defines as "the possibility for specific commands to find obedience from a specified group of people" (ES.,vol.1, p.207). The study of power requires recognition that it is not a quality intrinsic to a person; rather, it is *relational* and *specific* in nature. It is *relational* because it springs from the relationship between those who command and those who agree to obey. It is *specific* because the circumstances, conditions and limits of a power relationship must always be established.

Power has two essential features. The first is that if it is exercised continually it must be *legitimated*; or rather, it must be accepted as legitimate by those subordinate to it. An individual act of power may be obeyed simply because brute force is used (an act of extortion or personal violence). But if a power relationship develops over time, and does so in regular and stable manner, brute force is not enough to sustain it, and the relationship will have to be based on some form of legitimization accepted by the subordinates. The second characteristic is that, for its exercise, even legitimate power requires an *administrative apparatus* to mediate between the superior and his/her subordinates. This apparatus varies greatly according to the type of legitimization enjoyed by the power. Hence, more than power itself, sociological research is interested how it is legitimized. Weber identifies three pure forms or types of legitimate power: charismatic, traditional, and legal or rational.

Charismatic power takes its name from *charisma* (Greek *charisma*, divine favour) and is grounded on exceptional and sometimes superhuman characteristics attributed to a leader by his or her followers. Charismatic power involves devotion, faith and enthusiasm in an emotionally charged climate. Yet charismatic power is often short-lived, for it must constantly prove itself to its followers (with miracles, successes, victories, conversions of the skeptical). If it does not, it may disappear. In its pure form, Weber emphasizes, charismatic power is irrational, because it lacks pre-established rules, and it is revolutionary because it overturns the past. It springs from a radical break with the current institutions, and it affirms itself by preaching either a new order ('Jesus preaches: The law says... but verily I say unto you...') or a return to the origins of an institution condemned for its decadence (for example, Luther and the Protestant Reformation).

The administrative body of charismatic power is rudimentary, in that it consists of disciples, the leader's inner circle of trusted men, who stood on his side during the most difficult times and who have proved their devotion and loyalty, thus obtaining a 'halo' of charisma from their closeness to the leader. Although in its purest form charismatic power is to be found in the religious sphere, it is also manifest in the political sphere (great revolutionary leaders) and in the economic one as well (business leaders). But traces of charisma can be detected in all situations in which obedience to a leader is due more to the latter's personal ability to assert him/herself than to the official rank of his/her job. The typical shortcomings of charismatic power are the difficulty of exercising it over time and of finding a successor to the leader. Charisma is typically tied to moments of high emotion which by definition are exceptional. When the movement subsides, and especially when the leader dies or retires, his successors cannot prevent the gradual transformation of charisma into daily routine (Weber calls this the 'routinization' of charisma), which then transforms it into bureaucratic or traditional power.

Traditional power bases its legitimacy on ancient systems perceived as 'having always existed'. The holder of power demands obedience by virtue of the personal dignity attributed to him/her by tradition. S/he may not have personal gifts of command, but his/her subordinates must nonetheless obey and revere him/her because s/he represents what tradition holds to be sacred. A typical example of traditional power is the king who reigns by virtue of his bloodline and because he belongs to a dynasty. But traditional power is not found in ancient societies alone. Traditional forms are still apparent today: for example, in the great business dynasties, and in cases where inheritance or membership of a privileged group legitimates the exercise of power. In the case of traditional power, the principal criterion for the assignation of a job is not competence, but the fact that the person belongs to a privileged group. Yet this selfsame criterion constitutes the weakness of traditional power, which is constantly threatened by the advent of a local charismatic leader who will rebel against tradition, or by the objection that leaders must be chosen for their competence, not according to tradition.

Legal or rational power is thus termed because its legitimacy is based upon the presumption that those in command exercise their power by virtue of legal appointment, that they are competent, and that their orders accord with a system rationally oriented to the achievement of specified goals. It is also presumed that the system is based on abstract and universal criteria which apply equally to all similar cases. Also the holder of legal power, therefore, is expected to abide by the same impersonal system that s/he imposes upon his or her subordinates. The universal nature of legal power makes it a prerogative of the rule of law, where the subordinates are citizens with recognized rights (including the right to vote) and not the subjects of a leader who exempt from respect for the laws that s/he himself imposes.

3. THE TECHNICAL SUPERIORITY AND AMBIVALENCE OF BUREAUCRACY

The administrative apparatus typical of legal power is bureaucracy. Although imperfect and occasional forms of bureaucracy have already existed in the past – especially in the great empires of antiquity – the phenomenon has acquired its most complete form in modern societies. Weber insists that bureaucracy is technically superior to any other form of administration. He writes:

> Precision, speed, unambiguity, knowledge of the files, continuity, discretion, unity, strict subordination, reduction of friction and of material and personal costs – these are raised to the optimum point in the strictly bureaucratic organization.... . (ES vol.II,p288)

Those who have in mind the commonplace complaints about the inefficiency of bureaucracy might be surprised on reading this eulogy. To clarify the reasoning behind it, two points must be made. The first is the distinction that Weber draws between value-oriented rationality and goal-oriented rationality. Value is something ethically good, and thus desirable, whilst a goal is something that one or more persons pursue without consideration of its ethical value. Weber does not believe that bureaucracy is geared to values, or in other words, that its goals are always beneficial and desirable. A bureaucracy may also be used to exploit, to oppress, or to kill. Weber's contention is that bureaucracy, owing its intrinsic rationality, is *as a technical instrument* superior to any other type of administration in human history.[1] His opinion on the advantages deriving to humanity from the advent of bureaucracy is therefore problematic and ambivalent. The second point is that Weber draws a historical comparison between bureaucracy and previous administrative apparatuses (feudal, hereditary, patriarchal), and the comparison is made in terms of the ideal model. Weber does not deny that specific bureaucracies may be inefficient and corrupt. His attention, however, is focused on the reasons why a pure model of bureaucracy is better than other pure models of administration.

Owing to this superiority, Weber sees bureaucratization as a general trend in modern society, one aspect of the broader process of rationalization that characterizes it. The original feature of Weber's line of thought is that, in an era marked by the advent of great political projects such as socialism, liberalism or Christian communitarianism, it is not these that will prevail, but *bureaucratization*, a universal process which accompanies the realization of any socio-political project in the contemporary world. (Bendix, 1960).

But bureaucratic power has one peculiarity. Unlike charismatic or traditional power, it is *acephalous*, by which is meant that it does not contain

1 Weber's analysis dates to the early 1900s. Since then various post-bureaucratic forms of administration have been devised to overcome the intrinsic limitations of bureaucracy (see below)

within itself the supreme political command that determines the general decisions of a country or an organization. Bureaucracy is always at *the service* of political power, which may be based on various forms of legitimization: charismatic, traditional, or rational, in the sense that it conforms to the principles of the rule of law (and is therefore legitimated by popular vote in accordance with a constitution).

The most authoritative member of a bureaucratic apparatus is the official who implements orders issued by a political leader, whether he is a king, a dictator, a prime minister, a minister, or a mayor. Yet, whilst leaders change with political circumstances, the officials remain.[2] A complex relationship consequently arises between the political leader and the administrators whereby each need's the other. On the one hand, the officials need orders upon which to act; on the other, the political leader needs the officials so that s/he can obtain information and fulfill his/her political programme. As the officials implement the politician's programme, however, they interpret it and adapt it: they may dilute it, delay it, or even sabotage it should they believe that it will introduce changes against their interests. The paradox is that the more absolute the power exercised by a political leader, the more closely he depends on the bureaucratic apparatus to exercise that power: it is this apparatus that filters information on what can or cannot be done, what the costs will be, how long it will take, and so on. Weber shows that the Russian Czar of the *ancien régime* was rarely able to achieve long-lasting reform if the bureaucracy disagreed with it to an even minimum extent.

But the bureaucracy may even be hostile to a democratically elected parliament which seeks to exercise its normal powers of control. Weber observes that "an ill-informed and therefore impotent parliament is naturally liked by the bureaucracy, since this ignorance is compatible with its own interests. (ES, p.305). The problem, therefore, is how bureaucratic degeneration in the workings of the state can be prevented by establishing a correct relationship between political and bureaucratic power. The manner in which Weber examines the matter reveals his liberal-democratic convictions, these being contrary to any authoritarian regime, whether on the right or on the left. His thesis is that control of the bureaucracy is most likely to succeed in countries where two conditions have been fulfilled: freedom of the press and speech, and a professional political class with sufficient technical and administrative knowledge to control the bureaucratic machine.

2 This happens in Weber's model. However, there are cases, for example the United States, where the instalment of a new president brings with it a new executive administration (the so-called 'spoils system').

4. BUREAUCRACY BETWEEN IDEAL TYPE AND HISTORICAL VARIANTS

Weber develops an ideal model of the constitutive principles and workings of a modern bureaucracy – understood as both public administration and private enterprise. The features of his model can be summarized by the following ten points:

1. *loyalty to the office:* officials must obey superiors as the incumbents of formal roles, not as specific individuals. Their superiors may change, but the obligation to obey remains, contrary to the case of traditional or charismatic power, where loyalty is owed to the person and not to the role.
2. *Disciplined expertise:* each official is assigned specific and specialized tasks to perform in accordance with pre-established norms which guarantee the highest degree of formalization and standardization;
3. *Hierarchy of offices:* as a rigid system in which the authority has power of management and control over subordinates; the hierarchy is both a structure which governs top downwards and a channel of communication which operates bottom upwards:
4. *Specialized training:* working in a bureaucracy requires a specific course of study which prepares for the tasks to be performed but also affords social prestige;
5. *Public competitive examinations*: entry into or promotion within a bureaucracy is conditional on success in examinations which assess the candidates' preparation using objective criteria.
6. *Career development:* an official usually works for a bureaucracy throughout his or her working life, and as s/he accumulates seniority and experience, s/he is offered opportunities to work in positions carrying more responsibility and better remuneration;
7. *Full-time activity:* work in a bureaucracy is permanent and cannot be a sinecure or a second or occasional job.
8. *Secrecy:* A bureaucracy mandates the non-disclosure of official affairs and a strict separation between private life and life in the office.
9. *Fixed monetary salary*: this is paid by the administration for which the official works. In a pure bureaucracy, the clients or customers of the administration do not pay the officials for their services. Rather, they pay the administration, which then remunerates the officials.
10. *Non-ownership of work instruments:* Employees do not own the instruments that they use for their work. These are allocated to them by the administration and the employees are accountable for the use made of them.

It should be borne in mind that the above ten points delineate an ideal model of bureaucracy which does not exist in pure form. The sole purpose of the model is to enable evaluation of how and to what extent the bureaucracies of history have been similar to or different from the pure form.

Described thus far has been the standard version of Weber's thought set out in texts which explain his theory. However, further exploration of Weber's influence on later studies on bureaucracy requires more than the content of these popular texts. Two other considerations apply. The first is that, although Weber describes the ideal type of bureaucracy as an abstract and universal model, he was a German intellectual who lived in the late nineteenth and early twentieth centuries. Given his personal experience, therefore, it was the German bureaucracy of the time that served as his main empirical reference (Bendix 1960). Thorough understanding of his model requires one to try and *imagine* the *imaginary world* that he had in mind: a world that was profoundly male and made up of civil servants loyal to the Prussian state. They were observant of the law, scrupulous, methodical, aware of their importance, and always careful to uphold the image of an efficient and dedicated state system resembling what Bendix has called "bureaucratic absolutism". We may presume that Weber had a specific conception of the way in which these executives worked, their language, mode of dress, their private lives, and their opinions of themselves. Just as the European literature of the past two centuries contains enduring characters personifying the bureaucratic world of their eras, those depicted by novelists like Balzac, Dickens and Musil, so too Weber was conditioned by this world, not as a novelist but as a social scientist, and as such he replaces literary metaphor with the ideal and abstract type of the bureaucrat of his time.

The second consideration is that precisely because this model is pure and extreme, its ideal features can be taken to be aspects that vary according to the concrete situation. That is to say, they can be considered as *variables* which assume values that may differ greatly from those indicated by Weber (consider, for example, the growing number of women who work in bureaucratic organizations). The changes show that it is possible to construct not only pure types of institutions but also pure types of the variants of those institutions, with a ceaseless shuttling between empirical observation and theoretical reflection. This operation has been performed numerous times in post-Weberian sociology, bearing witness to the immense potential of Weber's model for research.

In what follows, all the points listed above are discussed from this perspective, taking account of the explicit features of Weber's model and the *imaginary world* implicit to it, and how far we have today departed from that model. We shall see that Weber's model enables examination of much more than the senior civil servants in a public bureaucracy, for it can be extended to an extremely broad array of work situations. We shall also see that many of the features identified by Weber are today obsolete and thus shed light on how the bureaucratic organization of work has changed in the course of the past century.

5. LEADERSHIP IN BUREAUCRACY: RATIONAL, CHARISMATIC OR TRADITIONAL?

The pure bureaucrats imagined by Weber are empowered to give orders because their role gives them authority, and because their colleagues assume that they are competent, in the twofold sense that they issue orders in accordance with the law and which match with the purposes of the organization. Pure bureaucrats neither want to be liked, nor to be feared for their personal traits. Their authority derives solely from the fact that they represent the law, and their every action is intended to reaffirm this fact to themselves and to others. Charisma and tradition have no place in pure bureaucracy, because it is only loyalty to the office that matters.

But can such a perfect, impersonal individual as the Weberian bureaucrat exist? Could he be so colourless as to never reveal his personality, emotions, or his human preferences and inclinations? Certainly not, and Weber was very well aware that he was depicting a pure type devoid of any human depth. But the problem is not how to fit diverse personalities into the model of the perfect bureaucrat; it is instead to determine the consequences for sociological analysis when there is obedience in a bureaucratic organization for reasons other than those described by Weber.

Of help is the analysis by an Israeli sociologist, Etzioni (1961), of the concept of charisma. Etzioni observes that charisma does not only spring from rejection of a pre-existing order, and therefore outside and in opposition to the institutions; it may also arise within institutions insofar as the leader is able to reinforce and renew it. There are other forms of charisma in the Catholic Church than the original charisma of Jesus Christ, which was routinized by a long sequence of popes: there is the charisma of specific popes who have gone down in history as having restored power, prestige and grandeur to the Church. The same process can happen in any other institution: a business, a political party, a trade union, a hospital, a research institute, a charitable association. Charisma may be apparent even in an organization which performs everyday tasks of routine administration. At times, the prestige and personal influence of a superior condition a subordinate's decision to obey more than the superior's official position requires. Charisma may also be exercised over people external to an organization. Nicole Biggart (1989) has described the 'charismatic capitalism' of sales personnel able to achieve high sales with their powers of persuasion. In all these cases, charisma has beneficial effects on the workings of organizations. However, this is not always so.

Etzioni observes that charisma is not only to be found at the apex of an organization. There may be charismatic individuals occupying middle level positions, and whose charisma derives from their exceptional ability in a specific field. This typically occurs in professional organizations (for instance, hospitals, schools, research institutes) where it is not necessary for management to be charismatic, but where the charisma of a doctor, professor or scientist brings prestige and economic benefits to the organization. In these cases, obedience to the charismatic professional more closely resembles the rational obedience found in pure bureaucracy. Yet it is different, and it is so because of the emotional attachment normally felt by the employees towards the professional, an attachment which does not occur in a pure bureaucracy. Problems may arise when the charismatic professional is replaced, or even worse, when he disagrees with management or other members of the organization. Internal conflicts may ensue, damaging the entire organization and requiring extraordinary measures to be taken from above. However, the most harmful conflicts caused by local charisma are those that occur in purely hierarchical organizations like the armed forces or the Catholic Church. These organizations only permit charisma at their summits, so that local charismas become a source of tension and conflict. In the army, the final result may be mutiny; in the Church, heresy or schism.

Another delicate problem arises in prisons, where the detention system is usually based on merely bureaucratic criteria. But amongst the prisoners there are often leaders who have acquired charisma during their criminal careers (Mafia bosses, gang leaders etc.) and have active support in criminal circles external to the prison. Order within the prison is often ensured by the silent consent of these leaders, who negotiate with the management to reach an ambiguous compromise consisting of complicity and covert privileges. No serious organizational study of a prison could omit analysis of the prison population and its relationship with the formal hierarchy (Cressey 1961 and 1965; Morris 1963).

Finally, there may also be traditional aspects of a bureaucracy which give rise to interpretative problems of no less interest. Managers, executives or office workers hired and promoted because they belong to a certain social group, and not because they deserve it, represent an instance of traditional bureaucracy. There are striking cases where 'daddy's boys' have passed public competitive examinations solely because of who they are, not because they fulfill meritocratic and objective criteria There are also cases where corporatist trade unions have accepted the principle that a percentage of job vacancies should be allocated to the relatives and children of employees. Usually, however, matters are managed more covertly. Recommendations made because an applicant belongs to a certain political party or church, or because he is a friend, or comes from a certain area, or because he belongs to a Masonic lodge, are typical traditional practices. They are as actively sought as they are verbally condemned as signs of nepotism or favoritism, and for these same reasons it is difficult to obtain documentation for research. On the other hand, it is also difficult to prove that the choice was made solely because of 'string-pulling' and not because the person was best qualified for the position.

Research on social mobility is easier to conduct. Such research examines, for example, how many relatives and family members of managers have been hired by the same organization or by others connected with it. In this case too, however, it is often difficult to separate traditional criteria from rational criteria based on qualifications. The percentage of doctors whose fathers are doctors, or university lecturers whose children are lecturers, is usually higher than what one would expect from a random distribution. (Goode, 1966; Cobalti and Schizzerotto 1994; Hout 1989). Yet the fact that someone follows in his father's footsteps does not necessarily mean that his career advancement is due exclusively to his family connections. Usually the advantage is subtle one to do with early socialization within the family which favours his professional development in that field. In this case the traditional criterion of belonging to the right group add to the rational and meritocratic criteria, even if it has provided an initial advantage.

Academic careers are further situations in which traditional criteria combine with rational and meritocratic ones. Here, a professor 'presents' of one his students at a public competitive examination for an academic post. In many societies like Italy's this custom is viewed as legitimate because of cultural affinity, and because of the research that the junior and senior academic have conducted together over the years. Often, however, professors are suspected of excessively favouring their candidates, so that other, more deserving ones from other cultural backgrounds are not evaluated fairly. The charisma exerted by the most senior professor on the selection board also plays an important role in legitimizing the choice. This case from academe highlights how analysis based on the Weberian categories of rationality, charisma and tradition can be complex and replete with ambivalence.

6. PROFESSIONAL BUREAUCRACY OR MECHANICAL BUREAUCRACY?

The chief of police or a messenger boy, a manager or a shop-floor worker, a chief consultant or a stretcher-bearer, a university professor or a janitor, a prelate or a sacristan: all these belong to bureaucracies, and they all have their specific duties and tasks. They are supervised to different extents and have careers which carry greater or lesser power and prestige. What criteria can be used to weigh the differences on a scale comprising such a wide variety of jobs and professions? Weber does not address the problem because he is concerned to outline the general characteristics of a pure bureaucracy. However, the need to distinguish between diverse types of bureaucracy based on different types of work done has repeatedly arisen in post-Weberian sociology

Gouldner (1949) pointed out that the Weberian principle of *disciplined competence* is based on a tension that makes it intrinsically unstable. Competence contrasts with discipline. Those who are assigned roles which require a high level of competence and responsibility act with the autonomy deriving from their command of the requisite professional knowledge. They see any external intervention, even by a superior, as interference which jeopardizes their autonomy. Any criticism of their work creates a conflict between professional competence and loyalty to the organization's hierarchy.

Yet only in extreme cases does the choice between acting according to one's own competence and accepting the suggestions of a superior becomes a major dilemma. Most bureaucracies are organized so that a clear distinction is drawn between highly professional jobs where competence is institutionally recognized as more important than discipline, and less professional jobs where the principle of discipline overrides competence. Examples of highly professional jobs are those of judges and doctors (as executives in bureaucratic systems like the judicial system and hospitals), whereas employees with routine tasks and factory workers on the assembly line belong to the second category.

Gouldner's thesis is that the Weberian model of bureaucracy must be replaced with a dualistic model which distinguishes between a bureaucracy based on the principle of competence and another based on the principle of discipline. This distinction extends Weber's analysis and poses new problems for sociologists. Can both models exist side by side in the same organization? What is the threshold above which the discipline principle gives way to the competence principle, and vice-versa?

Another way to conceptualize the differences between the two types of bureaucracies has been suggested by Mintzberg (1979), who distinguishes between professional and mechanical bureaucracies. Professional bureaucracy requires wide margins of discretion and personal initiative. Mechanical bureaucracy includes repetitive and standardized tasks which follow pre-established procedures at both the blue-collar and white-collar levels. Mintzberg maintains that the organization exercises control over both bureaucracies. While control is exercised over *the way tasks are done* in mechanical bureaucracy, in professional bureaucracy control is exercised over *the initial education and training* of the officials, who are hired only after their abilities have been verified, as well as over *the results that they achieve* during a given period of time. These different criteria of control can also be related to the fact that those who work in a mechanical bureaucracy usually do so in open areas under the surveillance of a supervisor, while the members of a professional bureaucracy usually work enclosed in their offices, or at least in greater privacy, where direct control by their superior, even less their colleagues, is not envisaged. However, there are also occupations that are undertaken in public, so that the norms which protect the official in his office may coexist with criticism and attacks from outside. It would be an extremely serious matter if a university lecturer took over a colleague's lectures; yet, this behaviour can be severely criticized by the students. In the same way, a judge's rulings are subject to rigorous control procedures by the judicial authorities, but at the same time they may be the subject of violent criticism in the press.

An original criterion with which to evaluate the different degrees of professionalism in a bureaucratic organization has been suggested by Jaques (1976), who pointed out that the greater the discretion and professionalism required for a job, the longer "the period for an employee to make decisions concerning a given amount of resources belonging to the organization". Thereafter, the decisions taken are examined. A factory line worker may be controlled various times in one shift, so that his or her autonomy is very brief. The supervisor is controlled no more than once or twice a month by the plant manager and thus has an intermediate level of autonomy. The plant manager's work is checked no more than two or three times a year, and so on up to the general manager, whose work is normally subject to evaluation and control by the shareholders only at the end of his term. The advantage of Jaques' model is that it offers a scale with increasing levels of professionalism, and therefore yields a picture more well-defined than that offered by the simple polarization between mechanical and professional bureaucracy. In addition, its concept of professional bureaucracy is not restricted to the 'educated' professions (medicine, university teaching, engineering, etc.), but also includes all those occupations, even manual ones, that require a significant amount of discretion and skill. The importance of middle-level employees becomes particularly evident.

Jaques' model was developed in the 1960s, and it is now in need of revision. The use of electronic monitoring devices in complex occupations (air pilots, air traffic controllers, laboratory technicians) requires reconsideration of Jaques' hypothesis that that the frequency with which work is checked is inversely proportional to its professional job content Today work that is highly technical is constantly supervised in order to avert the risk of catastrophic accidents. In other words, Jacques' premise that the degree of responsibility coincides with the amount of autonomy granted no longer holds true. There are now highly responsible technical jobs in which increased responsibility means less autonomy, because the worker must know and scrupulously comply with all the procedures laid down for the use of equipment (Klein 1991). Also the emergency procedures to follow in critical situations must be decided according to second-degree procedures. Memorization of procedures so that they become automatic is increasingly important in jobs where complex technology is used.

Finally, this section cannot be concluded without discussion of the relationship between the process of bureaucratization described by Weber and the scientific management of work developed in the same years by Taylor (who gave his name to *Taylorism)*. If Weber considered bureaucratic rationalization to be the process distinctive of modern society, then the 'Taylorization' introduced into factories during the first half of the twentieth century was certainly the most coherent and extreme expression of that process. On the basis of the principle that there is only *one best way* to solve every problem, which can be identified and pursued with scientific criteria, everything in the factory is subject to measurement, control, order, detailed planning, and the specialization of tasks at all levels. Not only were factory and office workers taylorized, but even the technicians hired to taylorize the factories underwent the same process of standardized planning according to pre-established procedures.

Taylorism can be considered the extreme manifestation of a mechanical bureaucracy. Taylor calculated that it was possible to make a factory three or four times more productive if technical work was completely separated from executive work, and if latter was standardized by meticulously specifying times, physical movements, and the tools to be used. In this way human work became simply an appendix to the machine. The factory worker was not required to think, only to obey, performing tasks that were little more than gestures obsessively repeated thousands of times a day (Braverman, 1974).

The human costs of Taylorization, the resistance raised against it in factories, and attempts to restore the human dimension to work were the central concerns of twentieth-century industrial sociology (Friedmann 1949). Finally, the combined effect of new technologies, labour unrest, and new management techniques attenuated the harshness of early Taylorism, so that some sociologists today maintain there has historically been a plurality of Taylorisms (Littler 1982). Just as the distinction between professional bureaucracy and mechanical bureaucracy was introduced into the Weberian model of bureaucracy, so it seems appropriate to distinguish between original and extreme Taylorism and moderate forms of Taylorism, and the so-called 'computerized neo-Taylorism' today found in numerous technologically advanced production systems.

Yet in recent years another singular phenomenon has become manifest: whilst extreme forms of Taylorism have been abandoned in factories, in the service industries Taylorism has suddenly begun to flourish. McDonalds, with its organization of fast food, is not the only company to symbolize rigorous neo-Taylorism (Leidner 1993; Ritzer 1996); call centres, too, can be termed 'neo-Tayloristic': dozens of employees (usually young women) contact potential users, following rigorously pre-defined communicative codes (Frenkel et al. 2000). Even certain traditional professions have undergone a process of bureaucratization and Taylorization, as anyone who has attended a modern doctor's or dentist's surgery or a legal office will testify. During just one appointment, various technicians come and go, all of them impersonal, smiling and highly specialized. Their assistance is brief, specific and focused. The old-fashioned offices run by a single professional with at most the help of an assistant are disappearing, so that young professionals at the beginning of their careers can only find work as bureaucratized employees with fixed salaries paid by the office, and not proportional to the fees paid by clients. At the same time their skills grow more and more specialized, so that the contemporary professional seemingly confirms the ironic dictum that an expert is someone who knows more and more about less and less until s/he knows everything about nothing.

7. HIERARCHY OF OFFICES

Weber's pure bureaucrats occupy specific positions in a hierarchy. They have superiors who give them general orders, colleagues with their same status with whom they may discuss their orders, and subordinates to whom they transmit those orders, adapting them to circumstances and to their competences. In a bureaucratic organization, orders and controls always pass through the ranks of the hierarchy; but the forms that this hierarchy may assume are countless. Consider the difference between the hierarchy of a military garrison and a convent, where orders are followed unquestioningly, the hierarchy of a factory where the unions negotiate the extent and form of orders, and the hierarchy of a public authority where the orders issued by the division head may be quite liberally interpreted by those receiving those orders. The hierarchy in a scientific laboratory differs even more, for the project supervisor give not so much orders as suggestions and advice, the purpose being to coordinate those working on the laboratory's various research projects.

Mainly between the 1930s and the 1950s, management studies long examined and discussed the different forms that a hierarchy may assume (for a survey of the literature see Massie, 1965). There are *long* hierarchies, with numerous levels, and *short* hierarchies with only a few; hierarchies which require scrupulous control from above, and hierarchies which give discretion to underlings; hierarchies based on formal authority and hierarchies based mainly on competence; hierarchies with only one superior for all the work performed by inferiors, and hierarchies which allocate responsibilities for each type of control to be performed; hierarchies which operate only vertically and ones organized with lateral staff for technical consultation.

To understand the differences among these various patterns, consider an organization with one thousand employees and suppose that they can be grouped into one hundred 10-person teams, or into ten 100-person teams. The difference is enormous in terms of levels of hierarchy, control, work content and overall coordination. In the former pattern, control over each employee's work is extremely close (it is easy to supervise ten people), but it entails the slow and laborious coordination of one hundred teams. In the second pattern, overall coordination is rapid and efficient, but supervising the work of one hundred people is almost impossible. Which is the better solution? The answer is that there is no best solution; rather, the choice must be made according to the tasks which the organization must perform.

Weber does not address the problem of hierarchies which are more appropriate to the various types of bureaucratic organization. In the 1960s and 1970s, the matter was examined in the management literature, as well as by an important strand of sociological analysis known as the contingency school. Of British origin, this school took its name because it maintained that Taylor's *one best way* to construct organizations, be these factories, offices or others, does not exist; rather, there are numerous options, and the best choice depends on the circumstances or *contingencies* in which the organization operates: its sector and business, size, technology, external environment, etc.

The strategic variable highlighted by numerous studies influenced by contingency theory (see e.g. Burns and Stalker 1961; Emery and Trist 1965; Miller and Rice 1967) is the one on the *tranquility-turbulence* dimension of the environment in which the organization operates. A tranquil environment means that events which occur are routine and repetitive and therefore easy to plan for. A turbulent environment, on the other hand, is one in which surprises may constantly occur to disturb routine management.

The organization best suited to management of a tranquil environment is one with a traditional bureaucratic structure: that is, a *long* hierarchy, with well-defined boundaries among competences, precise procedures, regular verification of method and merit, jobs which are largely individual, and vertical communications which flow from the top downwards and vice versa. Order, precision, obedience to orders, and reliability are the qualities expected of employees. Should change occur so that the routine is altered, employees must go to their direct superior to be told what to do, because they are not expected to act on their own initiative.

A structure of the opposite kind is required for turbulent environments. Necessary in this case are a *short* hierarchy, the maximum rapidity of communication, adaptation and response, non-predefined roles and areas, an openness to change, a willingness to learn, an aptitude for team work, and the ability to take initiatives by developing what is known as 'exploratory behaviors'. In other words, it is necessary to change from simple and repetitive tasks to complex ones in which employees undertake a wide range of self-regulated and flexible activities.

An important result of inquiries by the contingency school was Lawrence and Lorsch's (1967) discovery that various types of structures may coexist within an organization, which may have to deal with multiple environments characterized by different degrees of turbulence. In a study conducted on a sample of plastics manufacturers, Lawrence and Lorsch found that production was the most tranquil environment, while the most turbulent one was research and development; sales and marketing stood at intermediate levels.

Production, sales offices and research and development departments emerged from Lawrence and Lorsch's study as separate worlds, where profoundly different criteria are used to reason and act. The world of production is the most bureaucratic and formal, bound to tight deadlines, and with controls carried out according to established and periodic procedures. By contrast, the world of research is the most flexible, with more team work, less attention to levels of hierarchy, longer-term plans and more problematic controls. In order to coordinate such diverse worlds, the companies examined had appointed staff to ensure integration among the various parts of the organization: indeed, it was only through the interfacing activities of this staff that those parts were able to communicate with each other.

Another solution devised to deal with particularly complex situations is the matrix structure (Martino and Sinatra 1972: Benedetto 1989), thus called because superimposed on the vertical hierarchy is a structure which horizontally cuts across the hierarchical divisions (Table 1) The horizontal lines correspond to projects to be concluded within various time periods, and which require personnel with different competences from various sectors. The subjects involved in a project are thus part of two company structures: the institutional structure in which they normally work and the project group where they are working temporarily.

Table 1.1. Simplified diagram of a matrix organization

	Division 1	Division 2	Division 3	Division 4
Project 1				
Project 2				
Project 3				

The advantage of a matrix organization is that it is flexible, articulated, polymorphous, and designed to be dissolved when its objective has been achieved. Its success, however, depends upon its ability to overcome the resistance that may arise when the traditional structures are required to loan personnel and resources for tasks which are not usually their own. Moreover, project leaders are usually chosen solely for their professional competence, and when the project is completed they return to the divisions to which they originally belonged.

The matrix organization pertains to an organizational model that some authors (see Heckscher and Donnellon, 1994) have termed *post-bureaucratic* in that it relies on widespread communication and team work to manage technical, social and managerial problems much more complex than those that existed in Weber's time. Yet, from a conceptual point of view the post-bureaucratic model, too, can be considered a variant of the Weberian model.

8. SPECIALIZED TRAINING

The pure bureaucrat has attended schools, obtained qualifications and followed training programmes and courses in order to acquire profound knowledge of all the organization's regulations, which s/he applies unhesitatingly and appropriately. Specialized training, Weber maintains, is indispensable for the performance of any task within a bureaucracy. But what is meant by 'specialized training'? The question raises a number of important issues.

In the 1930s, Merton, one of the acutest critics of the Weberian model of bureaucracy, directed attention to the fact that the professional training given to bureaucrats may not be sufficient, using in this regard the expression 'trained incapacity' to denote the unexpected consequences that arise when "the actions based on training and technical ability, which in the past had produced good results, can be inappropriate in changed conditions" (1966, p.320) The bureaucrat is trained in a certain procedure on the assumption that the reality confronting him or her will never change. But when the situation changes and unprecedented problems arise, the entire apparatus of techniques, habits, procedures or decisions is thrown into crisis. The excessively specialized training received by the official turns into a lack of sufficient flexibility in applying the rules and therefore into an inability to achieve the objectives for which the bureaucratic organization was created. Merton thus called attention to one of the most widespread deficiencies of bureaucratic organizations, and in particular the civil service.

The shortcoming highlighted by Merton reflected a attitude widespread in the society of his time: that the technical and cultural preparation acquired before entering a specific occupation was enough to perform it for an indefinite period of time. This was a static conception of culture and competence. The slow pace of technical and scientific development and the reluctance of the bureaucracy's governing bodies to change consolidated practices gave rise to the belief that 'the piece of paper' awarded on conclusion of formal studies was a guarantee of professional competence which was valid indefinitely.

But today a radical change has come about. Consider the medical profession: in the space of only seven years the knowledge acquired at university becomes obsolete. The same applies to every field in which there is increasingly rapid technical and scientific innovation. Training courses, on the job training, seminars, conferences and access to electronic networks are now common practices among those who intend to remain competitive and well-informed in their field.

Even public bureaucracies, notorious for their rigid and suspicious attitude toward change, are increasingly influenced by innovations which oblige them to reconsider the way in which they deal with the public. The age of computers has indubitably had an impact on the civil service, and in Italy the 'revolution' of self-certification has eliminated hundreds of documents previously considered indispensable. Terms like continuing education, human resources management, the learning organization are now part of common parlance, and they bear witness to a transformation in the attitude toward the relationship between work and the specialized training required to perform it. Innovation has had the greatest impact on professional bureaucracy, but also mechanical bureaucracy has had to adapt; suffice it to consider the revolution engendered by the advent of computers and electronic communications systems.

The level of investments, the contents, forms and frequency of training programmes, the categories of workers involved, the effect of training on their work, the possible involvement of trade unions in the management training are some of the variables to be considered by comparative research on how the various types of bureaucracies today manage the relationship between work and human resources.

9. PUBLIC EXAMINATIONS, CAREER AND FULL TIME

Pure bureaucrats enter organizations by passing a competitive examination. They then begin careers which will last for the rest of their working lives. They will work full-time and must not take on part-time or second jobs. This constraint is typical of the civil service, but it also applies in the private sector, although there it is not quite so rigid or formalized.

The public competitive examination is the institution that in principle guarantees fairness in the assessment of the candidates and in the selection of those that deserve to win. This is possible because the calls for applications establish eligibility to participate, because the members of the selection board are appointed according to rules which stipulate competence, and because the procedures ensure that the first part of the examination (the written paper) is anonymous. It is normal that there should be complaints about the results of the examination – such legal disputes are part of human society – but in principle they do not make the legal-formal nature of the institution of the competitive examination less perfect.

Today, such examinations are not used solely to regulate the hiring of new intake from outside. In both the private and public sectors, numerous internal examinations are held to decide, according to the fairness criterion, the career advancement of personnel already working for the organization. Internal examinations are an important part of the creation and coordination of the internal labour market (Doeringer and Piore 1971). The latter expression is used to refer to what happens when a position remains vacant and the organization looks internally for a suitable employee who might be interested in filling it. The internal labour market has the effect of legally sanctioning the precedence for certain posts given to those who already work for the organization. The trade unions have played an important part in the growth of the internal labour market, in that they are concerned to protect their base made up of workers already in employment.

Althoug internal labour markets are a legal source of social inequality, they nevertheless favour employment stability, and thus the development of careers, team spirit and group identity within the organization. We shall see in the next chapter that these are important factors in obtaining efficient performance and cooperation within an organization. In particular, controlling people by offering them career opportunities is one of the most effective means at the disposal of a work organization (Consoli 1991). Internal labour markets also foster mobility among locations or sectors of the same organization, with the consequence that people recruited to a particular department to perform tasks requiring distinct competences can later be transferred to other departments, where they develop new competences that were not necessary in the previous job.

However, a feature of contemporary societies is that the development of internal labour markets has been flanked by the increasing frequency of temporary jobs. This is an era of *flexible work*, an expression that first came into use in the private sector but is now spreading to the public one as well. Research has identified three different types of flexibility: *functional, financial* and *numerical* (Atkinson and Meager, 1986); Harrison and Bluestone 1990). Functional flexibility is exemplified by a worker able to perform numerous different jobs and who can be transferred to other offices within the same company. Financial flexibility is used by companies to introduce greater individual competition among workers, the purpose being to overcome the constraints imposed by collective agreements. And numerical flexibility enables a company to hire or fire according to its needs.

Under the combined effect of these three types of flexibility, recent decades have seen the advent of a dual labour market consisting of a central market occupied by *strong* workers with a high level of professional competence and low risk of unemployment, and a marginal market with *weak* unskilled workers at high risk of unemployment (Paci, 1982). This duality is one of the main causes of present-day social inequality. Compared to the society that existed in Weber's time, when the main social distinction was between those who owned the means of production (the middle class) and those who did not (the working class), one of the significant social distinctions today is that between workers with vocational training demanded in the jobs market and unskilled workers.

There are further exceptions to the full-time job envisaged by Weber as distinctive of a pure bureaucracy. On the one hand, the number of dual job-holders is increasing (Gallino, 1985); on the other, part-time work is becoming increasingly common, especially among women with families, and among students.

10. OFFICE SECRECY AND SEPARATION OF PUBLIC AND PRIVATE LIFE

Pure bureaucrats scrupulously observe office secrecy, because it guarantees the authority and effectiveness of the decisions taken. They know that only by maintaining secrecy on what is done and decided in the office is it possible to avoid interference and undue pressure from outside. For Weber, the distinction between public life and private life is closely connected to secrecy. Bureaucrats take their decisions within their offices; they then go home, and as a rule do not divulge to anyone, not even those closest to them, what they have done or decided in the office. This discretion governs the rigid division of the bureaucrat's quotidian life.[3]

Also these aspects of the workings of a bureaucracy have changed greatly since Weber's time. Three main changes can be identified. The first is the development of the mass media, which has required radical revision of the regulations and practices that protect office secrecy. The concept of secrecy has been refined, with various degrees of confidentiality being defined – official, confidential, reserved, secret, top secret – and the sanctions imposed vary according to the secrecy of the information disclosed. On the other hand, organizations themselves may want to have certain news leak out in order to create a climate of expectation, to distract attention from more important business, to sound out the market for possible competitors or partners, or simply to do a favour to a newspaper or a television station so that they will reciprocate in the future. The calculated use of information and the development of close

3 This reserve is congruent with the tradition which dictates that women must not be involved in problems outside the domestic arena.

exchange relations with the mass media are increasingly frequent strategies used by organizations to create their public image. It is for this reason that it has become important for officials to be skilled in managing relations with the press, calculating carefully what should be openly announced, what should be leaked, what should be mixed with misinformation, and what should be kept absolutely secret.

The second change is the increased use of computers and the creation of a worldwide network of users who can be contacted in just a few seconds. The technical ease of communications has increased the volume of communications itself and lowered the threshold of control over communications. Also to be noted is that the rigorous division between home and office described by Weber as guaranteeing secrecy is now almost entirely ineffective.owing to the development of both telework and computer piracy.

The third change concerns manufacturing in particular, and it is the fundamental re-definition made to the notion of industrial secrecy. In the past two centuries, the development of industrial society has been accompanied by the close attention paid by companies to the problem of preventing information on their projects and innovations from leaking out. A technical innovation in a product or a process may give a company decisive advantage over its competitors. It is consequently understandable that over time, little by little, authoritative and comprehensive laws have been enacted to protect firms against industrial espionage.

Today, matters are changing rapidly. It is the increasing practice of companies to use networks of suppliers and experts who also collaborate with the competition. (Prahalad and Hamel 1990). Suppliers and experts move from one firm to another, and even if they disclose nothing about the specific projects on which they are working to another company, their *know-how* is always the same, so that the projects of rival firms are inevitably similar. As a consequence, secrets are increasingly short-lived, and the advantage of the 'first comer' soon disappears when the innovations are introduced in the other companies as well. Moreover, competing firms frequently set up joint ventures for specific projects (Poyago-Theotoky 1997). It may thus happen that two or more firms conduct research on new products in the same laboratories, knowing that those products will compete against each other. This choice is understandable, given that today innovation is increasingly more transparent, open and accessible. Firms might as well join forces and obtain results beneficial to both parties from the joint venture. All this has given rise a radical re-definition of the notion of industrial secrecy. Secrets less frequently concern *hard* technical-productive aspects and more often *soft* aspects, such as marketing. At stake in competition among firms is the image evoked by the product, much more than the intrinsic qualities of the product itself, given that these are largely similar.

Finally required is brief discussion of the demise of the division between work and home Not only has this division disappeared because the increased use of telework and the spread virtual business (Ettighoffer 1993; Nohria and Berkley 1994) but also the physical division between home and work is fading. Highly variable demand requires employees to have a mobile phone constantly switched on so that they can be at work in the space of a few minutes. This happens in professional bureaucracies (for example, the emergency services of a hospital) and in mechanical bureaucracies (sudden increases in the number of customers in a large store).

11. FIXED MONETARY SALARIES

Pure bureaucrats receive regular and constant salaries from their administrations, and this is their only source of income from work. No form of direct payment is made for their services by the users of the administration for which they work. Citizens pay the administration directly with their taxes or fares, or indirectly with income tax, and the administration then pays its employees. Weber posited the division between salary and the cost of a service as a prime condition for preventing favors to wealthier users and guaranteeing the office's impartiality. This is an essential feature of every bureaucratic organization, and it is integral to the modern rule of law, where favouritism in exchange for direct compensation to the employees of the administration is considered bribery or extortion.

A further important consideration applies to this principle: the bureaucratic or non-bureaucratic nature of a service does not depend on its professional content, but rather on the institutional context in which it is supplied. A doctor working in a hospital or a medical centre has a bureaucratic relationship with his patients (from an administrative point of view), but he has a professional relationship with the same patients if they make an appointment to be examined at his private surgery. The same applies to teachers who give private lessons or magistrates who supply legal services or arbitration outside the courts.

However, there are jobs and careers in which this dual legal status is not possible, either for material reasons (for example, railroad workers, airline pilots) or because it is prohibited by law. For example, law enforcement personnel and customs officials cannot legally supply private services. Once they have left the public administration, however, they can use what they have learned during their service to start a business (sometimes, however, this seems morally improper, as in the case of former tax inspectors who became tax consultants and then worked for the same taxpayers that they had been investigating just before they left the service.).

There are also a wide range of jobs which pertain to *hybrid bureaucracies*. They are usually in the private sector and offer a fixed wage, although this is only a part of the pay (usually the smaller one). This type of remuneration is usually offered when the job contract explicitly considers the employee's direct interest in total sales of the product (for example, sales representatives, insurance agents, stockbrokers).

A particular instance of a hybrid bureaucracy is a service where tips are received. These are typically personal services, and although the employee's remuneration is stipulated by his or her contract, s/he receives further unofficial remuneration from the client. As Whyte pointed out (1948), tips are ambiguous in nature. Tips are only given to lower-level personnel (waiters, porters, etc.), but they may amount to quite considerable sums; indeed, they may amount to more than the salary received by the employer. Tips are symbolic because they tell those who receive them that their service has been appreciated. On the other hand the nature of a tip, an arbitrary donation, is indicative of an explicitly unequal relationship between the giver and the receiver, so that it has often been suggested that tips should be 'rationalized' within an area of fixed and generalized service and added automatically to the client's bill.

Labour economics studies (e.g. Tarantelli, 1986) have shown that pay policies have an important bearing on the differences among bureaucratic organizations. Such policies have at least four significant dimensions:

(*a*) The pay level compared to market values. It may be assumed that where pay is higher, a company has opted for an excellence policy which enables it to select the best workers available on the labour market.

(*b*) The pay curve in time. An organization may decide to pay relatively low salaries at the beginning of careers and raise them according to years of experience. This policy motivates the organization's employees to remain with it for their entire working lives.

(*c*) The difference between minimum and maximum salaries. The smaller the difference between the maximum and minimum salary, the more the company believes in social equality, and vice versa, the greater the difference, the more evident the social difference is between the top and the bottom of the organization.

(*d*) Monetary and/or symbolic incentives (bonuses, certificates of merit) for productivity, efficiency, commitment, product or service quality, low absenteeism, etc. In such cases incentives may operate, explicitly or otherwise, as anti-strike rewards. Incentives may be offered to individuals, groups or corporations.

A particular form of incentive in for-profit organizations is the offer to the workforce of shares in business earnings, or what is known as 'employee shareholding': the trade unions are often suspicious of this type of incentive because it gives unpredictability and instability to incomes which they instead want to be stable and protected against business risks.

Another form widespread in the 'industrial districts' or small firms' networks (e.g. the so-called 'Third Italy') is the possibility for employees, after a given period, to open small businesses of their own, and work with their former employer. It has been stressed that in these cases the prospect of working for themselves may tempt employees into accepting immediate earnings significantly lower than those that they would have received from other companies not offering the opportunity. (Brusco 1982; Bagnasco 1988; Beccattini 1998).

12. NON-OWNERSHIP OF WORK INSTRUMENTS

Pure bureaucrats do not own the instruments of their work, and they use only those provided by the organization. Marx identified non-ownership of the means of production as a salient feature of the industrial working class, but Weber considered it to be a distinctive feature of modern society which concerns not only the working class but anyone who works for a bureaucratic organization.

Amongst the affluent in pre-modern societies, when the distinction between private property and public property was not as clear as it is today, it was necessary to own one's tools in order to work; indeed, it could be said that the job and its tools were practically the same thing. This was particularly evident in war and education. In feudal societies noblemen and knights were obliged to serve the king, and they brought their own arms. It was also usual for scientists and scholars to construct their own research equipment (as exemplified by Galileo and his telescope).

With the advent of the modern state and increasing technological progress, the distinction between the ownership and the use of work instruments has become necessary and conventional. The cost, complexity and social significance of certain apparatuses, from scientific laboratories to weapons requires them to be government property, or the property of other large organizations. Bureaucratic management entails that employees must periodically account for the use that they have made of the tools allocated to them.

Yet it is also well known that when employees are provided with work instruments, they may use them for their own purposes (Blau 1962). In many organizations, the personal use of stationery, telephones, fax machines, cars and other items is tolerated within certain limits; in some cases, it is formalized and may even become a status symbol. Indeed, at the highest levels of an organization it is unclear when an executive is using these instruments for work or for private purposes.

When an organization collapses, the distinction between private and public property disappears entirely. An example is provided by Russia in the early 1990s. When the Soviet Union disintegrated, numerous military personnel took over army installations, moving into military barracks with their families and even selling arms and equipment to third parties.

Generally speaking, the tolerance shown towards the private use of office equipment, the extent to which it is officialized, the categories of employees to which it applies, are aspects on which a comparative study of bureaucratic organizations can yield useful information on the internal climate and the extent to which rules of behavior are formalized. As in the case of tips, the private use of organizational resources is ambiguous. Up to a certain point it can be considered indicative of tolerance and a lack of pettiness. However, beyond that threshold, the private use of office resources tends to be considered indicative of permissiveness and laxness which may foster organizational cynicism among employees. The problem for research is to identify what limits and conditions determine how the phenomenon is perceived.

13. CONCLUSIONS ESSENTIAL FEATURES OF A PURE BUREAUCRACY

The ten characteristics discussed above constitute in their pure forms what Weber considers to be the ideal model of a bureaucracy. The model is coherent and complete and offers a rational means with which to achieve particular ends.

This rationality has an important implication: *a pure bureaucracy attempts to eliminate, or at least to control as closely as possible, every extra-organizational influence over its members' behaviour.* Such control comprises aspects both within and without the organization. Within the organization, bureaucrats are selected and trained so that they will satisfactorily fulfil their roles at the exclusive service of the organization. Their behaviour is not influenced by feelings, intentions or strategies foreign to the organization for which they work. They have no individual rationality; they reason in the same way as the organization. Three further conclusions may be drawn from this thesis: the pure bureaucracy is a centralized structure; it is standardized; and it is rigid.

1. The bureaucracy is a *centralized structure* because crucial decisions are taken only by the central management, while routine decisions are delegated to inferior or marginal levels. The efficiency of a bureaucracy depends upon the ability of its workers to manage the tasks pertaining to their hierarchical level, so that their subordinates are not left without instructions, while at the same time they themselves do not have to consult superiors on routine decisions.

2. A bureaucracy is a *standardized structure* because it follows precise procedures. The employees must comply with such procedures because:
   (*a*) it is assumed that they are best suited to achieving particular objectives;
   (*b*) uniform behaviour makes it possible to replace workers: if everyone works in exactly the same way, then anyone who performs a particular task will achieve the same results. Standardization of procedures and results means *depersonalization* of the service, and it is an integral part of bureaucratic rationality.
3. Finally a bureaucracy is a *rigid structure* because it does not contemplate innovation. Not coincidentally, when describing his ideal model of bureaucracy Weber made no mention of organizational change undertaken in order to adapt to innovations in the outside world. The reason for this is that a bureaucracy is an intrinsically rational instrument intended to achieve particular objectives. The bureaucracy itself is the source of changes that arise in those areas influenced by its action; otherwise one has to admit that the bureaucracy is influenced by factors alien to the criteria of perfect rationalization that inspired it.

These are the essential characteristics of a pure bureaucracy. However, the observations and comments relative to each of the ten characteristics examined above tell us that actually existing bureaucratic organizations assume forms which may be very different from Weber's model, differences that would be a useful basis for further research.

DISCUSSION

The information in this chapter is not enough to provide the basis for fieldwork or research. It does, however, allow us to begin discussion on what might be of interest to such fieldwork or research.

First let us consider what the subject of our research project could be, a work organization with a bureaucratic structure, possibly not too large, so that it can be examined in a relatively short time: for example the branch of a bank, a small municipal department, a small manufacturing plant, a supermarket, a small police station, a school, a parish church, an athletics club, a voluntary association, and so on. Once the selection has been made, it will be necessary to find out how to gain access to this structure, who can give information, and in what form; whether written materials are available, whether interviews can be made and with whom, whether questionnaires can be distributed, or whether it is possible to observe daily routine directly. Let us imagine that we have acquired this access.

We then take the ten features listed above and see whether they exist in the organization selected. It is not necessary to follow the order in which they are given in this chapter. A first step might be to compile an organizational chart of the internal hierarchy, or to write down all the formal positions in the organization, beginning with the person occupying the highest-ranking position, his or her assistants, down to routine staff.

An organizational chart is like a map. It gives essential information (the levels of the hierarchy, the presence of lateral staff, the degree of decentralization, relationships among the various positions), but above all it is an instrument which enables the collection of further information so that one can move within the organization, knowing where to go and with whom to speak.

Secondly we might determine the professional contents of each role present in the organizational chart: Who is it that manages, who has a technical role, who simply carries out routine task? Depending upon the institutional objectives of the organization and the technology used, we can then examine areas of competence, who decides what, who assists in decision-making, who verifies that the decisions taken are implemented. If both men and women work in the organization, it might be interesting to see how they are distributed within the hierarchy.

A third step could be to verify whether at the top or within the hierarchy there are people with particular charisma, meaning that they have a certain prestige or a reputation due more to their personality than their role. It is necessary to be cautious when collecting information about charisma. It would be odd to ask the person him/herself: Excuse me, do you think you're charismatic? One could do so, as long as the question did not sound ironic but as asking for confirmation. However, it would be better to obtain the opinions of the people who work with him or her first. Perhaps you could use indirect questions, having these colleagues tell stories about their experiences with the person. It is also necessary to bear in mind that in small private organizations (typically for-profit) those who issue orders are often the owners or co-owners. In this case Weber would say that the authority is traditional (the owner commands). Yet traditional authority does not exclude the existence of a legitimate bureaucracy (orders are also obeyed because they are rational and suited to the objective), or of a charismatic bureaucracy as well.

Other subjects for research are: the criteria used for hiring and internal promotion (competitive examinations or other methods), career prospects, the training necessary to perform various tasks, whether vocational training is encouraged, who it is that attends courses, and whether attendance on courses brings career advancement. Another subject could be pay levels, although generally speaking this is a highly sensitive subject and personal questions are difficult. It is easier to obtain general information, salary charts with pay scales, the criteria used to award raises (experience or merit), if bonuses are paid and of what type. It might be important to find out whether there are unions in the organization, and their role in relations with the management. So-called fringe benefits relate to income: what fringe benefits do they employees enjoy – the use of the telephone, fax machine, photocopier, or others? Are there any rules on their use and are they obeyed?

At this point it might be asked why we need this information. It is clear that an investigation of this type is useful only for research based on certain theoretical assumptions: for example, comparing two similar organizations, examining the differences and seeking to explain them in light of factors which for some reason are considered important, for instance the leadership of the person in command, technology, the degree of turbulence in the environment, the professionalism of those who work in the organization, and so forth.

In general, however, this type of research falls far short of fieldwork. Here, we have discussed only some institutional aspects of bureaucratic organizations that could be observed hypothetically after reading this chapter. We have yet to deal with the entire subject of relationships between people and organizations and the role of power in an organization, both internal and external. These aspects will be discussed in the chapters that follow.

REFERENCES

Atkinson Anthony Barnese Meager Nigel, *Changing work patterns :how companies achieve flexibility to meet new needs*, National Economic Development Office London 1986.

Bagnasco Arnaldo, *La costruzione sociale del mercato*, Il Mulino Bologna 1988.

Bendix Reinhard, *Max Weber: an intellectual portrait*, Methuen, London, 1966.

Benedetto Richarde Benedetto Beverly Jones *Management concepts for the '90's: matrix and project management*, Kendale Hunt, Dubuque Iowa, 1989.

Biggart Woolsey Nicole, *Charismatic capitalism: direct selling organizations in America*, University of Chicago Press, 1989.

Blau Peter *The dynamics of bureaucracy*, 1962.

Braverman Harry, *Labor and Monopoly Capital* Monthly Review Press, N.Y. 1974.

Brusco Sebastiano, *Piccole impresee distretti industriali. Una raccolta di saggi*, Rosenberge Sellier, Torino 1989.

Burns Tom e Stalker G.M. *The management of Innovation*, Tavistock Publ., London, 1961.

Cobalti Antonio e Schizzerotto Antonio, *La mobilita' sociale in Italia*, Il Mulino, 1994.

Collins Randall, *Weberian Sociological Theory*, Cambridge Univ. Press, Mass. 1986.

Consoli Francesco *Carriere professionalie governo delle imprese*, Rosenberg e Sellier, Torino 1991.

Cressey Donald, *The prison studies in institutional organization and change*, Holt Rinehart and Winston, N.Y., 1961.

Cressey Donald *Prison Organizations*, in March James (a cura di) *Handbook of Organizations*, Rand & Mc Nally, Chicago 1965.

Doeringer Peter e Piore Michael, *Internal labour markets and manpower analysis* , Lexington Mass., 1971.

Doeringer Peter, *Explorations in low pay, collective bargaining and economic mobility*, Cambridge Univ. Press, Mass, 1973.

Doeringer Peter e Bruce Vermuelen (eds) *Jobs and training in the 1980s: vocational policy and the labour market*, M. Nijhoff Boston, 1981.

Emery F.E. e Trist E.L. The causal texture of Organizational Environments, *Human Relations*, 1965 n. 18, pp. 21-32.

Ettighoffer Denis, *L' impresa virtuale: i nuovi modi di lavorare* , Muzzio, Padova 1993.

Etzioni Amitai *Complex Organizations*, Free Press, N.Y. 1961.

Frenkel Stephen e coll., *On the front Line.Organization of work in the information economy*, Cornell Univ., Press, Ithaca, 1999.

Friedman Georges, *Problemes humains du machinisme industriel*, Gallimard, Paris, 1946.

Goode William, *Family and mobility*, in Bendix Reinhard e Lipset Seymour Martin (eds.).

Class, status and power; a reader in social stratification, 1966 Glencoe , N.Y.

Gouldner Alvin, *Patterns of Industrial Bureaucracy* ,The Fee Press, N.Y. 1954.

Harrison Bennet e Bluestone B. *Wage polarization and the flexibility debate*, Cambridge Journal of Economics, n,14, pp 351-373, 1990.

Heckscher Charles e Donnellon Anne (eds.) *The post-bureaucratic organization, New Perspectives on Organizational Change* Sage, 1994.

Hout Michael *Following in father's footsteps:social mobility in Ireland*, 1989.

Jaques Elliot, *A General Theory of Bureaucracy*, Heinemann London, 1976.

Klein Janice A reexamination of autonomy in the light of new manufacturing practices, *Human Relations*, n. 44, pp. 21-48, 1991.

Lawrence Paul e Lorsh Jai, *Organization and Environment* , Harvard Univ. Pres, Cambridge Mass. 1967.

Leidner Robin *Fast Food, Fast Talk:service work and routinization of the everyday life, Univ. of California Press*, 1993.

Littler Craig *Development of the labour process in capitalist societies*, Heinemann London, 1982.

Martino F. e Sinatra A, L' organizzazione a matrice, *L' impresa* n.5, sett. ott. 1972.

Massie Joseph, *Management Theory*, in March James (a cura di) *Handbook of Organizations*, Rand McNally Comp., Chicago, 1965.

Merton Robert Social, *Theory and Social Structure*, Free Press, Glencoe 1949.

Mille E.J. e Rice A.K., *Systems of Organizations*, Tavistock Publ., London, 1967.

Mintzberg Henry *The structuring of organizations*, Prentice Hall Englewood Cliffs, 1979.

Morris Terence, *Pentonville: a sociological study of an English prison*, Routledge 1963.

Nohria Nitin e Berkley James, *The virtual organization: Bureaucracy, Technology and the Implosion of Control*, in Heckscher Charles e Donnellon Anne (a cura di) *The post-bureaucratic organization, New Perspectives on Organizational Change* Sage, 1994.

Paci Massimo, *Mercato del lavoro e clasi sociali in Italia. Ricerche sulla composizione del proletariato*, Il Mulino, Bologna 1973.

Poyago-Theotoky Joanna, *Competition, cooperation , research and development :the economics of joint ventures*, Houndmills, Basingstoke, MacMillan, N Y, 1997.

Prahalad CK e Hamel G The Core Competence of the Corporation, *Harvard Business Review*, May June 1990.

Ritzer George *The Macdonaldization of Society: an investigation into the changing character of contemporary social life*, Thousand Oaks, Calif., 1996.

Weber Max, *Economy and society.*

Weber Max, *L' etica protestante e lo spirito del capitalismo*, Sansoni, Firenze, 1965.

Max Weber, *Il metodo nelle scienze storico-sociali*, Einaudi, Torino, 1958.

Woodward Joanne, *Industrial Organization: theory and practice* Oxford Univ. Press, 1965.

Whyte William, *Human Relations in a restaurant industry*, Mc Graw-Hill, N.Y. 1948.

Whyte William, *Money and motivation*, Harper & Brothers, N.Y. 1955.

Chapter **3**

ORGANIZATIONS AS COOPERATIVE SYSTEMS : THE ACTOR'S ROLE FROM BARNARD TO CROZIER

The chapter examines the relationships between organizations and people. It explains Barnard's definition of organizations as cooperative systems and then describes Simon's theory of bounded rationality. It finally discusses two research studies, respectively by Roy and by Crozier, which shed light on the extremely broad and ambiguous range of relationships between organizations and their members.

1. BARNARD: BEYOND THE PURELY RATIONAL AND FORMAL ORGANIZATION

The legacy of Weber, Taylor and the classical management school is that firms are considered rational means to achieve specific ends. Bureaucracy, with its rigid and formal hierarchy, is the highest expression of that rationality. With the exception of supreme heads, and especially charismatic leaders, there is no room left for individual initiative. Actors must only obey the rules and conform to the roles assigned to them. As there is no rationality beyond the organization, any individual initiative that does not comply with that rationality causes a loss of efficiency and is considered a deviancy that must be repressed. This is reflected in everyday life, where a firm is compared to a machine of which the employees are only its cogs. The evolution of social sciences, and business studies in particular, starts with a critique of that theory and addresses the problems that it does not deal with, such as the role of people, the unexpected consequences of their strategies, the boundaries of organizational rationality, and the dynamics of power.

Chester Barnard (1886-1961) was the first to broach these new topics. American, a senior executive at the Bell Telephone Company, where he worked for nearly forty years, in 1938 Barnard published *The Functions of Executives*, whose originality and depth of intuition were to make it a classic of organizational thought. Arguing contrary to the purely formal and rational vision of firms, Barnard maintained that it is not possible to understand their function without considering the motives that induce individuals to contribute to those organizations. The relationship created between organizations and the people that contribute to the pursuit of their aims is therefore the central subject of his inquiry.

Two points help us understand the rationale of this approach. The first is that during the years when Barnard was at work, capitalism saw great changes take place in forms of corporate governance. The traditional figure of the 'boss', both owner and manager, was being replaced by the 'executive', a professional who ran the business but was not its owner. The rise of the executive made company strategy more complex as the owner-employee dichotomy was replaced by the owner-management-employee trichotomy. In this new scenario, executives had an autonomous role that did not always coincide with the wishes of the owners. Executives were to identify themselves with the interests of the company to the extent that they were part of the organization; but this commitment did not require them to relinquish their identities: on the contrary, a strong and independent personality was a prerequisite for being a successful executive. Reflecting on his own experience as a senior executive, and on the central role played by his personality in determining the success of his company, Barnard became aware of the shortcomings of an approach to organizations which does not take the human factor into account.

The second point is that Barnard was writing at a time when management theory was beginning to be influenced by the so-called human relations school. In the late 1920s and early 1930s, a number of studies and experiments by a group of psychologists and sociologists at the Western Electric company in Chicago highlighted the importance of human factors in employee productivity. Arguing against the Taylorian doctrine that work should be organized purely according to engineering criteria, and with no consideration made of the workers' individuality, these researchers (including Mayo, Roethlishberger and Dickson) discovered that a variety of psycho-sociological factors, such as group harmony and morale, friendly and cordial supervision, dialogue and direct interest in people, and understanding of their problems, powerfully influenced workers' motivation, and were often more effective than purely economic incentives. These factors were identified as the *informal* relations that management must use to off-set the insufficiency of merely formal relations deriving from an entirely engineered organization imposed from above.

The human relations school was later viewed (Gouldner 1962) as the antithesis to Weber's and Taylor's conceptualization of firms. Rather than considering firms as rational machines running according to pre-defined programmes set from above, human relations scholars saw them as natural, spontaneous and adaptable systems influenced by the actors working within them and by the surrounding environment. The view of the business as a machine in which people were merely its cogs was thus replaced by a view of the business as an organism whose cells are people and the groups that they form.

These two points are the premises for Barnard's work. Existentially, politically and morally, Barnard finds his main subject in the work of executives, individuals with responsibility and charged with the task of constant mediation between the interests of the company and those of its members variously involved in its workings (owners, shareholders, employees, customers, suppliers). Barnard stresses that theory must go beyond the antithesis between the formal and informal aspects of the firm, developing a more complex conception which takes account of both of them.

2. THE PARABLE OF THE ROCK. THE ORGANIZATION AS COOPERATIVE SYSTEM

The problem that Barnard seeks to solve is purely theoretical, and it can be stated as follows: how can it be that people with their own lives and private interests, who do not know each other and have nothing to do with the aims of a given organization, at a certain moment decide to devote their time and energy to achieving those aims? And how does that organization obtain their consensus and commitment? In the case of work organizations, the commonsense answer is that individuals are employed on the basis of a contract which obliges them to supply their labour in exchange for monetary recompense, and perhaps certain other advantages as well. But this is an answer that only scratches the surface of the problem.

First of all, Barnard is not talking about work organizations alone, but all possible types of organization: political, cultural, recreational, religious, military, and so on. His aim is to furnish a model that can be applied to any category of persons who collaborate with an organization. The employees, executives, shareholders, customers and suppliers of a firm can be conceptually grouped into the category of cooperating members, and so too can the leaders, officials and members of a political party or a trade union, the priests and believers of a church, etc. Secondly, Barnard examines the conditions under which an organization can pursue its own ends while satisfying at the same time the interests and aspirations of the individuals willing to contribute to the pursuit of those aims. Barnard's inquiry is, therefore, pitched at a high level of conceptual abstraction.

Barnard begins his discussion with a parable. Let us suppose that a man travelling on a deserted road comes across a rock blocking his way. After finding that he cannot move the rock on his own, he waits for other people to arrive who also want to clear the road. By combining their efforts, they manage to move the rock. Thus, whilst the limitations of one person prevented a goal from being achieved, cooperation among several people interested in the same outcome brought success. Now let us imagine that the rock is so large that the four people are unable to move it. They have to call for help from a fifth person, say a farmer who brings his tractor. The farmer has no direct interest in moving the rock – he does not use the road – but on being offered a sum of money, he has agreed to use his tractor. For the moment, moving the rock becomes his goal as well. With the mediation of money, the farmer seeks to achieve an objective that is not his own, but that of the group who called him and in which he has agreed to take part.

The parable of the rock has various implications.

The group managed to move the rock because they were organized. An organization, writes Barnard, is created when there are people able to communicate with each other and who wish to collaborate to achieve a common purpose. This statement already contains the two elements Barnard sets out to combine: the *informal* element, represented by the fact that individuals communicate with each other, swapping opinions, ideas, proposals, thereby getting to know each other and testing out the possibility of doing something together; and the *formal* element represented by their decision to cooperate in achievement of a common purpose.

An organization therefore arises from a combination of these two elements. Organizing means forming a *cooperative system* whose purpose is no longer that of the individuals concerned but of the entire organization that they have created. All human beings have physical, biological and intellectual limitations. But the organization, as a cooperative system, is an instrument which enables those limitations to be overcome and otherwise impossible objectives to be achieved. The organization is not just the simple sum of the efforts of single individuals; there is an extra *quantum* than arises from cooperation among its members. And this is the cooperative coefficient that makes the difference between a grouping of unconnected people and an organization with a specific aim. Studying an organization is to examine how a cooperative system works when that extra *quantum* is created from the sum of each individual contribution.

It is fallacious to suppose that an organization can be based solely on the unilateral adherence of individuals to its system of values, because those individuals have their own unchangeable personalities that must be expressed.

In other words, a distinction must always be drawn between organizational aims and personal motives. In the parable of the rock, the aim of the organization of five people was to clear the road. The farmer who came with the tractor was willing to collaborate towards that end, but his motive for doing so was not to move the rock but to obtain the monetary reward agreed upon. Distinguishing between organizational aims and personal motivation implies that the heads of organizations cannot merely pursue organizational goals; they must also consider the motives that induce single members to participate. Because an organization is a cooperative system, participation by its members must be based on consensus. Consequently, the fundamental problem for managers is how to mobilize a group of people in pursuit of a goal that is not theirs by offering them satisfactory incentives to do so.

A third aspect concerns the distinction, but also the close relationship, between formal and informal elements within an organization. Some of the five people who cooperated to move the rock might have already known each other. They might have already formed relationships, but these would have been informal because they did not comprise specific ends, structures or internal ramifications. It is only when shared aims are established (even if they are occasional and ephemeral like moving a rock) that an organization is created, with all the consequences that the division of tasks and the designation of responsibilities entail.

But once an organization has been formed, new informal relationships may arise within it. People who did not previously know each other begin to meet. Osmosis takes place between the formal and informal levels of human relations. One level links with the other, and the success of the former becomes the premise for the success of the latter, and vice versa. It may also happen that an informal group arises out of a formal organization to pursue a specific aim, becoming a new formal organization. It may remain within the first organization (e.g. a company sports group) or it may become totally independent and leave the original organization (e.g. former employees who set up a new company which competes with the one that they have left).

A distinction must therefore always be drawn between the formal aspect relating to the pursuit of the objectives for which the organization was created, on the one hand, and the informal aspects relating to the relationships established among individual members on the other. The two aspects are not mutually exclusive. On the contrary, the formal aspect cannot exist without the informal one, and vice versa. By proposing this reciprocal nexus, Barnard distances his theory from both the classical school, which concerned itself solely with the formal aspects of an organization, and the human relations school, which was concerned with only the informal aspects.

3. EFFECTIVENESS AND EFFICIENCY. THE RELATIONSHIP BETWEEN CONTRIBUTIONS, INDUCEMENTS AND PERSUASION

Barnard rejects both a purely ethical foundation of the social order (as the outcome of the 'internalization' by individuals of the predominant values system[1]), and the purely utilitarian explanation for it based on calculation of personal profit. Barnard points to a possible third way to reconcile the needs of the organization with those of individuals.

The distinction between organizational aims and personal motives forms the basis of Barnard's theory to the effect that every member of an organization has a dual personality: an organizational personality and an individual one. The former concerns the way in which an individual performs his or her tasks, which in principle pertains to an impersonal and replaceable role. The individual personality, on the other hand, concerns the individual's motives, the delicate and changeable balance created between his/her contribution to the organization and the benefits that s/he receives in return. The relationship between the two personalities may vary profoundly. There are cases where an individual's commitment to an organization is so strong and complete that his/her individual personality tends to merge with that of the organization. There are other cases where the individual personality is very different from, or even opposed to, the organizational personality (Barnard cites the example of a pacifist conscripted into military service during a war). Whatever the case may be, the relation between organizational and individual personality is a problem, and recognition of this problem is one of the points around which Barnard's theory rotates.

The distinction between organizational aims and personal motives prompts Barnard to identify two different dimensions in organizational action: effectiveness and efficiency. Effectiveness measures the extent to which the organization achieves its objectives, whilst efficiency measures the extent to which personal motives for joining an organization are satisfied. It should be pointed out that Barnard uses the term 'efficiency' in a sense different from the conventional one. In common parlance, efficiency has to do with the relationship between the cost of an investment and the profits deriving therefrom. Barnard uses the term to denote the degree of satisfaction that individuals gain from the relation between the contribution that they believe they are making to the organization and the moral and material payment that they receive in return.

Although effectiveness and efficiency are not necessarily linked, their combination can give rise to four different patterns, so that an organization may be:

1. effective and efficient, which is the optimum result;
2. effective but not efficient, when the organization achieves its objectives but does not satisfy its members;

1. *In particular, this is the explanation given by Talcott Parsons*

3. not effective but efficient, when the organization does not achieve its objectives but satisfies its members;
4. neither effective nor efficient, which is the worst situation.

These four patterns suggest that the optimum solution of maximum effectiveness combined with maximum efficiency is extremely difficult to accomplish. The most common situation is the one in which the quest for effectiveness and efficiency generates tension and problems. Barnard consequently views reconciliation of the two terms as being the crucial task set for the management of any organization. Barnard's awareness of the difficulty inherent in creating a satisfactory cooperative system induces him to conclude that stable cooperation is not normal but abnormal:

> "Those that we see from day to day are the survivors that have been successful among innumerable failures...... The majority of cooperations fail in the attempt, or die in infancy or are short-lived. In our Western civilization only the Roman Catholic Church has reached a considerable age. Some universities, a few national governments and some formally organized countries are a little more than 200 years old. Some communities are a little older, but very few other organizations have existed for more than 100 years." (pp. 16-17).

In the light of the precariousness of the lives of organizations, Barnard develops a model which he calls the economy of incetives and persuasion. He writes: "the net satisfactions that induce a man to contribute his effort to an organization derive from weighing up the advantages and disadvantages of that contribution" (p. 130). If the benefits that individuals believe they will receive outweigh the costs, they will continue to participate and contribute; if not, they will decide to leave the organization. The organization has two instruments with which to secure the efforts necessary for its existence: the incentives system, and the persuasion system. Incentives are objective factors intended to fulfil people's expectations, and they may be both material and moral: pay, career opportunities, physical conditions, and the social environment in which work takes place are the more common examples of material incentives. Among moral incentives Barnard lists the prestige of the organization, and what he calls attractive association' that is, the absence of racial, social or religious discrimination.

But incentives are not always sufficient for an organization to obtain its members' stable contribution. It must therefore also use persuasion. This operates on the subjective side of the relationship between people and organizations, because it seeks to alter existing expectations and to instill new motives in individuals. The purpose of persuasion is "to change the desires of a sufficient number of people so that the incentives offered become adequate" (p. 137). Thus, the organization not only has the possibility of fulfilling existing motivations; it can also act upon personal motives – that is, change people so that their desire to collaborate is increased. Among the instruments of persuasion, Barnard cites coercion, ideological or political mobilization in pursuit of certain general objectives, schooling, and personal education. He points out that coercion is the least efficient of these means, while his sympathies lie fully with education.

4. THE SUBJECTIVIST FOUNDATION OF VALUE AND THE "SOLVENCY" OF THE COOPERATIVE SYSTEM

Three aspects of Barnard's model should be stressed. The first is that calculating the relationship between costs and benefits is never a purely rational operation. Barnard warns that "only occasionally is the determination of satisfaction and dissatisfaction the subject of logical thinking". There is much subjectivity in the perception of the relationship between contributions and incentives, since what is a satisfactory balance for one person may not be so for another. Involved here are what he calls the 'utility functions' of individuals, by which he means their inclinations or propensities. There are people with greater propensities to take risks and others who are more inclined towards security; people who prefer material advantages and others who seek moral satisfaction, and so on. The 'objective' situations of external reality, such as opportunities to find other employment, are always filtered through the individual's subjective perception.

The second aspect of Barnard's model is that it is not only valid economically and materially, but it also emphasizes the importance of non-material incentives in work organizations :

> "Material compensation beyond the level of subsistence is inefficient except for a limited percentage of people.....even in strictly economic organizations where you would least expect it, money without distinction, prestige or position is so clearly ineffective that it can rarely be used, even temporarily, as a stimulus for greater earning if it is accompanied by a loss of prestige.." (pp. 133-4).

Barnard's emphasis on non-material incentives should not be seen as an argument in favour of a low-wage policy. The problem is more complex, and Barnard seeks to explain it as follows:

> "Efficiency means giving money up to the point when it has greater value for the employer than for the employee, and giving further incentives that cost the employer little but have greater

value for the employee; and refusing those which damage the employer the least." (p. 226).

Barnard's model does not refer to work organizations alone, however; it has wider application to any organization based on transactions between the contributions of its members and the incentives that they receive in return. There are organizations in which the incentive to members consists in the moral satisfaction of making a contribution: in a humanitarian organization, for example, the members work gratuitously to help the needy, and they find their gratification, and therefore their motivation for continuing as members of the association, in the act itself of helping others. But in their relations with for-profit organizations, those same people may evaluate in materialistic terms whether or not to maintain those relations, and they may consequently change or cease their participation.

Finally, the third aspect concerns the 'solvency' of the cooperative system with regard to its members. It might be objected that if the members of an organization expect from it an equal or greater contribution than the incentive they receive, then the organization is destined for early insolvency. Barnard meets this objection with two arguments. The first, of a more economic nature, is that the overall weight of an organization is not the sum of the contributions of its individual members, but rather that sum multiplied by a certain coefficient related to the fact that the organization is a cooperative system. Cooperation multiplies the value of individual contributions and enables the organization to give individual members more than they have given. The second argument concerns the subjective nature of the value attributed to the contributions made and to the incentives received. Apart from the fact that it is extremely difficult to give an 'objective' value to a particular job, Barnard's emphasis on non-material incentives enables him to deal with the question of the solvency of an organization in terms that not are strictly economic, but more broadly symbolic and moral.

5. AUTHORITY AND "AREA OF INDIFFERENCE"

A cooperative system and an effective balance between contributions and incentives do not arise spontaneously within organizations. Creating them is the task of an authority, which to be recognized as such must be legitimate and competent. Legitimacy is greatest when the authority does not resort to the coercion of subordinates but instead uses incentives with moral value. At the same time, competence entails that subordinates recognize that the orders which they receive conform to codes of effectiveness and procedural correctness. In particular, the order received must:

- be understood;

- not seem to be at odds with the general and recognized aims of the organization;
- be compatible with the legitimate interests of the people to whom it is addressed;
- the people to whom the order is given are able to execute it.

(Note the difference between Weber and Barnard on this point. Like Weber, Barnard regards competence and compliance with formal orders as the prerequisites for an order to be recognized as legitimate. But Barnard goes further than Weber in specifying the conditions under which subordinates can actually execute an order. This specification is indicative of the close attention that Barnard pays to the relationship between organization and employees).

Barnard then investigates the specific terrain on which authority is exercised, identifying it as the distinction between the goal of the organization and the motives of the individual. However intense the motives that induce an individual to cooperate may be, Barnard believes it unrealistic to expect individuals to identify completely with an organization. He maintains that executives must set themselves the practical objective of managing the relationship between contribution and incentive in such a way that subordinates extend their area of willingness to obey the orders of their superiors. This is not an easy task, however, because the tasks that an organization requires of its members may provoke different responses. Barnard writes:

"If we set out all the orders for reasonable jobs according to their acceptability to the interested parties, we can imagine that there are a number of clearly unacceptable ones, that is, that they will not be obeyed; then there is another group on a more or less neutral line, that is either just acceptable or just unacceptable; then there is the third group of undeniably acceptable. This last group is in the "zone of indifference". This will be larger or smaller according to the degree in which the incentives outweigh the obligations and sacrifices that determine the individual's adherence to the organization;" (p. 153).

Expanding the area of 'indifference' – that is, the area of willingness to obey orders – is therefore the realistic objective that those in authority must seek to achieve with regard to their subordinates (in modern terminology we might say that the objective of a business is to maximize work flexibility). Barnard thus avoids basing the individual/organizational relationship on a utopian 'corporate mystique', a mix of organizational ends and individual motives.

It is true that cooperative action must be based on the primacy of moral incentives; but such primacy does not entail that individual motives must be subordinated to organizational ends. It is not necessary for employees to love their work; only that they do it out of a sense of duty and professionalism. This realistic choice is flanked with recognition that individuals have private spaces, interests and multiple loyalties; and that they therefore reject the totalitarian demands of a single organization, at work or anywhere else. The broader the area of employee willingness to obey orders, the more effective the authority becomes. But the area of consent also expresses the degree of efficiency (in Barnard's sense of the term): the greater the extent to which individual motives are satisfied, the wider the range of jobs that individuals are willing to undertake.

6. THE FUNCTIONS OF EXECUTIVES AND THEIR PERSONALITY

Having established that expanding the area of willingness to collaborate is the main task of authority in an organization, Barnard moves to the examination of the specific functions that an executive must perform.

First and the most important function is ensuring that an efficient communications system is in place. This priority is consistent with Barnard's view of organizations, where, as we have seen, communication among people is the prime requisite for the existence itself of a social group. Not only must the executive ensure that communications circulate, s/he must also create a general structure of roles, and therefore appoint employees able to guarantee the flow of communications. Establishing an efficient communications system is to lay the foundations for the smooth operation of the organization.

The executive's second function is to guarantee a regular and constant flow of the resources necessary for the organization's operations. The most important resources are human ones, that is, the members collaborating with the organization. But the members are not only the actors within the organization – employees or those enrolled with it – but all those who have relations with the organization, such as suppliers, customers, shareholders, and so on.

The third function of the executive is to define the aims of the organization. It may come as a surprise to find that Barnard puts in third place a function generally considered to be the main task of an executive. His decision to do so can be explained in the light of the meaning that he attaches to the concept of aims, which he defines as all actions in which the effectiveness of the cooperative system is verified. Barnard sees the goal of an organization as being, not a single act of will imposed from above, but a process which involves all the members of organization. The members are mobilized in pursuit of increasingly specific aims until defining the goal is the same as specifying the work to be done. Determining the aims therefore becomes a widely distributed function, of which only the most general part pertains to the management.

This view of the purpose of the organization as a widely distributed process involving the cooperative system in its entirety is linked to Barnard's emphasis on the pre-eminence of communicational aspects over decisional ones in the executive's role. A good executive chooses to ensure the balance of the cooperative system by means of discreet actions, instead of laying down the law. Barnard writes that:

> "The executive's delicate art of decision taking consists in not deciding which problems are not important now, in not deciding pre-maturely, in not taking decisions that cannot be taken effectively, and in not taking decisions that others could". (p. 174).

The figure depicted by Barnard is a 'gray' executive, less inclined towards self-promotion with attention-grabbing decisions, and more aware that managing is not only deciding but communicating, mediating, representing, coordinating and motivating. Barnard also places great importance on what he calls non-logical qualities: intuition, creativity, the ability to discern hidden connections. But what sort of personality does an executive of this kind have? Contrary to the belief that impartiality and cynicism are required for command, Barnard stresses that the gifts of command are a moral complexity and an above-average sense of responsibility. By 'moral complexity' he means reliance on a variety of codes of behaviour governing different spheres of public and private social relations. However, the more moral codes there are in the personality of an individual, the greater the likelihood of interior conflicts and dilemmas. Being in charge and behaving consistently require a sense of responsibility which Barnard defines as "the ability of an individual to render whatever morality he possesses effective in his conduct" (p. 235).

The sense of responsibility is therefore a 'meta-code' (that is, a code governing other codes) which guarantees adherence to a principle during inevitable moral dilemmas. In the case of an executive, the sense of responsibility can also be seen as the expression of a marked 'organizational personality', as opposed to the 'individual personality' with its inevitable doubts and hesitations. This again reflects the dualism between the aims of the organization and individual motives that characterizes all of Barnard's thought: he identifies the capacity to mediate among the conflicts arising from this dualism as the basis for the leader's legitimacy.

It was said at the outset that Barnard's thought reflects his professional life as an executive. It is precisely the distinction between organizational aims and personal motives that can be considered the most important expression of that experience. Barnard, an executive working for the success of a company he does not own, describes the complexity deriving from the constant tension between the organizational personality that induces him to identify with the company and the individual personality that passes impersonal judgment on his work and himself. Barnard's implicit reference to his work as an executive helps us understand why he prefers mediation and the search for consensus over autocratic decisions. Barnard knows from direct experience that executives may have to deal with both employees and the owners, and that they consequently require constant legitimization if they are to carry through their ideas and maintain their autonomy. The theory of organization as a cooperative system in which all the members are governed by the logic of an equal relationship between contributions and incentives provides the basis for that legitimization.

7. SIMON: BOUNDED RATIONALITY AND DECISION MAKING PROCESSES

Barnard laid the foundations for what would become one of the most widely debated and studied themes of organizational research – the relationship between organizations and the actors that constitute them. An author whose work can in many ways be seen as a development and completion of Barnard is Herbert Simon (1916-2001).

A Nobel laureate in economics, a sociologist, one of the founders of cognitive psychology and the analysis of decision-making processes, as well as one of the first analysts to recognize the revolution that information technology would bring to the management of complex organizations, Simon acknowledges his debt to Barnard on two points: (i) organizations must be viewed as cooperative instruments with which to extend the range of achievable goals in human actions; (ii) the balance between contributions and incentives is the essential condition for the existence of organizations.

But Simon does not restrict himself to consideration of the motives that induce actors to cooperate. He shifts the focus of analysis to a higher and more abstract level: that of decisions or, more precisely, decision-making processes within organizations. Decisions, he maintains, are taken on the basis of *bounded rationality*. This is a universal condition that applies to both the decisions that actors take in the name and on behalf of the organization in which they operate, and the decisions that they take in private life, including those relative to their membership of that organization. Thus, the motives that induce actors to contribute to organizations, which Barnard identified as the chief subject-matter of organizational analysis, are linked by Simon to the broader category of decisions.

The notion that decisions are taken on the basis of bounded rationality is, therefore, a highly unifying concept. Firstly, it posits the continuity of the human condition from the most complex and formal organizations down to the most intimate and private sphere. The instruments and procedures of decision-making change according to the situation; but the fact remains that, as a rule, any decision, be it public or private, is taken in recognition that absolute rationality is impossible, and therefore with acceptance of a margin of risk, conjecture and subjectivity. Second, the view that decision-making processes should be the principal concern of organizational analysis entails that study of what happens within the organizations must begin with the actions of individuals.

The continuity of Simon's theory with respect to Barnard's, and also its development by the latter, is thus apparent. When studying organizations, it is not enough to consider individual motives for participating; the researcher must start from the consideration that it is the actors themselves who construct organizations, doing so in the most rational way possible but also with all the intrinsic limitations of their rationality. Simon's views can also be read as warning against considering organizations to be entities with lives of their own independent of human action. This cannot be so, because organizations, however big and complex, are always the result of human initiative. This must be borne in mind when one seeks to understand their successes, defects and failures.

Simon's point of departure (1947) is a criticism of the management literature of his time, which he accuses of not furnishing valid tools with which to analyze organizational behaviour. That literature viewed organizations as structures made up of numerous roles inter-linked by formal channels of communication and command. Its main concern was to prescribe the work content of roles, and to describe organizations by means of hierarchical diagrams consisting of numerous little boxes, each corresponding to a role. Simon points out that such organizational diagrams say nothing about the real life of an organization, and that the concept of role is too generic to furnish any information on the actual behaviour of actors. For example, all the responsibilities of a personnel manager can be itemized, but, however, detailed the list may be, it cannot convey the concrete choices that specific managers make in the everyday management of their role.

Understanding real organizational behaviour requires us to alter our point of view and start, not from the formal organizational structure, but from the persons who work within it, viewing them as actors who constantly take decisions.[2] The prime subject of organizational analysis is not the role but the decision. The decision, writes Simon, is a much smaller and subtler analytical unit than the role, and it depends on a great many factors that must be examined. Studying how a group of people behaves within an organization requires us to view the latter as "a structure that provides everyone belonging to the group with a large part of the information, bases, objectives and attitudes that influence their decisions" (1947, p. 14). It is, therefore, necessary to create a theoretical framework within which to study how information, constraints, procedures, and individual motivations all contribute to decision-making.

2. The central importance of decisions as the object of analysis is not in contrast with Barnard's thesis that the art of the executive lies in not taking premature decisions that cannot be effective or that cannot be taken by others. Simon works on a general theoretical level, Barnard on the level of practical opportunities in the exercise of authority.

Simon places the principle of *bounded rationality* at the base of this framework. Barnard insisted on the physical limitations that induce people to cooperate in achieving goals otherwise impossible for single individuals (the parable of the rock). Simon resumes Barnard's discussion of human limitations but shifts its emphasis to mental limitations. In contrast to classical economic theory, which views humans as perfectly rational, aware of all possible choices, and endowed with a system of certain preferences, Simon underlines the factors that restrict human rationality.

There are objective limitations deriving from the fact that, although we may wish to weigh up the pros and cons of a decision, it is not possible to foresee all the consequences once that decision has been taken, because many of the consequence are indirect and remote. There are cognitive limitations in that humans have preferences and convictions which induce them to choose from a restricted range of solutions, ignoring *a priori* others that may be more effective but are not appreciated or familiar. There are then the ethical, cultural and emotional limitations apparent in the uncertainty and ambiguity of the criteria used to take decisions. And there are social limitations deriving from the fact that when several people are involved in taking a decision, compromises between different, and sometimes opposing, criteria and preferences must often be made; and compromises are contrary to the criteria of pure rationality.

The result is that the majority of decisions are taken in accordance, not with the criterion of greatest efficiency but with that of sufficiency. And this is the only criterion that allows action to be taken, whereas obstinately continuing the search for the optimum solution almost always leads to paralysis. Simon explains:

> The choice of the optimum alternative requires processes that are much more complex than the ordinary processes for choosing the satisfactory alternative. For example, think of the difference between looking in a haystack for the sharpest needle and searching through the same haystack for a sharp enough needle to sew with." (1958, p. 176).

This criterion holds true for both the micro-decisions that actors take in their private lives and for the more complex decisions that they take in the name and on behalf of organizations. There is no difference in principle from this point of view: humans act on the base of criteria of bounded rationality in all situations.

8. THE ENDS-MEANS CONTINUUM

It is necessary to examine how the decision-making process actually evolves. Simon's first step is to distinguish between two broad categories of judgments: those of fact and those of value. Factual judgments concern events that have happened or are predicted in the real world, and it is always possible to verify whether they are true or false (e.g. yesterday in Rome the minimum temperature was 16 degrees; rain is forecast for tomorrow). Value judgments instead express a preference for a certain situation. The preference may be ethical, aesthetic, ideological or emotional, but whatever the case may be, it is not possible to verify empirically whether these judgments are true or false. They can be accepted or rejected only on the basis of other value judgments, not on the basis of scientific verification.

The distinction between factual judgments and value judgments seems straightforward. But as soon as we begin to observe real human behaviour, we find that the two types of judgment are so closely interconnected that distinguishing between them becomes difficult, if not impossible. And it is in the study of decisions that the link seems indissoluble. In principle, decisions can be divided between those concerning the means to achieve an end, these being based on factual judgements, and those concerning the ends, which are based on value judgments. To give a simple example, the decision to take a plane instead of a ship to go on holiday in Greece is based; on the factual judgment of the convenience of the means (a plane is quicker, cheaper, etc.). But the decision to go on holiday in Greece rather than Sweden concerns an end, and it is based on a value judgment (I prefer the Mediterranean sea to the Scandinavian forests and lakes). Whilst a judgment on the convenience of means can be disproved, the judgment of preference for one place rather than another belongs to the sphere of taste, not to that of truth or falsehood.

In real decision-making processes, the distinction is not so simple, however. Simon maintains that there is always a continuum between ends and means, in the sense that a given end achieved on the basis of a value decision is then transformed into a means to reach the next end. To take an example from student life, taking the bus in the morning is a means to attend lectures at the university. Attending lectures is a means to pass examinations. Passing examinations is a means to acquire a degree. And a degree, usually considered the end of the course of studies, can be seen as a means to find a job. But the chain does not end there, because even the job can in its turn be considered a means to achieve financial security, social standing, personal satisfaction, and so on. Every action always has two sides to it: it is the end of the preceding action and at the same time a means for the next, in a largely continuous chain.

The ends-means continuum prompts some important considerations. The first is that the merit of an aim cannot be evaluated by separating it from the means necessary to achieve it. The ends do not justify the means, warns Simon, and the desirability of ends cannot be defined by removing the means chosen to reach them. If the available means are too costly, dangerous or illegal, actors may decide not to pursue the ends. Value judgments on ends can thus be changed into more general judgments on their context, and new ends may emerge as the ends-means continuum advances. The continuum should be seen as a process that constantly redefines itself as the actors evaluate the consequences of their actions.

A second consideration (which does not contradict the first but supplements it) is that acting in a chain of decisions where the preceding ones are instrumental to the ones that follow gives coherence to human behavior and enables the claim that it is oriented by rational criteria. Simon defines rationality as "the selection of alternatives of preferred behaviour in relation to a system of values on the basis of which it is possible to evaluate the consequences of that behaviour" (1947, p. 137). But coherence between ends and means is not only an expression of rationality; it also moulds the social identity itself of the individual, his/her character, and his/her image. There is a great deal of subjectivity in human rationality. Simon puts it as follows: "What a person wants and loves influences what a person sees, and what he sees influences what he wants and loves" (1958, p. 189).

A third consideration is that, because of the boundedness of human rationality, the end/means chain is always vague and incomplete. The chain may be quite precise over a relatively short period, but the more distant the end, the weaker and more elusive the concatenation among actions becomes. The connection between everyday activity and final ends is often unclear. Rationality illuminates only a part of the continuum, which then enters the darkness of the unsaid, the ambiguous, the not yet decided. This is true of both actors and organizations. In the latter, people nearly always work on limited programmes with mid-term objectives whose overall rationale is rarely questioned. Often, everything is known about a given procedure but nothing is known about the wider continuum of which it is part. It is not only employees in routine jobs that are ignorant; also managers, who have a view of the ends-means connections broader than of their employees, have only limited understanding. The limitation is rooted not so much in the division of labour as in the human impossibility of achieving total understanding of the ends-means continuum.

9. CRITICAL AND ROUTINE DECISIONS: THE IMPORTANCE OF PROCEDURES

Simon's discussion concerns both individual and organizational decisions. But what is it that makes organizational decisions distinctive ? What is the difference between how actors take private decisions and how they take decisions in the name and on behalf of an organization? One could answer in principle that the main difference lies in the complexity of organizational decisions, in that these normally involve more people, are more formal, follow set procedures, and have socially more important consequences than decisions taken in private life.

But if we are to ground these differences in theory, we must take account of the preceding discussion on organizations seen as instruments to extend the area of goals achievable by human action. We may say that whilst Barnard concentrates on the physical limitations that induce people to cooperate, Simon mainly considers the mental limitations that do so. This differing emphasis on human limitations has an important consequence for organizational analysis. For Simon, the organization is a cooperative system which not only coordinates the tasks of its members in achieving certain goals but also conserves and accumulates the memory of that coordination, together with the decisions taken, the results achieved, the experience acquired, the errors committed, and so on. An organization is a cooperative system that exists and evolves over time. Time is essential for the development of a learning process which makes it possible to select and codify the stock of knowledge useful for dealing with the various types of problem that the organization encounters.

One of the most effective ways to expand bounded rationality is to draw upon past experience. If complex goals are to be set, it is not enough for actors to work in a group. It should not be necessary to take new decisions for every single act, and actors should be able to rely as far as possible on procedures: that is, predefined decision sequences based on experience and calculation. This applies just as much to routine activities like using a machine according to the technical instructions as it does to more critical situations where strategic decisions are taken only after a series of feasibility studies and analysis of the economic pay-off from the project.

Procedures are important so that decisions are as programmed as possible. In the case of routine decisions, it suffices to decide at the outset which programme to activate, bearing in mind that there are norms which regulate the passage from one programme to another, and secondary procedures with which to continue and revise programmes. But even in the case of critical decisions, which by definition are less programmed, organizations possess an inventory of predefined guidelines with which to establish the minimum criteria to apply in the decision-making process. Even in the extreme case of entirely new decisions, which must be taken in unknown or exceptionally complicated circumstances, the decision-makers try to keep to methodological procedures.

Thus apparent is a second function of procedures. Their purpose is not only to provide frameworks within which to address the problems that arise in the lives of organizations; but also to serve to *cushion the uncertainty* of those who must decide. Uncertainty exists when there is no certain proof of the validity or reliability of the data available: an unpredictable market, an unexpected increase in costs, an unusual malfunction, etc. In these cases, behaviour intended to maximize certainty would require decisions to be suspended until all the factors which provoked the anomaly have been analyzed. But more often than not, complete exploration is not possible because it would entail intolerable costs and delays. Consequently, a decision is taken on the basis of indicators that stand in the stead of certain proof but which have been shown to be acceptable by previous calculations and experiences. Simon writes that "rational behavior requires simple models that contain the essential elements of the problem without reflecting the whole complexity" (1958, p. 212). Procedures serve precisely this purpose.

All this provides important insights into human behaviour. Decisions are taken in order to find a satisfactory solution, not an optimal one. Decisions are taken progressively, one problem at a time. Decisions are taken by choosing among the options for action already available in the organization's inventory. Finally, the action programme selected is executed in semi-independence from other programmes. Loose connections among the various parts of an organization are indispensable for it to function. If all the parts were rigidly interconnected, the resulting complexity would paralyse all activities. Although beneficial, organizational coordination must never go beyond the critical threshold where it turns into rigidity. Nevertheless, this threshold is often exceeded, or at least very closely approached, which illustrates the complexity of the principle of bounded rationality. Actors seek to act in the most rational way possible; but at the same time organizational rigidity and dysfunctions manifest the boundedness of their rationality; it is like looking at a curve from both sides, concave and the convex.

10. ROY: A CONTRIBUTION FROM INDUSTRIAL SOCIOLOGY

Barnard explains the functioning of organizations on the basis of the relationship between contributions and incentives. Simon integrates Barnard's theory by underlining the boundedness of human rationality and the predominance of criteria of sufficiency over those of optimality when decisions are taken. Both authors are convinced that it is impossible to study organizations unless the analysis begins with the actions of the actors who contribute to the lives of those organizations. The generality of their arguments takes Barnard and Simon to an extremely abstract level of thought. But it is precisely their capacity to offer general theoretical models that has made their contribution milestones in organizational theory. It is no exaggeration to say that nearly all research in the second half of the twentieth century made more or less explicit and direct reference to their theories.

Unlike Weber, Barnard and Simon do not propose ideal-typical models of how an organization works. They do not envisage pure types of bureaucrats or executives; they are more concerned to reflect on the general conditions that render the existence of an organization possible. Consequently, in their case there is no need to raise the question, as we did with Weber, of the extent to which their theories are viable, or requires modification, in the light of subsequent historical developments. Nevertheless, it is opportune to extend the discussion to certain studies that fill out the above theories with both the depth of empirical research and the extent of new theoretical developments. The first study comes from industrial sociology and concerns the various ways in which workers respond to financial incentives to increase production.

Industrial sociology – a constant source of information and insight for organizational theories – flourished in the middle decades of the twentieth century, in parallel with the maximum expansion of the Taylorist-Fordist production regime. As already mentioned in Chapter 1, the central research concern of industrial sociology was the workers' response to Taylorism and whether it was possible, first to attenuate, and then go beyond that production regime. Accordingly, the limitations of Taylorist rationalization, and the extent of worker resistance to/acceptance of management's endeavor to obtain maximum production, are two themes that lend themselves well to interpretation using Barnard's and Simon's models. The intensity of the situations examined, often with the crude and spontaneous language of the factory, gives dramatic life to the information, affording the reader an extraordinary conceptual bridge between the world of toil and subterfuge and the rarefied academic purity of the theoretical models.

Of the many industrial sociologists who studied factories, Donald Roy (1911-1980) is certainly among those who give the most vivid descriptions. Spending a year as a worker in a machine production factory enabled him to be a participant observer and to gather extraordinarily rich ethnographic material (1952, 1953, 1954, 1960). In those years, there was no automation at the factory, and workers operated single machines (lathes, milling machines, grinders, etc.) which required dexterity and constant effort. To obtain maximum production, the management had adopted an individual piecework system by which the workers, if they exceeded a certain level of daily output, received a bonus approximately proportional to the extra pieces produced. In theory, this system was fair and rational, rewarding the best and stimulating the others to imitate them. It was founded on two assumptions: that fair and precise measurement can be made of all jobs and of the corresponding pay, and that employees work only for financial reasons. Consequently, it was assumed that that only social relationships that counted were formal ones, and that management could expect a homogenous and continuous flow of reliable information.

Roy's research uncovered a much more complex world, one far removed from the above assumptions. Four important points can be identified in his analysis. The first is that the piecework system was the source of constant conflict and a deep-rooted, radical, lack of trust between workers and management. Particularly hated by the workers were the timekeepers who recorded work times and were seen as servants of the owners out to 'swindle' the workers by setting excessively high rhythms. The workers and the time-study men waged an underhand war which consisted of reciprocal ruses and cheating ("I'll cheat you because you want to cheat me"). The workers invented pointless movements so as to appear busy while the timekeepers were watching them, and the latter spied on the workers in order to compare their work rates. Roy reports the advice that Starkey, a veteran in the factory, gives to Tennessee, a recently hired worker, on how to defend himself against the time-and-motion men:

If you expect to get any kind of a price you got to outwit that son-of-a-bitch! You got to use your noodle while you are working and think your work out ahead as you go along! You got to add in movements you know you ain't going to make when you 're running the job! Remember if you don't screw them, they are going to screw you....Every movement counts!"

"Another thing", said Starkey, "You were running that job too damn fast before they timed you. I was watching you yesterday . If you don't run a job slow before you get timed, you won't get a good price. They'll look at the record of what you do before they come around and compare it with the timing speed. Those time-study men are sharp..........

"I wasn't going very fast" exclaimed Tennessee "Hell, I was going as slowly as I could without wearing myself out slowing down"

" Well, maybe, it just looked fast, because we were going so steady at it" said Starkey

"I don't see how I could of run it any slower" said Tennessee " I stood there as I was practically paralyzed!".

Remember that these bastards are paid to screw you" said Starkey. "And that's all they got to think about. They'll stay up half the night figuring out how to beat you out of a dime. They figure you're going to try to fool them, so they make allowance for that. They set the prices low enough to allow for what you do".

" Well, then what the hell chance have I got?" asked Tennessee.

"It's up to you to figure out how to fool them more than they allow for " said Starkey....

Always keep in mind the fact that you can't make money if you do not do the job that way it is timed. They time jobs just to give you your base rate if you kill yourself trying to make it, no more...

Yeah, but what if they make you speed it up to maximum speed? What are you going to do then? asked Tennessee.

You got to be tough with them ! said Starkey. "Remember those guys don't know their ass from a hole in the ground as far as these machines are concerned. When they tell me to speed up to about what I figure I can run the job, I start to take my apron off, and tell them: All right, if you think it can be run that fast, you run it! They usually come around ... (1955, pp. 15-16).

Elsewhere, Roy describes a group of workers mounting a metal framework. They had discovered that by tightening some bolts first, the frame twisted so that it took longer to screw up the other bolts. Naturally, the workers used this strategy only when the timekeepers were watching. But it is wrong to believe that their aim was only to work less; their principal motive was to keep management in the dark about real work times and so be able to obtain the piecework bonus. If the timekeepers had discovered the real times, management would certainly have raised the piecework rates, with a consequent reduction in pay.

The second important point is that the workers' response to the piecework system was very different to what the management envisaged. In the production statistics, the workers' performances were clustered at two points, a very high one above the threshold for the bonus, the other much lower. This meant that the workers were responding in two very different ways to the same piecework system. On one hand they accepted it to the extreme limits of their abilities; on the other they rejected it and stayed well below the quotas fixed.

How can we explain these different behaviours? Roy looks for the answers in both the imperfections of the system and the differing attitudes of the workers. The piecework system was imperfect mainly because of the blockage of information caused by worker resistance. Because the workers did everything possible to conceal real work times, the time-and-motion men evaluated the work done in the workshops approximately, and using unequal criteria. Consequently, the workers had divided the work into two broad categories: greavy and stinker jobs. The stinker jobs were those where it was difficult to earn the bonus, while the greavy ones were those where it was relatively easy to fulfil the piecework rate. The workers knew that they would not fulfil the quota in the stinker jobs, so they refused *a priori* even to try, and took things easy; in the greavy jobs, on the other hand, they were motivated to do the maximum to earn more pay.

But there was another influential factor, this one to do with the individuality of the workers, who Roy divides into two categories: the *rate busters* and the *goldbrickers*. The former constantly sought to earn the bonus, while the latter preferred a more relaxed work rate to extra money. Because the foremen knew the different attitudes of their workers, the rate busters were assigned the jobs in which it was easier to earn the bonus, while the goldbrickers were given the other jobs. The result of this practice was a further separation between the workers' two responses to the piecework system.

The third point to stress is that the differences in the use of the piecework system did not arise solely out of individual conflicts between workers and timekeepers; they also sprang from a complicity network involving other actors. Maintenance staff, trolley-pushers, sometimes even the foremen, informally conspired to justify delays and help the workers get the bonus. Anticipating or delaying the supply of material, declaring a longer repair time for a machine than necessary so that the worker could produce more pieces, and hiding already-made pieces under the bench, bringing them out on the next shift, were some of the ruses used to meet production rates, while at the same time making life in the workshop more human. The foremen played a decisive role by constantly mediating between the demands of the management and their desire to maintain the workers' support. Roy describes one foreman who altered working times so that his workers could earn the bonus, or declared stoppages for technical reasons so that they could make up for lost production. This complicity was not merely an act of personal generosity, it was part of a continuous negotiation of production in return for favours.

Finally, the fourth point concerns the entire system of worker motivation. Roy discovered that, although the workers constantly talked about their works in terms of money, the reasons for their commitment were not purely financial. As he worked with the machines for nearly a year, Roy acquired some tricks of the trade and was able to work at rates that he had at first thought impossible. Consequently, the job that he had initially found unbearably boring became a sort of pleasant competition against himself, where the prize was fulfilling the quota within a certain time.

Roy conducts long and subtle analysis of the forms that these 'production games' took and their consequences on relations in the workshop. A combination of formal and informal rules, material and symbolic incentives, and legal and illegal cooperation enabled the workers to 'make out', that is, fulfil the production rates in a sort of obstacle race to be completed within a certain time limit. The production game consisted in maneuvering among rules and regulations so as to reach the final goal as quickly as possible, but still respecting the quality standards imposed by the hierarchy, which the workers accepted as one of the difficulties in the game. These sporting aspects show that the piecework contract was not just an economic incentive, but a much more complex mechanism that comprised not only gain but also the pleasure of transforming the job into a game of skill. Winning the game meant having a few extra minutes of free time, acquiring importance in the eyes of colleagues and, above all, exacting revenge against the factory hierarchy, especially the hated time-and-motion men..

11. RE-READING ROY IN THE LIGHT OF BARNARD AND SIMON. FURTHER DEVELOPMENTS IN INDUSTRIAL SOCIOLOGY

Roy's analysis raises an important theoretical problem: how can his results be interpreted in the light of Barnard and Simon's models? As far as Barnard is concerned, the results seem to be a surprising refutation of the view that the factory is based on cooperation and consensus. Roy emphasizes the importance of the informal sphere, but formal and informal aspects would seem to be much more in conflict than Barnard suggests. The informal does not appear to be the harmonious counterweight to the formal, but rather the arena in which workers mount their resistance. The profound reciprocal mistrust between workers and timekeepers (I'll cheat you because I know you want to cheat me) conflicts with the image of the factory as a cooperative system. Barnard views communication as the prerequisite for cooperation, but Roy underlines the workers' desire to block information in order to conceal the ruses used to slow work down when times were being recorded, and also to speed it up when there was no supervision. The piecework system, which should have been be the hub around which the entire relation between contributions and incentives revolved, seems to have been an inefficient and unreliable system subject to constant manipulation from both sides.

Certainly, Roy's description belies any idyllic conception of the factory. The place he depicts is a place of forced labour, in many ways similar to a jail, where rigid bureaucracy and the bending of the rules, complicity and coercion, favours and pretence, are intertwined. Between a management pushing for maximum production and workers resorting to every device to limit their exploitation, there was an irremediable conflict of interests.

But who ever said that Barnard proposes an idyllic vision of organizations, and of factories in particular? This is a superficial reading of Barnard, for he repeatedly stresses the extreme difficulty of creating cooperative systems, and he is careful not to give the impression that cooperation is the same as altruism and sentimentality. Fundamental to Barnard's conception is recognition that actors have personalities and interests unconnected to the aims of the organization of which they are members. Consequently, management cannot expect them to be totally dedicated to the achievement of those aims; it can only seek to widen what he calls the area of consent conditional on a satisfactory balance being struck between contribution and motivation. It should also be noted that Barnard's insistence that incentives are not merely financial is entirely congruent with the production games described by Roy. Roy's research is a major advance in understanding the world of the factory; it does not gainsay Barnard's theoretical model but prompts a re-reading of it.

It is easier to relate Roy's analysis to Simon's theory. Everything in Roy's factory seems to be performed under bounded rationality: approximation, compromise, ambiguity, and impromptu adjustment characterize everyday production practices. All together, these practices form a cooperative system with its regulations and procedures; and it is a system that works, despite its defects, because it continues to exist. It is especially interesting to conduct a reading *à la* Simon of Roy's analysis of the endless shuttle between attempts by management to impose tighter controls on the production process and the workers' attempts to evade them. Commenting on Roy's analysis, Whyte writes (1955):

> The management imposes a system of incentives. The workers do not respond according to theory. So the management sets up new rules in the effort to meet that response. But because the new rules upset consolidated ways of working, the workers, and sometimes the foremen, look for shortcuts. When management issues its orders from above without understanding the real shopfloor situation and without consultation, the workers always find a way of responding, even with sabotage. When management discovers that the problems are still there, it often reacts by imposing new rules. New rules lead to new ways of evading them, which in turn lead to more new rules in an apparently endless game.

What Roy's analysis confutes is the ingenuous view, sometimes put forward by diehard Marxists, that the factory is the place where Capital, as a personified entity, reproduces itself with unrelenting rationality. Roy's endeavour to analyze the organization of a factory starting from people – be they workers, foremen, timekeepers or executives – investigating their interests, resources and strategies, is entirely in harmony with Barnard and Simon, and so is deducing dynamics and social structures from this analysis.

It should not be forgotten that Roy's analysis dates to the middle of the last century. In subsequent decades, changes in technology, social relations, and managerial culture have profoundly altered the world of the factory. Thirty years after Roy, another researcher, Michael Burawoy (1979) repeated the same research in the same factory. Burawoy rediscovered the production games examined by Roy and confirmed that they were still the main factor inducing workers to produce. But this happened in a world that had changed almost entirely. The fixed wage had increased so that the increments deriving from the piecework system were less decisive than before. The distinction between lean jobs and fat jobs had diminished and workers were easily moved to jobs with higher rates. Disputes were not settled on the shopfloor but discussed in special offices. Foremen were less common than before and had less power and were more indulgent. Timekeepers were less of a worry because new technologies meant that many jobs had set times. Overall, the importance of hierarchy had diminished and the number of self-sufficient skilled workers carrying out jobs previously checked by management had increased. All this had given rise to more relaxed relations between workers and managers, but also to a more evident individualism and a greater likelihood of conflict among the workers themselves.

Burawoy published his research at the end of the 1970s, just before a new technological revolution. Since then, the advent of flexible automation, the mass diffusion of information technologies in the production process, and the use of 'intelligent machines' needing supervision, has changed workers progressively into technicians (Zubof 1984, Hirschon 1986, Bonazzi 1993). As the direct ratio between the quantity produced and the effort necessary to produce it has diminished, the equation that a firm gains more if the worker earns less, and *vice versa*, has diminished in importance. Work has become more transparent, the stratagems used by workers to defend themselves against exploitation are no longer as necessary as they were in the past (indeed, many of them can be 'sold' to management as suggestions on how to improve the production process). Obviously, differences, disputes and negotiations have not disappeared, but machine work, *as such*, is increasingly less an intrinsic source of conflict. The end of the industrial question as an acute social problem stems from the reduced number of manual workers in industry, and also from the improved working conditions of those who remain in the factories.

12. CROZIER: ACTORS' POWER AND STRATEGIES

This chapter has been devoted to the importance of individual action in understanding how organizations work, and it would not be complete without paying due attention to the work of Michel Crozier. A Frenchman, Crozier is the founder of a flourishing school of organizational studies in his country, and he has made an enormous contribution to reform of the French administrative system. If today that system is much less bureaucratic and inflexible and much more business-like and dynamic than it used to be, it is thanks to the huge influence exerted by Crozier's thought and work on the French political-administrative class.

A sentence by Crozier's is indicative of his thought: 'a man is not just an arm and not just a heart. A man is a mind, a project, a freedom'. The sentence is replete with theoretical implications. Crozier believes that the classical school's conception of employees as simple executors of hierarchical orders (the arm) is not enough to understand the workings of an organization; nor is that of the human relations school, which restricts itself to the psychology and sensibility of people (the heart). One must consider the person's mind, and acknowledge that he or she is able to think, to plan, and to make choices unforeseen by the organization in which s/he works.

This assertion encapsulates the continuity, but also the innovation, of Crozier's thought with respect to that of Barnard and Simon. While Barnard stresses that individual motives should be satisfied so that they contribute to achievement of an organization's end, Crozier completes the reasoning by pointing out that actors (be they single individuals or a group or coalition) are able to develop *strategies* within the organization. In other words, actors negotiate their participation, seeking to protect what they see as their interests. And while Simon views human rationality as bounded, Crozier points out that rationality does not pertain solely to organizations, because actors too have their private rationality, which not only does not coincide with that of the organization but may also produce behavior unforeseen by the organization itself. Whence derives the possibility of *vicious circles*, that is, degenerative processes beyond the will of actors and which give rise to dysfunctions and problems in organizations.

Linked with strategy and vicious circles is the concept of *power*, which Crozier defines as the ability to control the margins of uncertainty in one's relations with other actors. To understand this definition, one should consider the attempts made by formal organizations to establish precise rules on the work behaviour of their members. The most extreme manifestation of this rationalistic project is Taylorism, where every productive action must be standardized according to criteria based on *the one best way*. Taylorism claimed to be a perfect bureaucracy, but it was in fact a utopia. Were it to be fully realized, Crozier observes, the *one best way* would dictate how an individual should behave no matter what hierarchical level he or she occupied. Freedom of choice would be entirely eliminated, and human behaviour would become defined and predictable, with the paradoxical result that even hierarchical relationships would be meaningless.

But that is exactly what Taylorism is: a utopia. In reality, unexpected situations constantly arise, and it is impossible to make actors behave like bees in a hive. According to Crozier, power lies in these margins of unpredictability in human behaviour. Suppose that one card player knows what cards the other players are holding, but they do not know his cards. It is obvious that he has an excellent chance of winning the game, because he can predict their moves whereas his are unpredictable. The other players are uncertain, whilst he is sure. Crozier uses the example of the card game to argue that power is rooted in unequal predictability relations between two or more individuals. An individual has power over others in any situation where s/he is able to predict their moves while concealing his own.

Three important consequences ensue from this definition of power. The first is that power is different to formal authority. The latter is connected with the hierarchical level in an organization, but there is no natural relation between hierarchical level and sphere of power. Crozier claims that if someone lower in the hierarchy is able to preserve the margins of unpredictability in the way that s/he works, this gives him or her the power to elude the control of his or her superior. (A typical example is provided by technicians. These have a monopoly on knowledge, so that it is often they who define the modes and times of their work, and their superiors can only accept them). The second consequence is that someone who achieves a margin of uncertainty in his/her behaviour seeks to preserve it, and those who suffer from it seek to eliminate it or to reduce it as far as possible. Organizations are thus constantly riven by more or less explicit power struggles where the prize is the margin of uncertainty in the behaviour of given individuals. The third consequence is that the overall systematic result of these strategies may be the vicious circles mentioned above. The road to hell, Crozier is wont to repeat, is paved with good intentions.

13. BUREAUCRATIC VICIOUS CIRCLES AND INDICATIONS ON HOW TO OVERCOME THEM

Crozier became internationally famous with *The Bureaucratic Phenomenon* (1963), the book in which he sets out his research on the functions of two state administrations, an accountancy at the Finance Ministry and the Tobacco Monopoly. In many ways, the two administrations recall the Weberian model of pure bureaucracy:

(*a*) they were acephalous administrations, in the sense that their main decisions depended on an external political power (the Finance Ministry);
(*b*) the management was appointed by the political power using solely legal and bureaucratic criteria;
(*c*) the structure was highly centralized with a pyramidal hierarchy;
(*d*) all functions were governed by strict, precise and impersonal rules to which management had to adhere, with no freedom of interpretation and no autonomous initiative;
(*e*) remuneration and the assignation of responsibilities were strictly regulated according to seniority criteria, and employment was guaranteed for life.

Despite these similarities, the bureaucracy studied by Crozier is far removed from Weber's pure type. Whereas Weber maintains that bureaucracy is technically superior to any other form of administration, Crozier depicts a ponderous, inefficient bureaucracy incapable of innovation. One reason for the difference is that while Weber is concerned to furnish an ideal (and idealized) bureaucratic model, Crozier's research is empirical. It is reasonable to suppose that an important factor in the low efficiency of the bureaucracies studied by Crozier was that they did not operate in market conditions.[3] Consequently, they were not obliged to make a profit, they had no competitors, and they were not stimulated to innovate by the threat of bankruptcy or redundancies. Without external challenges, everything proceeded according to a time-honored routine. Management, bound to norms and lacking charisma, had limited responsibilities:

3. Weber does not discuss the difference between bureaucracies that operate in market conditions and those that do not. Crozier does not explicitly deal with this difference either, although his proposal to give public administration greater business capacities can be seen as a suggestion that it should operate in more competitive conditions.

ensured discipline, guaranteed service regularity, informed the ministry of the institution's needs. Workloads were regular and homogenous, defined according to consolidated practices and in agreement with the trade union, which played an important role in protecting acquired rights.

Crozier lifts the lid on those bureaucracies and asks what social relationships might develop in the context described. At the Finance Ministry, he found a frozen, stratified microcosm with no explicit conflicts but also with very few occasions for communication and social contact. Employees performed their work as prescribed by the rules; the various hierarchical levels tended to become isolated while still maintaining formal courtesy relations; open conflicts were assiduously avoided and criticisms of office malfunctions were passed impersonally to the general management, the system of norms and the ministry. The command style was both impersonal and authoritarian, with little overall efficiency. There were no technical instruments or managerial capabilities with which to change the organization; every decision in that regard was referred to the ministry in accordance with strict bureaucratic procedures.

Employees worked in a disciplined and uniform manner, but dissatisfaction with monotonous work with no prospects led to high turnover, especially among younger women. Among intermediate-level executives, frustrations caused by long years of service with no major responsibilities or recognition found outlets in job security and broad personal freedom, but also in jealous defense of every minor prerogative. At all hierarchical levels, there was a marked distaste for direct dependence and face-to-face relations between superiors and inferiors. To avoid these relations, it was customary to use written and impersonal communications.

Despite widespread individualism, there was also the logic of collective defence. At the Tobacco Monopoly, production workers were aware that they had privileges unusual for French industry, and consequently endeavoured to protect their positions in order not to lose those advantages. The result was an attitude at once complacent and aggressive, consisting of hostility to new technologies and an ideological appeal to class solidarity with the maintenance workers, the purpose being to maintain the *status quo*.

For their part, the maintenance workers exploited a small amount of power deriving from their technical knowledge and from the irregularity of the breakdowns which they had to deal with. Their monopoly of factory maintenance had also been legally sanctioned by a rule obtained by the union which forbade production workers from interfering with the machines, even for the slightest problem. This gave rise to an attitude of superiority among the maintenance workers, and their paternalism towards the production workers.

The intermediate executives were the most frustrated. Reduced to simple observers of the regulations, with no personal choice in use of their employees, and no real technical skills, their reaction was to carve out niches of small favours for their workers. This situation influenced the workers' judgment of their superiors, where personal merit did not matter, only the degree of cordiality and tolerance.

Management, too, maintained a low profile. General objectives were set by the external political power. Production methods and processes were unchanging. It was not possible to hire or fire, and jobs could not be allocated by personal discretion because a rule of seniority was in force, so that "if a post becomes free and is sought after by more than one person, it will be given to the most senior, if nobody asks for the post, it will go the most junior".

The logic of reducing personal power distributed across the hierarchy to the minimum had led to the concentration of formal responsibility at its apex, but at the same time to the removal of any real power. Crozier writes:

> Everything converges on the director and only the director has legitimate power, but his authority is paralyzed at the same time as it is absolute. Certainly, the director is the only person in the factory to have kept the formal right to take decisions. But this right gives him little influence over staff members because they do not pay him much attention; in effect, the director can only take impersonal decisions that respect all individual conditions and privileges because the interested parties almost always know in advance the content and have no reason to worry about the intentions of who is taking the decisions. Therefore the director cannot manipulate his inferiors or influence their behaviour by using the power to agree compensation because he does not have that personal power. In practice, he is a prisoner of a system that decides for him (p. 87).

Crozier wonders whether change is possible in situations such as the one he describes, and his answer is 'no'. The impossibility of change, he observes, is intrinsic to the way in which such bureaucracies are constructed. Being acephalous, he deprives them of the financial, political and technical instruments with which to decide any innovation. But also the corporate culture is hostile to change. When the predominant values in a workplace are job security and equality, Crozier notes, there is no base from which to start an innovative programme.

This does not mean, however, that within those bureaucracies there was no dissatisfaction, frustration or pressure from below to introduce reform. But because internal management could not and would not change, it merely compiled reports on internal dissatisfaction for the political authority. Faced with problems they knew about only indirectly, the Ministry and the ministerial executives reacted with the only means available to them. They issued new general orders against any form of favouritism or discretion, so as to maintain, as far as possible, the balance among the various components of the system. But the measures had exactly the opposite effect to change, since this required the delegation of responsibility to lower levels and instruments of action along the hierarchical chain. The pressure for change was, therefore, bound to cause further rigidity and fuel the vicious circle.

Crozier observes that when organizations do not possess internal corrective mechanisms, their only hope for change is collapse. If the gap between the state administration and external society becomes intolerable, there is a general and traumatic crisis. Crozier is thinking of French history, where institutional breakdowns such as the Revolution of 1789 and the Napoleonic regime, the Third Republic of 1870 and De Gaulle's Fifth Republic in 1958 occasioned massive intervention by the central power to reform, amongst other things, the public administration. The reformed bureaucracy started functioning again but still had no internal mechanisms of self-correction. It was destined to stayed trapped in the logic of alternating between long periods of stability and brief periods of change caused by crisis.

On this note, Crozier concludes *The Bureaucratic Phenomenon*, a work that reflects the state of French bureaucracy in the 1950s and 1960s. He subsequently modified his pessimistic conclusions when, also as a result of his suggestions, the political class began to reform the public administration, giving functionaries and executives greater decision-making responsibility and powers to intervene. The French State therefore embraced Crozier's idea that it is better to risk cases of incapacity and waste rather than keep society blocked by the paralysis of its administrative class.

14. ACTORS, POWER, STRUCTURES: SOME CONCLUDING REMARKS

Crozier and Roy study opposing realities. Roy explores a private company afflicted with constant problems of competition and cost reduction, sweat and toil, conflicts, manipulation of the rules, widespread distrust and covert complicity. Crozier studies two marketless state bureaucracies, without innovation and open conflict, where everything is guaranteed, routine and regulated by impersonal rules. Roy describes a colorful and dramatic world, replete with human relations; Crozier gives us a bland and boring world of rarefied and ritual relationships among people more concerned with defending their niches of minor certainties and minuscule privileges.

And yet in the history of organizational philosophy, Crozier is more important than Roy, owing to the theoretical depth of his analysis of social dynamics within a bureaucracy. Although Crozier sees very small margins of uncertainty in inter-personal relationships in the bureaucracies that he studied, they are sufficient to have him believe that such margins can be considered the expression of strategy and power. His elaboration of the concepts of strategy, and of power as control over the margins of uncertainty, has placed Crozier in the restricted circle of the classics.

Roy only gives us an evocative ethnographic description of a past world, but this does not mean that reading his work is pointless. Apart from the intrinsic importance of his direct testimony of work in a Fordist factory, all the social dynamics that Roy describes in the quantity, regularity and methods of working can be read in the light of Crozier's theory as strategies to eliminate or maintain margins of uncertainty, and therefore as having to do with power. The fact that Roy's fieldwork observations can be interpreted on the basis of Crozier's conceptual model confirms that in sociological research, as in any other expression of the human mind, it is not the object represented that counts but the representation of the object.

Comparison between Roy and Crozier prompts a second consideration. The central concern of both their studies is individual behaviour in relation to the structures and organizational restrictions within which they act. Actors display such diverse behaviour not only because they have different beliefs and preferences, but also because they work in organizational environments heavily influenced by macro factors such as the level of competition, markets and institutional guarantees. These factors must be borne in mind when seeking to make sense of actors' actions. Stressing the importance of a 'micro' approach to individual strategies is not to exclude a 'macro' approach to the institutional structures in which those strategies are to be found. On the contrary, it is precisely this shift between macro and micro analyses that yields sociological knowledge and enables it to evolve. This is the subject of the next chapters.

DISCUSSION

This chapter has introduced some important concepts: actor or subject, balance between contributions and incentives, bounded rationality, strategy and power as control over margins of uncertainty in social relationships between two or more interlocutors.

Returning to the organizations discussed in the first chapter, we can try to use these concepts to understand the dynamics observed in them. For example, let us think of a workplace, or even a voluntary association, that we know well. What contributions are the members asked to make and what incentives are they offered? Is the balance between contribution and motivation satisfactory, and why? Or is there tension and dissatisfaction which may provoke a crisis in the organization or the decision to leave it? Which actors are more or less satisfied by the balance? Are the differences personal or more general ?

We have also seen that humans act with bounded rationality and that factual judgments and value judgments are mixed in human decisions. Think about Simon's phrase: "What a person wants and loves influences what he sees, and what he sees influences what he wants and loves".

Have you understood the important episodes in the life of an organization that can be interpreted according to Simon's terms? And again: the imperfect decisions that had to be taken, and which were 'rationalized' in retrospect using reasoning different to that which led to the original decision? Can you analyze more exactly the various steps in that decision, who took part and with what role, how positions changed, in what way the final decision differed from the original hypothesis? Were there repercussions on the internal power structure of the group taking the decision?

Another point for reflection is procedures, be they bureaucratic or technical. Simon says they are an important element for extending the boundaries of rationality and for tackling complex problems. Can you give examples?

But procedures also serve to protect the actors who use them against the risk of being accused of incorrect behaviour in the case of accident. Can you think of events that can be interpreted according to Simon?

To conclude, Roy and Crozier give us brilliant examples of how workplaces are often arenas where actors meet and fight in alliances, conflicts and ambiguous complicities. Actors can be single or collective: groups, internal alliances, professional levels, formal representative bodies and lines of conflict that are normally much more complicated and changeable than those of the class war of classical Marxism.

All these phenomena can be seen in the organizations you examine. What protagonists will you find, what strategies will you discover, what objectives, what successes and what compromises and alliances? Or does the concept of strategy seem too complicated for you to find coherence in the actors' behaviour? Are there more or less explicit conflicts where the prize can be described as control over the margin of uncertainty with which certain members of the organization carry out their job? Do you have any examples of the malfunctioning of an organization caused by a cure which actually makes the situation worse and which can therefore be defined as a vicious circle?

Can you find situations where formal authority is different and distinct from power as control of one's own margins of uncertainty? For example, technicians with specific know-how or simply people in strategic positions where they can informally control a flow of information or resources? What big or small advantages can they obtain and what strategies do they use to keep those positions? And do those positions damage the overall efficiency of the system or can they be of some help?

Finally, can you compare two or more organizations to see which has the most conflicts and why, and which is the most efficient and why? Roy suggests that the tighter the structural restrictions, the great the probability of serious conflict. But Crozier warns that the absence of external stimuli and too many job guarantees can easily become the source of frustration: do you have any examples of this?

REFERENCES

Barnard Chester, *The functions of the executive*, Harvard Univ. Press, 1938.

Bonazzi Giuseppe, *Il tubo di cristallo. Modello giapponese e fabbrica integrata alla Fiat Auto* Il Mulino Bologna 1993.

Burawoy Michael, *Manufacturing Consent*, Univ. of Chicago Press, 1979.

Crozier Michel, *Le phenomène bureaucratique*, Editions du Seuil, Paris, 1963 –

\- *La societé bloquée* , Editions du Seuil, Paris, 1971.

- *Ou va l' administration francaise?* Editions de l' organisation, Parsi, 1974.

Crozier Michel e Friedberg Ehrard, *L' acteur et le système. Les contraints de l' action collective*, Editions du Seuil, Paris, 1977.

Gouldner Alvin, Organizational Analysis, in *Sociology Today* Merton Robert , Boom Leonard e Cottrell Leonard eds. Basic Books, N.Y. 1962.

Hirschhon Larry, *Beyond Mechanization*, Cambidge Univ, Press, Mass., 1986.

March James e Simon Herbert, *Organizations*, Wiley, N.Y. 1958.

Roy Donald, Quota Restriction and Goldbricking in a Machine Shop, *American Journal of Sociology*, 1952, n.57, pp. 427-442.

- Work Satisfaction and Social Reward in Quota Achievement: An Analysis of Piecework Incentive, *American Sociological Review*, 1953, n. 18, pp. 507-514.

- Efficiency and The Fix: Informal Intergroup Relationsin a Piecework Machine Shop, *American Journal of Sociology*, 1954, n.60, pp. 255-266.

- Banana Time: Job satisfaction and Informal Interaction, *Human Organizations*, 1960, n. 18, pp. 156-168.

Simon Herbert , *Administrative behavior*, Mac Millan N.Y, 1947.

Wolf William, *The Basic Barnard*, ILR Paperback Cornell University 1974.

Whyte William Foote, *Money and Motivation*, An Analysis of Incentives in Industry, Harpers and Brothers Publ., N.Y, 1955.

Zuboff Shoshana, *In the Age of the Smart Machine*, 1988.

Chapter 4

INSTITUTIONS, POWER AND SOCIAL CHANGE : FROM SELZNICK TO POWELL AND DIMAGGIO

The chapter follows the development of institutionalist thought from Selznick to contemporary neo-instituionalist theories. It explains that in the second half of the twentieth century, the perception of the influences exerted by the external environment on organizations changed profoundly from Selznisck's pessimism to realization that they are normal and common phenomena.

1. GENERAL CHARACTERISTICS OF INSTITUTIONALISM

In the last chapter we saw how the role of the actors and their relationships with organizations have grown increasingly complex. After Barnard, who examined why individuals co-operate in order to achieve an organization's goals, Simon emphasized that the interests and convictions of these actors limit the rationality of an organization. Then Roy, with a powerful empirical analysis, showed that conflicts may be deeply embedded within an organization, and finally Crozier went one step further by recognizing that actors are able to develop strategies inspired by a rationality other than that of the organization. It is this capacity, Crozier argues, that is the unsuspected source of informal power, which he defines as control over the margins of uncertainty present in organizational channels. Consequently, an organization, caught in vicious circles which cause inefficiency, may go into a downward spin. Furthermore, it may be the reason for the gradual change that has taken place in the perspectives adopted by organizational studies. From Barnard to Crozier there has been growing disenchantment in organizational studies, and the analysis has shifted from the conditions that enable an organization to function normally to the factors that cause dysfunction and pathologies.

It can be said that the intellectual path from Barnard to Crozier exhausts study of the direct relationships between organizations and their actors. To go beyond and to examine other types of problems, requires one to break through that conceptual format and include other variables, and to consider phenomena which have thus far been neglected. Those authors who have adopted the institutionalist approach have undertaken this operation. Institutionalism is a school of thought with numerous branches, in economics as well as in the political and social sciences.[1] All its branches, however, refuse to consider society as a simple aggregate of individuals seeking to maximize their utility according to the criteria of rationality, bounded or otherwise. This refusal is due to the fact that institutionalism emphasizes the material and symbolic conditioning exerted by long-standing institutions (the state, church, justice system, armed forces, banking and financial systems, universities, etc.) on human behaviour and attitudes. Taken as a group, these institutions constitute the social and cultural environment which must be borne in mind when explaining specific types of human behaviour, be these individual or collective. In recognizing the importance of the environment as defined above, institutionalism differs:

- from the rationalist schools of thought which claim that they are able to explain human behaviour on the basis of universal and abstract principles of human nature (for example, utility, interests, rationality),
- from a reductive view of the environment which defines it solely as a group of production factors with different degrees of turbulence (for example the contingency school mentioned in the first chapter).

The environment to which institutionalism refers is broad and comprehensive, and requires one to conceive human nature as historically defined and shaped by the action of particular institutions. People create institutions, but in their turn these institutions act upon people, imposing constraints on them and establishing their norms of behaviour. Thus it is the institutions which shape the mental maps of individuals in their cognitive and normative components; or rather, the institutions indicate how people should behave, as well as how they should know and interpret the world. This is not to imply that there are no deviations; rather, that their nature and gravity are defined by the institutions themselves when they establish those norms.

In the social sciences, institutionalism has been of particularly importance for organizational studies. Developed mainly in the United States, organizational institutionalism can be divided into two phases: the first between the 1940s and the 1960s, and the second from the end of the 1970s to the present. The differences between the two phases will be examined more closely later.

1. Weber is generally considered a percursor of institutionalism in the social sciences because of the importance he places on institutions as legitimate sources of rules and regulations.

However, it may initially be pointed out that the feature shared by them is an endeavour to explain both order and change in organizations by reference to the wider institutional framework, this being understood as the social and cultural environment.

2. PHILIP SELZNICK: A FUNCTIONALIST AND HIS PESSIMISTIC APPROACH

Philip Selznick is commonly considered to be the founder of the first phase of institutionalism in organizational analysis. His thought comprises the following three main aspects:

- *functionalism*, which defines organizations as social systems which must satisfy a set of fundamental needs if they are to survive,
- *emphasis on the influences* exerted by external power centers, perceived as institutions, on organizations so that they conform with their desires;
- *the pessimism* of his analysis, which sees organizational change as essentially due to degenerative processes in organizations in that they agree to compromises with the external institutions in order to survive, yet as a result of those compromises diverge from the purposes for which they were created.

Understanding Selznick's position requires one to bear two points in mind. The first is that Selznick was profoundly influenced by Roberto Michels, the Italian sociologist who at the beginning of the twentieth century studied the degeneration of the representation system in the Social Democratic Party of Germany. Even though this party claimed to be inspired by the values of democracy, the numerous problems caused by its complex organization had generated an apparatus of bureaucratic functionaries. Little by little, this apparatus consolidated into an élite with no turnover in its personnel and more concerned with its self-preservation than with protecting the interests of the party's members. Michels maintained that this degenerative process sprang not from the executive's opportunism but from impersonal mechanisms which made defense of the party as an instrument of action more important than pursuit of the goals for which it had been created.

The second point is that Selznick's subject of study is not private firms, these being relatively unconstrained in their pursuit of profit. He examines other types of organizations in which it is possible to detect degenerative processes similar to those studied by Michels. These are public or semi-public organizations statutorily obliged to pursue goals in the general interest. Yet when these organizations are caught in a network of external influences, they drift away from those goals. It is in this regard that a certain similarity can be found between the research conducted by Selznick and Crozier's later studies on vicious circles in French bureaucracy.[2] Selznick, however, differs from Crozier in that the latter identifies the origins of the degenerative process in the strategies of individual actors working within the organization, whereas Selznick attributes them to the actions of external power centers.

At the young age of thirty, Selznick published a study (1949) on the Tennessee Valley Authority (TVA) which became a classic of organizational analysis. In a previous article (1948), which anticipated various themes of his subsequent research, Selznick specified that his subject of study was formal organizations, which he defined, following Barnard, as " tools rationally oriented at achieving defined objectives" . Every organization has its own chain of command, technical and managerial competences, and a division of labour. An act of fundamental importance is the delegation of tasks, which requires the creation of formal mechanisms for the coordination and control of the activities delegated. In order to ensure that the organization's workings are regular and constant, the management standardizes jobs, and seeks to make workers as interchangeable as possible regardless of their personal characteristics. Thus the formal nature of an organization is guaranteed by its ability to replace actors in various roles without incurring significant problems. This is the ideal picture of a rational organization as drawn by the classical management literature.

However, Selznick points out, this picture omits two features important for understanding how organizations actually behave fact. The first is that the formal organization is only one aspect of a *concrete social structure*. The latter is made up of actors who act as *total* human beings, not just as performers of the roles assigned to them, and it is therefore the result of reciprocal influences between the organization's formal and informal aspects. The second feature is that an organization is situated in an environment which is not neutral but instead applies pressures on it, forcing it to make constant adaptations.

These two features prompt Selznick to identify what he calls the inevitable paradox of every organization: people and the external environment are necessary for an organization's very existence, but at the same time they are a constant source of dilemmas and tensions, or even collapse. On the one hand, the formal model is unable to take account of real life in its totality; on the other, most important for maintenance and development of the formal organization is the real life that the model excludes. The interests and pressures of people and of the external environment are two non-rational dimensions to the organization which formal models by definition cannot include.

2. It should not be forgotten that Selznick's study on the TVA (1949) was puboished fourteen years before Crozier's *Bureaucratic Phenomenon* (1963).

3. TWO SOURCES OF TURBULENCE: INSTITUTIONALIZED CLIQUES AND EXTERNAL POWER

This, therefore, is the task that Selznick assigns to sociology of organizations: to study how formal structures are unhinged by internal cliques and external power centres. Although Selznick's interest in cliques aligns his theory with the strand of analysis examined in the previous chapter, he accentuates its problematic and pessimistic nature. Selznick's inquiry focuses on the paradoxes, tensions and dilemmas which ensue from the relationship between people and organizations. People tend to depart from the roles assigned to them, to participate as 'total' persons, to resist dehumanization. The formal model does not have the instruments with which to explain these deviations, so that the actors pose unforeseen problems which derive in part from their individual personalities and in part from often incompatible commitments with other organizations.

The deviations of formal structures may become institutionalized. This is an important aspect of Selznick's theory. Institutionalization is a process by which individual behaviour or social practices which are regularly and constantly repeated are perceived as *institutions*, by which is meant that they are relatively stable structures, whether they are formally legitimized or not (for example, Selznick would regard the Mafia as an institution). There, therefore, may also be institutionalized informal forms of behaviour, both within and without organizations, or ones that are 'transversal' in the sense that they are found in more than one organization.

One effect of institutionalization is that deviations from the norms are no longer considered as stemming from simple personal differences, but rather as structural aspects of formal organizations. One informal institution is the *clique* based on personal relationships which insider members of an organization use in an attempt to control the environment in which the organization's decisions are made. Cliques often have harmful effects on pursuit of the organization's formal goals; but in certain cases, Selznick points out, they may increase the number of resources available and contribute to fulfillment of the organization's objectives. No thorough sociological study of organizations can omit the actions of cliques.

In this regard, two points help in understanding the extent to which Selznick draws on Barnard, but also differs from him. The first is that recognizing cliques as informal structures highlights the importance of viewing organizations as cooperative systems, in Barnard's sense of the term. Cliques are also an integral part of the cooperative system, defined as a concrete system that goes beyond formal prescriptions. Changes in the formal system can only be understood and interpreted in relation to the informal and silent pressures applied by the cliques.

The second point relates to the functionalist approach used by Selznick, and it concerns the fact that the institutionalized nature of cliques requires study of the *functions* that they perform in organizations regardless of the personalities of the people who belong to them. Just like formal organizations, cliques act according to a logic of their own which extends beyond their members' personalities. A functionalist analysis of cooperative systems is based on the assumption that certain actions and certain consequences at organizational level are not related to the individuals involved. Selznick's position in this regard is quite different from the action-based approach examined in the preceding chapter, where the analysis was entirely focused on the relationship between the organization and the individual.

Another disruptive influence on the formal structure of organizations is exerted by external power centres which take action to modify the way in which they work. This prompts Selznick to conceive organizations as structures which adapt by reacting to these centers' influences. In accordance with his functionalist assumptions, Selznick views organizations as social systems. The way in which their internal components work can be compared to those of living organisms: they perform the functions necessary to keep the systems to which they belong alive. Selznick lists some of these functions:

- The organization's security in relation to the social forces active in the environment;
- The stability of internal lines of authority and communication;
- The continuity of policies and the sources of their definition;
- The projection of an image homogeneous with the meaning and role of the organization.

Selznick's thesis is that no social system can survive without satisfying the needs listed above, and that the activities observed within an organization can be interpreted in terms of the functions necessary to satisfy those needs. From a functionalist point of view, the reasons that induce people to act are relatively unimportant compared to the objective consequences that these action may produce on a large scale. The emphasis should be placed not on people's intentions but on the constraints imposed upon their actions. The problem for research is to discover why actions which were begun with specific intentions lead to unforeseen and often undesired consequences.

This emphasis on the unforeseen consequences of actions, rather than on the actor's intentions, is associated in Selznick's thought with a pessimistic view of organizational activity. His reasoning is as follows: the people interested in a given goal create an organization that will be used to achieve that goal. When the organization is set up, it requires resources to continue to exist and expand.

Yet it is not easy to obtain such resources. It is necessary to devote effort to acquiring them, make agreements, and reach compromises. Moreover, local power centres often apply pressures on the organization in order to condition the way in which it acts. To ensure the organization's survival, its leaders enter into pacts which dilute the ideals of the original programme. At the same time, they cite the organization's ideology to demonstrate that they have acted in keeping with its original goals, and to justify their decisions.

Selznick does not doubt the personal honesty and good will of leaders. But he stresses the dilemmas that they encounter when they have to act: in particular, the dilemma between whether they should pursue with no comprise and at all costs the goals for which the organization was created, or whether they should reach compromises with the external pressures. A crucial concept in Selznick's analysis is the recalcitarncy of means. By this expression he means that an organization is an instrument indispensable for achieving a goal, but at the same time it is an imperfect instrument which distorts the objective it seeks to fulfill. The reason that recalcitrancy exists is that the instruments created to achieve objectives have lives of their own, and their need for self preservation may clash with the very objective for which they were created. Selznick writes that we are inevitably bound to the mediation of the human structures which are necessary to achieve our goals but at the same time interpose themselves between us and those goals.

On the one hand, it is necessary to act in accordance with given objectives; on the other, it is necessary to strengthen the instrument created to achieve those objectives by giving it political continuity and protecting it against external risks. There thus arises a conflict between those who defend the goals of the organization's original programme and those who manage its organizational apparatus. The former accuse the latter of organizational cynicism, and in their turn are accused of being idealists with no sense of reality. Both sides are convinced that they are acting for the good of the organization. Selznick seems to be saying that the road to hell is paved with good intentions; a lesson similar to the one drawn in the previous chapter from Crozier's analysis. But Selznick's diagnosis is different, for he examines, not the strategies of actors concerned to preserve small or large margins of power, but the way in which, for the sake of the organization's survival, its managers accept gradual shifts away from its original objectives and rationale.

4. GRASS ROOTS. A STUDY ON INSTITUTIONAL PRESSURES

The discussion thus far has concerned Selznick's study of the Tennessee Valley Authority (TVA) conducted in the 1940s. Not only is this study Selznick's most famous work, it also influenced his successive intellectual development. To conduct his research, Selznick spent numerous months in Tennessee, analyzing archive material and carrying out extensive interviews with dozens of people, including TVA executives and staff, as well as local dignitaries. However, he went to Tennessee under the influence of Michels' pessimistic doctrine, with the consequence that the focus of his research was the degenerative processes provoked by the tyranny of means over ends.

The TVA was an agency created in the 1930s by President Roosevelt during the period of the New Deal, the government aid programme intended to promote economic recovery after the slump of 1929. The TVA was set up to implement a broad programme of large-scale public works in the Tennessee Valley, as well as to improve the living conditions of its residents. Selznick reports that Roosevelt wanted the TVA to have the power of a governmental agency and yet retain the flexibility of a private company. Besides constructing dams and electrical power plants, the TVA organized the production and distribution of low-cost chemical fertilizers, technical and economic assistance to local farmers, the opening of vocational schools, and the creation of social centres. The TVA was exempt from a series of administrative controls which would have hampered it activities. It was given an annual appropriation, and it could re-use the earnings obtained from the sale of electric power and chemical products.

Nothing similar to the TVA had ever been attempted in the USA before. The liberalist view of local autonomy still prevailed, and the federal government restricted its participation in state and local matters to the minimum. Consequently, the TVA was created amidst controversy. Its opponents maintained that the new body, which combined the power of a government agency with the advantages of a private company, constituted unfair competition in a free enterprise system, and consequently posed a threat to local democracy. The governing body of the TVA, therefore, had to develop a strategy which would overcome these preconceptions and win the trust of local agencies. Selznick writes that the TVA had two alternatives: it could either implement its programmes with direct action, or it could develop a method which would use local institutions as mediators. The executives at the TVA soon realized that a project imposed upon the local residents was doomed to failure. It thus decided to distribute its departments over the region, with the closest possible involvement of local agencies, professional associations, ethnic communities, the university, voluntary organizations, and all the state and federal offices willing to co-operate.

This strategy seemed all the more appropriate because it concurred with the popular American belief in 'grass roots' democracy, an expression of American political jargon which denotes a bottom-up democracy born in the frontier towns as opposed to the 'smoke-filled rooms' of the capital. Co-operating with local institutions in the name of the people's interest became the ideological watchword of the TVA.

But what exactly, Selznick asks, does 'in the interest of the people' and 'institutions committed to the people' mean? He replies that these are only indeterminate abstractions used for the purposes of ideological coverage. Because there were conflicting social interests in local society, the TVA had to choose which groups to side with: it could carry forward a radical project which safeguarded weaker or more marginalized groups, or it could adopt a more cautious and conservative programme which would not provoke the hostility of local dignitaries. And since the latter were better represented in local associations than the former, it followed that the TVA's decision to satisfy demand expressed through the local channels of representation favoured privileged social groups. The gap between the TVA's original position and its practices grew ever wider, and it was ideologically justified on the grounds that choices had to be made which reflected the concrete demands of the environment.

5. FORMAL AND INFORMAL CO-OPTATION

This introduces the notion of co-optation, given the TVA made much use of it to involve local authorities in implementation of its programme. Selznick defines co-optation as "the process of absorbing new elements into the management of its structure which determine the politics of an organization, as a means of warding off threat to its stability and to its existence". When an organization feels itself threatened by external dangers, one way to defend itself is to co-opt representatives of the environment from which the threat stems. Co-optation is a rational strategy with which to defuse dangerous conflicts, but in particular circumstances it may underline the rationale for an organization's existence.

Selznick identifies two types of co-optation: formal, and informal or essential. Formal co-optation exists when an organization officially absorbs new elements by enlarging its executive bodies or creating new roles. Formal co-optation becomes necessary when

(*a*) the legitimacy of a body or its executives is challenged by an important segment of the group affected;

(*b*) or when the need to promote the participation of wider segments of the population suggests that some form of self-government should be granted.

Formal co-optation can be considered the organization's reaction to a difficult situation which arises when the rank-and-file of the organization does not give its consensus. It does not, however, translate into an effective transfer of power; the invitation to participate is more symbolic than real, and at times involves the sharing of responsibility for unpopular tasks. With formal co-optation, the organization does not set out to increase the number of decision makers, but rather to broaden the social base of consensus for the decisions to be taken. A typical case of formal co-optation occurred in colonial countries, when the authorities of the occupying nation co-opted members of the native population into the local government. Another example of formal co-optation is provided by forms of participation in company management offered to the unions so that they can share responsibility for some of the strategic choices made.

Informal or essential co-optation follows a different logic. Its aim is not to broaden the basis of popular agreement with a company policy which remains unchanged, but rather to deal with threats originating from external power centres. Faced with a difficult struggle, whose outcome is uncertain, the organization may decide that it is more advantageous to reach agreement with those centres. This may come about in two ways: either by including some of their members in the decision-making bodies, or by acceding to their demands In this way the organization's survival is guaranteed, but its original programme must be changed. This type of co-optation, Selznick points out, usually remains informal (and at times it may even be officially denied), since the external forces are interested in the substance of the power, not in its form.

The two types of co-optation stand in different relationships to the organization's official ideology. Selznick considers ideology to be an important instrument used by organizations to legitimize their actions. However, whilst formal co-optation is easily legitimized by the organization's ideology, informal co-optation almost always contradicts its declared ideological values and orientations. Consequently, the more that informal co-optation is used, the wider the gap between the way an organization functions and its ideology.

Selznick uses this distinction between formal and informal co-optation to examine the overt initiatives taken and the covert compromises made by the TVA. At the outset, its executives promised the broad formal co-optation of representatives of local agencies and the community, including associations for the advancement of Afro-Americans. Yet these co-optations, which were coherent with the principle of grass-roots democracy, were soon overridden by essential co-optation, which conditioned the TVA's policies and greatly reduced the original innovative scope of its programmes. The essential co-optations took place mainly because of pressure applied by the larger landowners, and it was facilitated by the decentralized structure of the TVA. Owing to the nature of their work, the TVA executives responsible for agriculture developed close relationships with the landowners, who became akin to their personal 'administrative clientele'. But a clientele relationship Selznick notes, is no more than a disguised form of co-optation.

These relationships gradually induced the TVA's agronomists to adopt a favourable stance toward the landowners, even when this was in conflict with other TVA departments and government agencies. Decisions were taken which diluted or even reversed the social direction of the original programme. The large landowners managed to have the assistance to small farmers programme changed. By having the size of the farm eligible for aid increased, and consequently increasing the level of fertilizer consumption, they were able to corner almost all the low-cost fertilizers which the TVA had to sell. Another initial objective which was **subsequently betrayed concerned involved** the areas to be bought for reservoirs. Since the construction of reservoirs raised the value of the land around them, the TVA had initially decided that each reservoir constructed would be surrounded by a protective belt of land about 100 to 300 meters in width. These areas should have been for public use and for experimental agriculture. The large landowners, however, opposed this programme on the ground that it was "super-idealist" and their position was accepted by the TVA agronomists, who restricted the purchase of land for reservoirs to the minimum necessary, and abandoned the idea of creating protective belts.

The increasing number of compromises reached with the local powers caused such an involution in the TVA's policy that it clashed with other federal agencies created as part of the New Deal. Selznick writes that " the situation became politically paradoxical since the TVA, clearly set up under the principles of the New Deal, abstained from supporting organizations with similar political purport, and aligned itself with enemies of such organizations". At this point one may ask what remained of the TVA's original programme: Selznick answers that a distinction must be drawn between the technical and the social parts of the programme. Whilst the technical part (reforestation, construction of dams and electricity generating plants, production of fertilizers, etc.) was completed on schedule, the social part was substantially betrayed. It is true that, in the name of local democracy, numerous local voluntary welfare associations were formally co-opted by the TVA. Yet these association had no real power, unlike the lobby for established interests, which obtained substantial co-optations. In particular, decentralization, which should have produced the most democratic system possible and the adherence to grass-roots principles, ended up by favouring the formation of an external administrative clientele, well-organized and exerting strong influence on the TVA's decisions.

Selznick observes that it would be naive to blame the incompetence or corruption of the TVA executives for their relinquishment of the organization's original objectives. They, he writes, were morally upright and substantially honest. The contrast between moral qualities and political compromises indicates instead that the fundamental problem that sociological research must address is the unexpected consequences of the logic of organizational action. A Latin proverb runs *propter vitam, vitae perdere causam* : in order to save life one loses the cause one lives for. In short, this is the disillusioned message that Selznick conveys with his study on the TVA.

6. INSTITUTIONS AND FUNCTIONS OF LEADERSHIP

The study on the TVA leaves one basic problem still resolved: if the TVA was an organization subject to the pressures applied by external power centres, did not these power centres also have organizational structures? And if these power centres were also organizations, is the assumption that *all* organizations are subject to external pressures weakened? But if there are organizations which are subject to pressures and others which apply them, what is it that distinguishes between them?

Selznick answered these questions in a subsequent work (1957) devoted to the study of leadership in organizations. Here he apparently alleviates the pessimism of his study on the TVA. He gives this impression because, instead of studying the external pressure which the organization is forced to accept, he examines the initiatives undertaken by the leadership to define objectives for the organization and to create consensus among its members so that they can be achieved. Selznick acknowledges that an organization is not always obliged to relinquish its original objectives, because it can achieve them when its leadership is effective. But what are the conditions necessary for this to happen?

Selznick answers by identifying two types of organization. There are instrumental organizations which simply undertake technical services, and there are organizations, which he calls *institutions*, able to create policy. Whilst administrative effectiveness and the procedures rationally directed towards technical ends are what matter in instrumental organizations, of principal importance for institutions is defining and transmitting values, creating an identity, and developing a project which distinguishes them from simple technical instruments.

As a straightforward example, garbage collection agencies or city transport companies are instrumental organizations, while the city government is an institution because it establishes and implements policies (instrumental organizations may be sub-units within institutions). But the distinction raises complex problems. Using Selznick's terminology we can, for example, assume that a newspaper which refuses to be the mere conveyor of anodyne information, but instead sees itself as a means to carry forward a political and cultural campaign to influence public opinion and the centers of political decision making, is not only an organization but also an institution. The same applies to all those bodies – parties, churches, universities, companies etc. – which coherently pursue objectives which are necessarily of importance to the external context as well.

To clarify his argument, Selznick divides decisions into two categories: routine and critical. Routine decisions are part of ordinary administration. They concern service organizations and can be evaluated in terms of their technical efficiency. Critical decisions, on the other hand, are taken by the leadership because they involve the definition of values and objectives which characterize institutions. By definition, the political will to define and achieve objectives is embodied only in institutions.

Leadership is never merely passive adaptation to external pressures; it is always a creative activity which turns the institution into an actor able to take initiatives. Leadership, which can be carried out by one person alone or by a group of executives, is manifest in four basic functions.

1. *It defines the mission and the role of the institution*: it sets out a general plan of action which includes and subordinates all routine activities.
2. *It incorporates the objective into the institution*: it does not merely set objectives but propagates certain ways of thinking, feeling and acting. It seeks to create a group identity so that the institution's objectives become those of all its members.
3. *It defends the institutional integrity*: the leadership is expected to protect the ideals of the institution, to safeguard its values and its identity. This requires constant redefinition of its action by means of budgets, celebrations, critical analysis. By examining past events the leadership finds points of continuity with which to interpret its present problems, indicate new ways forward, establish objectives, identify the enemies to be fought. The more innovative a programme, the more the leadership must legitimize it by emphasizing its continuation of the institution's heritage, its battles, and its past successes. The leadership must, therefore, perform a function which is highly symbolic and communicative.
4. It *settles internal conflicts*: the leadership must also be able to mediate and settle conflicts which arise within the institution. Such conflicts cannot be solved simply by forcing the parties to accept a solution. The leadership must ensure that both parties agree on the solution and that they feel that their legitimate interests have been protected. Good mediation should always give rise to increased support for the leadership.

These are difficult tasks, and not always is there a leadership able to undertake them. Yet, Selznick adds, it is not indispensable for an organization to have a leadership; indeed, most organizations do not have true leadership or they have leaders who make mistakes or even fail. Selznick indicates three main risks in the exercise of leadership:

1. *Escape into technology* when the leadership lacks strategic objectives, it tends to concentrate on acquiring instruments as if they were an end in themselves. Often the escape into technology is accompanied by a non-problematic definition of these ends, which are taken for granted or seen as imposed by external forces.
2. *Opportunism* is a risk when short-term goals are pursued without a long-term vision or master plan. The main danger of opportunism is that the institution's identity will be lost if management selects disparate and incoherent objectives not rooted in the established environment;
3. *Utopianism* is a risk when goals which cannot be achieved are pursued in the name of ideals. As Selznick remarks, however, Utopianism may often give rise to opportunistic choices. When the goals are not realistic, but decisions must be taken in any case, it is likely that an opportunist line will be chosen for practical purposes as the alternative to inconclusive utopianism.

7. LEADERSHIP, INSTITUTIONS AND EXTERNAL ENVIRONMENT: SOME AMBIGUITIES IN SELZNICK'S REASONING

When Selznick distinguishes between organizations and institutions, he recognizes that the latter, given effective leadership, are able not only to resist external pressures but can also decide their own goals and pursue them successfully. How much power institutions exercise over the external environment depends upon the extent to which it is included among their goals. We may say that Selznick's pessimism has been attenuated, because he has extended his study from organizations alone, which are subject to external pressures, to institutions, or rather organizations of another type whose leaderships enable them to pursue their own goals by exercising power on the surrounding environment.

This development in Selznick's theory prompts a number of considerations. The first involves a re-reading of his study on the TVA in light of his subsequent work. If one bears in mind his notion of leadership, one may say that the centres of external power that conditioned the action taken by the TVA were no more than institutions with effective leaderships able to define and achieve their objectives of control. Symmetrically, the TVA's decision to abandon its original objectives of social change must be attributed to the fact that it was unable to become an institution itself and thus condition the external environment. Rather it allowed itself to be conditioned by stronger institutions.

If this is the case, a question arises: Is the failure of the TVA to be blamed on the shortcomings of its internal directors, unable to deliver true leadership, or should it be attributed to a series of macro factors in the environment which would have condemned any leadership to failure? In his study Selznick does not accuse the TVA executives of being unable to exercise effective leadership. Rather, his analysis is intended to show that the external institutions were powerful enough to prevent the TVA from fully implementing its programmes. Yet if this is Selznick's reply, one may legitimately ask another question: what are the conditions which require an organization to change its original objectives in order to survive, and what conditions foster the growth of true leadership, thereby enabling the organization to establish itself as an institution pursuing its goals as originally established? Is everything predetermined by the environment or are there degrees of freedom in organizational action?

Selznick does not give a satisfactory answer to the question, prompting Perrow's penetrating criticism (1986, p.170) that "when we get results we approve of, this is leadership; when we do not, it is a process of goal displacement". Perrow highlights the ambiguity in Selznick's analysis evidenced by the evolution of his research, first centred on the conservative action of the institutions in Tennessee and then proffering an attractive image of leadership in institutions which pursue goals that may even be innovative.

Despite this ambiguity, if considered together, we note that the two studies on the TVA and on leadership have one constant object of inquiry: the power relations among organizations and the changes caused by those relations. On the one hand, organizations can be the *subjects* of pressures applied by external powers and are consequently forced to change. On the other hand, if guided by leadership, they can become *actors* able to exert pressures over the external environment and bend it to their purposes. In this case Selznick calls them institutions.

At this point we can draw two conclusions. The first is that the ultimate source of institutional change is human initiative, provided it is able to establish itself as leadership. The second is that institutions themselves constitute the framework of strong powers to be borne in mind when studying what takes place in other organizations and in society in general This was one of the most significant insights that Selznick afforded to sociological research, and it was subsequently taken up and reformulated by neo-institutionalism.

8. 'FIRST WAVE' INSTITUTIONALIST RESEARCH: SOME EXAMPLES AND THEIR SPECIFIC FEATURES

Selznick's work profoundly influenced American sociology of organizations. In the 1950s and 1960s numerous studies analyzed the discrepancy between the original goals of a particular organization and the changes made to adjust to external pressures. The organizations examined were, for the most part, philanthropic associations, hospitals and schools: all organizations that depended heavily upon external funding or subsidies, and thus were particularly subject to external pressures.

Some examples follow.[3] An association initially set up to help poor immigrants gradually changed its target group until it had been transformed into a recreation centre for youths from outside the city, most of whom were from the suburban middle class (Zald and Denton, 1963). A vocational training institute for young blind persons, which according to its statute was to train them for labour-market entry, found it more profitable to persuade them to work indefinitely at the institute itself, because they could be employed at low cost without losing the grants for them (Scott, 1967). The junior college of a small town, which claimed that it guaranteed easy entry to university, had become in fact, because of the poor quality of its students, a mere diploma factory which did not give them any real chance of admission to university. The fraud had never been exposed because the students and their families themselves had every desire for the diploma to be recognized on the jobs market. (Clark, 1960). A hospital which had accepted private donations saw an increasing number of its benefactors demand that the funds be used, not for research, but to purchase technological innovations of little or no use, because this would create publicity for the hospital and for themselves (Perrow, 1961).

How original goals may become distorted has also been shown in a famous study by Sudnow (1964) of the justice system in the USA. Although the law proclaims that the purpose of trials is to ascertain the truth, defendants who could not afford to hire a lawyer were consigned to a bureaucratic system where the lawyers allocated by the public defender's office advised them to plead guilty in exchange for reduced sentences. This technique accelerated trials, giving the impression that the justice system was rapid and efficient. Perrow points out, however, that not all research on the deviation of objectives from those originally established have uncovered degenerative processes, and he cites a study conducted by Janwitz (1960) on the armed forces. This study showed that placing the army under the control of a civil bureaucracy appointed by the government resulted in the gradual marginalization of the more hawkish generals and favoured the growth of a military techno-structure much more prudent in its use of weapons.

These early institutionalist studies have a number of features in common:

1. A *discursive and holistic structure*[4]. Since the purpose of the research is to show that an organization gradually distances from its original objectives,

3 For a list of these researches see Perrow 1986, Chpt. 5

4 Holistic from 'holism' (from ancient Greek *olis*, whole), to denote an approach to a given reality conceived as a number of parts which are so closely integrated that no one part is more important than another.

the authors reconstruct the history of the organization beginning with the reasons for its establishment. They discuss the leadership of its founders and their successors; they illustrate the organization's successes and failures; they explore the origin and the dynamics of the pressures to which it is subject; they analyze the justifications given for compromises which gradually changed the organization's ends and its rationale. In general, their accounts do not identify specific variables as factor of changes; rather, they cover the entire range of events that indirectly and unconsciously contributed to the change (which is what is meant by *holistic* analysis). It should be noted that this analysis does not require comparison of the organization studied against an ideal model in the Weberian sense, but instead comparison between the original goals and those which the organization actually pursues.

2. *Emphasis on the external environment* as a group of institutions able to influence the choices of organizations. The pressures are not necessarily applied by potential enemies of the organization in question; and co-optation, which Selznick considers the main device with which transformation of goals is accomplished, frequently takes covert and unexpected form. The pressures are often exerted by members of the organization itself, who believe that adjusting to market forces or to consolidated social interests is necessary for its survival. Such was the case of the association created to protect the poor immigrants but transformed into a recreation centre for suburban middle class youths; and it was also the case of the institute for the blind which decided that it was more economical to put the young people to work for itself than help them find regular employment outside.

3. A third characteristic is that both the organizations which are subject to pressure and the institutions exerting it seem to have a *logic of action which transcends the will of single individuals*. This is a difference with respect to Selznick's theory. Selznick described institutions as animated by leadership which establishes objectives and which endeavours to have its members assume those objectives as their own. More often than not, the above-mentioned studies depict institutions as impersonal and detached entities which orient the action of individuals and the way in which organizations behave, with no need for leadership or conscious strategies. From this standpoint, the market is one of the crucial institutions to be considered if we want to understand the behaviour of organizations whose missions have apparently little to do with economics. Their drift away from their original goals always takes place for reasons that have ultimately to do with profit or the interests of the affluent.

Overall, these studies suggest that, in the USA, the mix of the market, competition and upper-middle class values pervades every area of social life, so that even organizations which by statute should be extraneous to this mix cannot survive if they do not adapt to its demands. One might object that something of the sort takes place throughout the entire Western world, but the USA is the country in which awareness of these institutional constraints is greatest – as witness the large number of studies of institutionalist inspiration.

9. THE NEW INSTITUTIONALIST SCHOOL. MEYER AND ROWEN: ISOMORPHISM AND RATIONALIZED MYTHS

In the late 1970s institutionalist research received new impetus from a number of authors who resumed study of organizations and the environment. Their studies, however, took an approach different from the one adopted by Selznick in the 1950s. To signal this change in perspective the proponents of the school gave it the name of 'neo-institutionalism'. Although the name indicates a linkage with the past, in that its main focus was on institutions, the key problem addressed had changed. Analysis no longer centred on why organizations modify their original goals but rather on why organizations of the same type (hospitals, schools, newspapers, companies) are similar to each other. Redefining the problem brought with it major changes in the way that hypotheses are structured. With respect to old institutionalism, the new school had the following features:

- *the disappearance of the functionalism* that viewed organizations as organic systems with basic needs which they had to fulfill in order to survive;
- the *diminished importance of power* which intentionally and purposefully seeks to dominate existing and new organizations;
- *the disappearance of the pessimism* which induced the view that organizations must inevitably relinquish their original goals:
- *a more articulated account* of the relationships among organizations subject to a widespread network of reciprocal influences, which are not always negative;
- *attention paid to the cognitive processes* of actors: that is, mental maps become important in the social construction of reality.

John Meyer and Brian Rowan were the first to launch neo-institutionalist research. Their article (1977) set out the concept of *isomorphism*[5], which denotes the reasons and processes by which the various units of a given population (whether these are single individuals or organizations) grow increasingly similar.

5 From ancient Greek, *isomorphos*, identical form

The article developed out of a study conducted by the two authors on the American school system (1975). Their research showed that since it was impossible to measure the influence of education on students' later professional lives, the school system had developed alternative procedures which presumably guaranteed the effectiveness of the academic programme. Teachers, students, educational materials, the type and quality of the schools were evaluated using specific parameters. But because the effectiveness of these parameters could never be verified directly, one deduced that they only reflected the socially prevalent beliefs of what constitutes effective education. And because they were not supported by empirical data, these beliefs constituted only a 'myth'. The criterion used to evaluate the quality and effectiveness of a school is nothing but the extent to which a school conforms with the formalities of the procedures established by this myth of educational quality and effectiveness. The more the school conforms, the better its chances of receiving financial support and symbolic recognition, and the better its students' job opportunities on conclusion of their studies. The circle is thus closed: the more a school conforms to the prevalent ideas on education, the more highly it is considered by other institutions of its type, and consequently the more the adoption of this prevalent form of education is rewarded.

On the basis of this research, in an essay of 1977, Meyer and Rowan sought to develop a broader theoretical model. They observed that organizations operate in highly institutionalized settings which establish criteria of rationality that the organizations themselves must respect in order to be considered efficient. Assuming that criteria of rationality are established outside organizations, however, introduces an entirely new perspective compared to that of more traditional studies. In the classical school, no one, not even Weber, had ever doubted that there was just one criterion which could be used to judge organizational behavior as rational, nor that this rationality was the same for individual organizations as for those institutions making up the external environment (schools, research centers, financial institutions, government agencies, etc). It is true that Simon talked of bounded rationality and Crozier suggested that people and businesses have different types of rationality. But in their analyses this boundedness and these differences derived from individual strategies forming behaviour are at odds with the canons of official rationality. Meyer and Rowan, on the other hand, put forward a revolutionary hypothesis, namely that organizations very often:

- do not have their own rationality criteria and adopt those suggested by the external environment,
- or they have their own criteria, but these differ from the criteria prevalent in the environment.

It follows from this hypothesis that the main focus of research is the pressures exerted by institutions on organizations until they adapt to the prevalent rationality criteria; in other words, how isomorphism processes come about. In their research on the American school system Meyer and Rowan had detected isomorphism in the advantages to schools of adopting rules of external origin as the criteria for their conduct. The two authors now go a step further, stating that in contemporary society isomorphism is caused not only by the tendency of existing organizations to conform to external prescriptions but also by the fact that institutions often endeavour to bring new organizations into being to pursue aims and objectives set by the institutions themselves.

Meyer and Rowan's thesis is that we have entered a world which is profoundly different from that of the past. Organizations (typically manufacturing enterprises) were once set up by an entrepreneur with sufficient enterprise, intuition, and propensity for risk-taking to be able to operate alone and be successful. He alone assumed the risk, and he alone decided how to lead and manage the business. Today this has changed. Society is densely populated with institutions of every kind – local, national and international agencies[6], banks, associations of various kinds, consultancy firms, schools, mass media, regulatory agencies – which all together form an institutional framework. This framework establishes a dense network of regulations with which organizations must comply in order to be recognized and successful (consider the number of regulations that must be obeyed to obtain a bank loan or a work order). Indeed, it is impossible today to understand the way in which an organization acts, or the very existence of individual organizations, if consideration is not made of the environmental (i.e. institutional) pressures intent on bringing them into being and have them operate in a certain way.

But what criteria govern the development of isomorphism processes? Meyer and Rowan define them as "powerful institutional rules" which act as rationalized myths. This expression is an oxymoron[7] which suggests the idea of an imaginary belief made plausible by a logical discourse. It denotes rules which are not based on empirical proof obtained scientifically but legitimized by the conviction that they are rationally effective or consistent with a legal order. Typical rationalized myths are, for example, the regulations on total quality for product certification, the technical requisites for exercise of a profession, the recent educational theories which recommend particular teaching syllabuses as more effective than previous ones. When a rationalized myth becomes established, it fosters the creation of new fields of activity, engendering a

6 Consider the growing role of the European Community institutions in regulating production and consumption.

7 Oxymoron: a rhetorical figure which combines two contradictory terms.

competition between old and new organizations to satisfy the business which the myth itself has created (the proliferation of business consultancy companies and vocational training agencies). It is not necessarily true that closer similarity always means greater efficiency. There is a threshold above which the spread of an innovation does not improve performance, but instead increases the social legitimacy of those who accept it.

It was said earlier that Meyer and Rowan identify two types of organizations: those that receive rationality criteria from outside and those that have their own criteria which may conflict with the external ones. Organizations with no criteria of their own with which to evaluate efficiency (schools, theaters, museums, churches, volunteer associations, etc.) belong to the former type, and are therefore founded on their ability to adapt to the formal expectations and needs prescribed by external institutions. Belonging to the other category are organizations which have their own criteria perceived as 'objective' in evaluating the efficiency of their production process (typical of the manufacturing industry). Such criteria must be respected for the success and survival of the organization, even if they are not entirely consistent with the predominant social standards.

Organizations of the second type raises the most interesting problems for analysis, given the conflict that arises between their efficiency criteria and those suggested by external institutions. The conflict is not so rare if one considers, for example, that the efficiency criteria established by banks to grant credit to a business are often different from those actually used by the business itself. There may also be differences between the public evaluation of a business and its actual productivity (a well-known case is the American company which earned a sought-after international award for total quality, and a year later went bankrupt because of the excessive expenses sustained in order to win the award).

Meyer and Rowan suggest that these organizations develop, as far as they can, two parallel structures: a formal and visible one which respects external formalities, and an informal one which is discreetly concealed so that the organization can use its own efficiency rules. This dual structure, they point out, is not hypocritical, for it recognizes that there are multiple and divergent criteria with which to evaluate the same performances, and it, therefore, belongs to the category of everyday problems of complex management.

10. POWELL AND DIMAGGIO. ORGANIZATIONAL FIELDS AND A TYPOLOGY OF ISOMORPHISM

An important contribution to the study of isomorphism processes has been made by Powell and DiMaggio in an article published in 1983, where they:

- develop the concept of *organizational field* and go beyond the distinction between organizations subject to pressures and institutions which exert pressures for isomorphism;

- observe that isomorphism processes are not always the same and indistinct; rather, they differ according to a typology based on the patterns and the rapidity with which they develop:
- stress that isomorphism concerns not only organizations but also individuals within and without organizations.

Powell and DiMaggio's study starts from Meyer and Rowan's conclusion that institutional pressures induce organizations to grow increasingly alike, without, however, their becoming necessarily more efficient. But the reasons for this phenomenon were not explained. Powell and DiMaggio find the explanation in the concept of *organizational field*, which they define as "those organizations that, in the aggregate, constitute a recognized area of institutional life: key-suppliers, resource and product consumers, regulatory agencies and other organizations that produce similar services or products" (p.64). In other words, an organizational field consists not only of units competing with each other but also of a multitude of actors that, directly or indirectly, consciously or unconsciously, contribute to a process of change, be this political, cultural, economic or technological. An organizational field should be seen as a broad and heterogeneous system with fluid and indistinct borders but close-knit and stable internal communications. The concept of organizational field has three important consequences for research.

The first is that study of a process of change cannot be restricted to examination of decision-making within specified organizations. It must be extended to the roles performed by all the actors involved in that process: academic communities, consulting agencies, the press, professional and consumer associations, labour unions, government authorities. The concept of organization is extended to encompass the manner in which the organizational field composed of many different types of organizations is organized. The second consequence is that the distinction between organizations subject to pressures and institutions which exert them disappears. Since the most important factors that organizations must consider are other organizations, all the organizations involved are both subject to and exert the pressures that traverse an organizational field. The problem to be addressed, therefore, is not what has adapted to what, but how the pressures are exerted, how they are received, and how rapidly they change. The third consequence is that research on organizational change becomes the reconstruction of the entire period of history of the society in which the change has taken place. And this reconstruction may cover a very long time span – years or even decades. Isomorphism, or rather the increasing homogenization of criteria and performances within a given organizational field, is therefore the result of the interconnected actions of all the actors present within it.

The second point made by Powell and DiMaggio is that isomorphism is not indistinct; rather, it varies according to the patterns and rapidity with which it develops. They identify three types of isomorphism: coercive, mimetic and normative. Isomorphism is *coercive* when the organization is subject to external pressures which force it to conform: typical examples would be legal obligations, or clauses in contracts with more powerful companies, i.e. the conditions that a company imposes on its sub-suppliers. Isomorphism is *mimetic*[8] when organizations begin imitative processes spontaneously in order to cope with uncertainty in the environment. Imitation, in these cases, acts as a surrogate for certainty, according to the typical train of reasoning to the effect that, if everyone is acting in a particular way, they must have good reason, so that it is better to conform. Finally, isomorphism is *normative* when it springs from processes of professionalization, or rather when the heads of the organization learn in specialized centers of the existence and advantages of new management methods, new technologies or new areas for research. In normative isomorphism, the choice of what is new is not prompted by coercion or uncertainty, but by certain knowledge of the superiority of the new practices over the old ones.

An important mechanism of normative isomorphism is the selection and hiring of personnel with closely similar characteristics. Organizations prefer to hire people who come from the same sector, from the same schools, and who have similar experience, skills and aspirations, and who even use the same format in compiling their curriculum vitae. Powell and DiMaggio write that "many career tracks are so closely guarded, both at the entry level and throughout the career progression, that individuals who make it to the top are virtually indistinguishable (p.71), adding that:

•• individuals in an organization field undergo anticipatory socialization to common expectations about their personal behaviour, appropriate style of dress, organizational vocabularies.. and standard methods of speaking, joking, or addressing others (ibid.)

The isomorphism of organizations is reproduced in the isomorphism of people who, in turn, become a powerful factor in strengthening the normative isomorphism of organizations. When those who hold positions of responsibility in an organization are profoundly convinced that certain modes of thought and action are correct, the result is a form of isomorphism in the organization which is not passively accepted like coercive isomorphism, nor copied like mimetic isomorphism, but takes the form of a deliberate search for ways to improve while remaining the same. It may be said that the key to success resides in an oxymoron: being able to absorb the prevailing pressures in the organizational field so well that a small degree of originality and innovation can be created while remaining socially acceptable.

8 Mimetic = imitative (from Ancient Greek *mimesis*, imitation)

Finally Powell and DiMaggio address the problem of the differing rapidity of isomorphism processes. They maintain that the more an organization depends upon external resources, and the greater the uncertainty and ambiguity of their objectives, the more rapidly isomorphism takes place. Similar factors operate in organizational fields. These are the more homogeneous, the more integrated they are, the fewer the alternative models of organization and the greater the professionalism of employees

11. A NEO-INSTITUTIONALIST RESEARCH STUDY: THE EVOLUTION OF ART MUSEUMS IN THE USA (1920-40)

The focus of neo-institutionalist inquiry is, therefore, on the great changes that take place in the organization of society, and in particular the institutionalization of new patterns of behaviour, new criteria for action, and new organizational forms. Given the breadth of this field of study, neo-institutionalist research entails:

(*a*) emphasis on organizational fields rather than on individual organizations;
(*b*) examination of a long period of history in which the changes under examination have occurred.

In the past twenty years a large number of studies with these characteristics have been produced, especially in the United States, where neo-institutionalism has developed to its greatest extent. These studies have examined extremely diverse fields: for instance, reform of the civil service (Tolbert and Zucker, 1983), transformation of American industry during the twentieth century (Fligstein 1985), the growth of philanthropic associations (Galaskiewitz 1991), changes in university alumni associations (Brint and Carabel 1989) and the development of different types of capitalism in the Far East (Orrù, Biggart and Hamilton 1988).

One feature shared by these studies is their recognition that the processes of institutionalism, and therefore isomorphism, are not painless; instead, they always involve a conflict of some kind between the defenders of an old social order and the advocates of a new one.

A good example of research in these matters is provided by DiMaggio's study (1986) of the evolution of art museums in the United States between 1920 and 1940. This research has been selected for three main reasons:

- the originality of its subject of study;
- the importance of the role played by the organizational field in the process of change;
- the outcome of the change examined, which prompts useful discussion on old and new institutionalism.

DiMaggio studies a typical case of normative isomorphism in which a successful innovation was introduced by professionals working within organizations. Yet the purpose of his analysis is less to emphasize this aspect than to examine the conflicts that the innovation provoked. He begins by pointing out a flaw in such institutionalist research: that it often studies isomorphism processes without considering the organizational field that created them, so that it views the evolution of organizational forms as a conflict-free and predictable process in which the actors involved have no direct part in the change. DiMaggio warns that this approach is misleading, because in order to understand how an organizational form changes, it is first necessary to understand how the organizational field in which that form arose was created. Organizational fields are not simple mental constructs created by researchers; they are also highly meaningful structures for those who are part of them and "include specialized organizations that condition, regulate, organize and represent the field itself" (p.360). Conflicts may develop within organizational fields between new actors who want to transform the existing organizational forms and old actors who control them and want to conserve them as they are. Institutionalization processes involve not only the new forms of organization but also the new category of authorized actors who win the struggle against the groups that controlled the organizations before the change.

More simply, it is wrong to believe that it is possible to study an isomorphism process as if it were the natural, peaceful and indistinct evolution of an old organizational form into a new one. The change in organizational forms is the consequence of transformations which concern the entire field of actors involved, and the transformations are often conflictual. New categories of actors, new agencies promoting the change, new activities, and new channels of co-operation and communication emerge. The group of actors and their initiatives define a new organizational field. Understanding which new organizational forms are legitimated by this field requires one to understand how the field was formed, the interest groups that supported it, and the conflicts that it caused. It is not possible to understand a new social order if the process which has generated it is ignored.

This is the initial premise with which DiMaggio begins his study of the change that took place in American museums between 1920 and 1940. He begins by describing the conflict which arose in the early 1920s between the supporters of two opposing conceptions of an art museum: one conservative and elitist, the other reformist and democratic. The conservatives, who initially prevailed, held that museums should be dedicated to the collecting of art, meaning rare and antique objects of indisputable value. They should be open to a select circle of connoisseurs, and should be controlled by patrons and art specialists and be housed in elegant buildings. By contrast, the reformists believed that museums should display beautiful objects even if they are not antique, they should be committed to the education of the general public, they should be controlled by museum professionals and housed in simple and accessible buildings (see Table 1)

Table 1

	Conservative model	Reformist model
Mission	Collection and conservation	Education, exposition
Definition of art	Art as such, rare objects	Useful art, well designed objects
Perception	Direct, for the knowledgeable	Learning, with aids
Education	Not a priority	Priority
Public	Elite, collectors	General public
Control	Patrons, art specialists	Museum professionals
Strategy	Fast growing collections	Fast growing number of visitors
Buildings	Elegant serious and classic	Simple and accessible
Living artists	Excluded	Included

DiMaggio examines the events which brought victory for the reformist model. His account sheds light on two main aspects. The first is the conflict that arose between the rapid growth of donations by private patrons, which favoured the conservative idea of museums, and the increased influence of museum professionals in favour of the reformist conception of museums. In the decade between 1920 and 1930, private donations rose from two and a half million dollars to 18 million, and the number of museums tripled, so that in the 1930s there was no American city with a population of more that 250 thousand without at least one museum.

The increase in the number of museums set off a chain of effects. Not only did the number of visitors to museums increase, but also the number of schools of fine arts at American universities also increased, with the consequence there was also an increase in the number of museum managers, art critics, and artists with university degrees. In turn, the growth of courses in fine arts induced universities to develop relations with museums and this changed the composition of museum personnel and their tasks. One of the effects of the increased number of museum professionals was that they began to apply for funding from government agencies, thereby reducing the dependence of museums on the power of private patrons. In short: the increased financial commitment by private patrons to the growth of American museums laid the foundations for the growth and institutionalization of a community of professionals who believed that museums should exist for reasons diametrically opposed to what the private patrons wanted.

The second aspect emphasized by DiMaggio is that the conflict between the professionals and the patrons was not manifest within the museums themselves, where a strong formal hierarchy was in force, and where the professionals were careful to comply with the wishes of the patrons. The conflict was evident outside the museums in the development of a dense network of parallel organizations and initiatives mounted to support the reformist cause. In this network, which was not governed by hierarchical structures but ranked its members according to competence, the museum professionals were particularly adept at obtaining support for their conception of what a museum should be.

The Carnegie Corporation played a decisive role in the institutionalization of museum professionalism. Although a private foundation, the Carnegie Corporation, under the charismatic leadership of its president Frederick Keppel, took up a determined stance in favour of the reformist conception of museums. Keppel has the merit of being the first to understand that the management of museum property can and must be regulated a national policy directed by a central agency: the Carnegie Corporation, which not only raised its museum donations to more than 13 million dollars (equal to 80% of all private donations in that period) but funded numerous fine arts schools and professional associations. The most important of the latter were the American Association of Museums (AAM) which brought together all American museum directors and mounted large-scale public education campaigns as well as coordinating museums, and museums with the universities, and The College Art Association, a consortium of regional associations of art teachers which became the official voice of American art historians.

The result of these endeavours was the creation of an organizational field consisting of a dense network of organizations dominated by museum professionals and academics: schools, professional associations, publishing houses and coordination bodies. An integrated and homogeneous professional elite was created, with an intense flow of communications, the publication of books, magazines, traveling exhibitions, and the sponsoring of training courses for museum professionals. In this way, DiMaggio writes, "the Carnegie Corporation programme reinforced the awareness of museum professionals and trustees that they were part of a collective enterprise, and thus the likelihood that they would look to one another as models and sources of innovation" (p.277).

A significant stage in this process of institutionalization was the decision to build decentralized branches of museums. Decentralized museums seemed the most coherent and advanced expression of the reformist intent to bring art to the suburbs – to the general public rather than persuading it to visit the central museums. The Carnegie Corporation also performed a leading role in the decentralization of museums. In May 1931 the first branch of an art museum was inaugurated in Philadelphia. Its success was greater than could have been imagined, although the programme had later to be downsized owing to the severity of the 1929 economic recession.

Overall, we may say that DiMaggio's study of museums is not just an example of organizational analysis but also a historical reconstruction of an unfamiliar aspect of American society which exhibits acute sociological insight. The main conclusions that DiMaggio draws from his research can be summarized as follows:

- The growth of museums was guided at national level by a network of organizations (the organizational field) created by actors who wanted to modify the museum's original structure and mission. The institutionalization of museums was not, therefore, a peaceful process; rather, it engendered conflict;
- The new organizational forms to be taken by museums were justified by appeal to the progressive ideology of democracy;[9]
- Creation of the organizational field was intertwined with the efforts of museum workers to define their profession and increase their authority. The museum professionals avoided conflicts within the museums, but they took action at an inter-organizational level and managed to achieve widespread national control within the organizational field.

More generally, DiMaggio points out that, in non-profit organizations like museums in particular, administrative professionals may occupy extremely powerful roles. When public organizations have little power to act, communities of professionals have greatest opportunity to transform themselves into powerful fields of professional power.

12. OLD AND NEW INSTITUTIONALISM: THE SENSE OF AN ITINERARY

In this chapter, discussion has ranged from the inevitable betrayal of an organization's original goals described by Selznick, to the more varied and problematic scenarios set out in neo-institutionalist studies. The world changes and so does the way in which the world is seen. Yet the way the world is seen does not change simply because the world today is not what it was yesterday. Indeed many studies, like DiMaggio's on museums, examine events from the

9 Although DiMaggio does not mention it, the victory of the reformist conception of museums took place in the 1930s during the period of Roosevelt's New Deal, and therefore under a political leadership which favored democıatic and progressive policies.

past. It is this aspect of the neo-institutionalist interpretation of society that differs most profoundly from those put forward by early institutionalism. How wide the gap is between Selznick's approach and DiMaggio's can be illustrated by the following exercise. Let us try to imagine what results we might obtain if we were to interpret DiMaggio's study on museums using the criteria suggested by Selznick.

The victory of the reformist conception of museums over the conservative one certainly shows how far the museum organizations had diverged from their original objectives: the patrons saw that their desire to celebrate art with no concession made to popular taste had been betrayed. The museums were no longer the sanctuaries of masterpieces reserved for contemplation by a select group of connoisseurs. In order that they might survive, their administrators had abandoned the solemn buildings that they once occupied and had gone to the suburbs; they organized traveling exhibitions, and contaminated masterpieces by mixing them with other objects appreciated by an uneducated public.

The traditionalist nature of this position is immediately evident. Denouncing the betrayal of the original objectives of museums can only spring from nostalgia for an elitist conception of art. But can we be sure that changing the mission of museums was truly a betrayal? And on the basis of what values? Is not using museums to enhance the aesthetic awareness of the general public more in keeping with the values of democracy and progress that Selznick himself seemingly embraces?

Furthermore, Selznick's model identifies the origin of this betrayal of an organization's original objectives in the pressures applied by powerful external forces concerned to maintain the *status quo*. The case of the American museums, however, contradicts Selznick's model. There was no informal co-optation, and the museum professionals were co-opted (meaning appointed) in formal and transparent manner. Moreover, the change arose from within, when the museum professionals began to mobilize themselves in order to change the institutional goal of the organizations that they administered. A pessimist might object that the reform of the museums led to their bureaucratization: before there were only disinterested patrons appreciative of beauty, now there were paid executives who sought to use the museums to increase their power and prestige. Yet is it not Weber who teaches us that bureaucracy is the most efficient way to direct a modern administration, and that an increase in citizens' rights requires strengthening bureaucratic apparatuses so that those rights can be satisfied efficiently and fairly? If this line of reasoning holds for doctors and hospital administrators, why should it not hold for critics, teachers of art and museum administrators as well?

These observations are not intended to gainsay the value of Selznick's work, only to remind us that his model is not universally valid. They are an invitation to reflect on the fact that researchers usually decides to devote their time and energy to subjects that match their personal convictions. Selznick's pessimism induced him choose a topic which confirmed his convictions. DiMaggio and many neo-institutionalists are more open and problematic in their vision of the world, and therefore select subjects which confirm their ideas on the intrinsic ambiguity of social relations.

Powell and DiMaggio discuss the continuities and differences between the old and new institutionalism in the introduction to a collection (1991) of neo-institutionalist essays. Forty years after the study on the TVA, Powell and DiMaggio re-examine Selznick's work, and more generally old institutionalism, and its validity. They find that, although the explanation concerning pressures from outside continues to hold true, the changed social context requires its reconsideration from a profoundly different point of view. Their thesis is that we live today in a society so densely populated by public and private institutions that it is entirely normal to discern an uninterrupted, widespread and interconnected system of regulations and controls on the activity of any organization.

Because the combination of influences in organizational fields is today accepted as normal, the external influences condemned by Selznick diminish in significance. His approach to organizations as if they were besieged by malevolent external forces seeking to distort their institutional objectives loses credibility. Today, organizations operate in a structured and recognized context of constraints and reciprocal influences, and the perception that these influences are normal removes from the action of external forces the dramatic aspect of conflict condemned by Selznick. Often, in fact, it is individual organizations that request external intervention in that they consider it as lending social legitimacy to their action. Selznick's theory is turned upside down. Far from being a risk to an organization's integrity, external pressures help shape the institutional structure which legitimizes them, as long as they conform with it. For neo-institutionalists, external pressures do not arise from obscure power centers but from rationalized myths, or at least from isomorphism processes which transmit socially approved convictions and practices on the assumption that they are intrinsically positive.

However, it would be wrong to take this concept of isomorphism as entirely reassuring, for the institutionalists themselves:

- recognize that institutionalization processes are not without conflicts between advocates of the old and new orders;
- admit that there are no guarantees that institutionalized practices will always have beneficial effects.

There are, then, two issues that invite the proponents of institutionalism to refine their theory. The first is whether Selznick's warning is less alarming because today the power of institutions is truly less brutal and intrusive than it once was, or whether we are so used to impersonal and widespread power that we are less sensitive to gross intrusions in our daily lives; have we become immune to them? The second question concerns the nature itself of isomorphism and can be formulated as follows: if isomorphism causes society to change by favouring what is similar and marginalizing what is different, from whence derive the critical voices that warn of the danger of this phenomenon, and who listens to them?

These questions have prompted various authors (Powell, Jepperson, Friedland and Alford: all in Powell and DiMaggio, 1991) to conduct a critical revision of neo-institutionalism which has attenuated the determinism of its early versions. On the one hand, these authors insist on the autonomy of people in elaborating their own cognitive maps; on the other, they recognize that the main shortcoming of neo-institutionalism is that it emphasizes homogenization to the detriment of diversification. The problem faced by institutionalism in its revised version is to give a satisfactory theoretical explanation for the fact that in human society there have always existed hidden spiritual resources able to generate a collective movement that refuses to accept not only the existing institutional framework but also the emerging one.

The concept of isomorphism must be reformulated so that it is not seen as conflict-free: conflicts not only lead to the success of a new order over an old one; they can also affect the way in which the new order comes about. This can be observed in the on-going process of globalization, a phenomenon so vast that it can be taken to epitomize isomorphism on the planet. It comprises not only the multinationals which seek to decide what we consume and to shape our ideals and lifestyles according to their interests; also isomorphic is the growth of social protest against multinational globalization. Even the ecological movement for the protection of bio-diversity on the planet can be seen as exhibiting a process of planet-wide isomorphism.

These, however, are problems on which the neo-institutionalists must still work if they wish to develop a comprehensive theory.

DISCUSSION

This chapter began with the micro approach in which actors interact and concluded with the macro approach which examines the institutional influences on the important process of organizational and social change. It is difficult to observe these processes because, generally speaking, they take place over long periods of time, and slow change escapes observation in everyday life. But it is not impossible to observe and reflect upon them.

As in previous chapters, once again we can apply these theories to organizations in our daily experience: voluntary associations, small businesses, schools, public services like libraries and museums. Many threads of the discussion can be untangled, beginning with leadership. When discussing Weber, we saw that the three pure types of power, charismatic, traditional and bureaucratic can be mixed to various extents in an empirical phenomenon. Now Selznick offers us other instruments of analysis. Let us look at an organization that we know and ask ourselves, using Selznick's criteria, whether it is only an instrumental organization, or an institution, in the sense that it has a leadership which identifies values and objectives, instills them in its members, protects the ideals of the institution, mediates and resolves conflicts.

Another topic of discussion concerns change and relationships with the external environment. How has the organization changed in the time that we have known it, and under what stimuli? Does the inevitable logic of compromise with pressures applied by external powers described by Selznick seem useful for understanding the change? Or are the more ambivalent and widespread processes of isomorphism described by neo-institutionalists more useful? And in this case, what type of isomorphism do we mainly see: coercive isomorphism, which obliges reluctant people, to accept unwelcome new ideas (in this case we are closer to the pressures described by Selznick); mimetic isomorphism, in which everyone hurriedly follows a fashion; or normative isomorphism, which enables one or more individuals, after they have learned new competences or practices, to choose those ideas, convinced of the advantages they offer? And where does one type of isomorphism end and another begin? At times this difference is very subtle (we shall see that the difference is only a question of a person's interior attitude).

In the previous chapter we examined the role of people, their strategies and their interaction. And we saw that many of the balances struck within an organization can be explained as the result, often unexpected, of those actions. In this chapter we have gone a step further. We have extended our study to the important changes prompted by the external environment. But we have also learned that these changes are, at times, promoted by subjects within the organization itself: by leaders as Selznick teaches us, but also by entire professional categories as in the case of the museums.

This is where the picture becomes more complicated. The same phenomenon can be dealt with at a level of individual strategies and at a level of institutional conditioning. There is no reason, however, to become disorientated. It is enough to remember that there exists an unlimited number of interpretations of the same event, and that the choice of viewpoint is simply a question of heuristic effectiveness: what we want to examine, what seems more interesting, more important or more original to us. And the two levels, micro and macro do not exclude each other; rather, using both levels is very often the best way to give value added to the inquiry. It is true that organizations have continuity and persistence, but it is also true that they only exist thanks to their members.

REFERENCES

Brient Steven , Karabel Jerome 1991 Institutional Origins and Transformations: The Case of American Community Colleges , in Powell e DiMaggio 1991, (trad. ital. 2000).

Clark Burton 1960, *The Open Door College : A Case Study*, Mc Grw Hill, New York.

DiMaggio Paul 1991 : Construction and Organizational Fiedl as a Professional Project:U.S.Art Museums 1920-1940 , in *The new Institutionalism in Organizational Analysis* W.Powell e P. DiMaggio eds. University of Chicago Press.

Fliegstein Neil 1991 The Structural Transformation of American Industry: An Institutional Account of the Causes of Diversification in the Largest Firms 1919-1979, in Powell e DiMaggio 1991.

Friedland Roger , Alford Robert, *Bringing society back in: Symbolism Practices and Institutional Contradictions,* in Powell e DiMaggio 1991.

Galaskiewics Joseph.

Making Corporate Actors Accountable:Instition-Buildingh in Minneapolis-St Paul, in Powell and DiMaggio 1991.

Janowitz Morris, 1960 *The Professional Soldier* Free Press, New York.

Jepperson Ronard *Institutions, Institutional Effects and Institutionalism,* in Powell and DiMaggio 1991.

Meyer John, Rowan Brian: 1977 Institutionalized Organizations :Formal Structure as Myth and Ceremony, *American Journal of Sociology,* 83, n.2, pp. 340-363.

1978 The Structure of Educational Organizations, in Marshall W Meyer et al. *Environments and Organizations, Rituals and Rationality* Jossey & Bass, San Francisco.

Michels Robert 1966 (1st edit. in German 1911) *La sociologia del partito politico nella democrazia moderna* , Il Mulino Bologna.

Orrù Marco, Biggart Woolsey Nicole, Hamilton Gary 1991, Organizational Isomorphism in East Asia, in Powell and DiMaggio 1991.

Perrow Charles.

1961 Organizational Prestige :Some Functions and Dysfunctions, *American Journal of Sociology* 66, n. 4, January pp. 335-341.

1986 *Complex Organizations, a Critical essay,* Random House, New York.

Powell Walter, DiMaggio Paul.

1983 The Iron Cage Revisited :Institutional Isomorphism and Collective Rationality, *American Sociological Review* 48, Aprile pp. 147-160, ripublished in *The new Institutionalism in Organizational Analysis* W,Powell and P.DiMaggio eds. University of Chicago Pres, 1991.

1991 *The new Institutionalism in Organizational Analysis* W.Powell and P. DiMaggio, eds. University of Chicago Press.

Expanding the Scope of Instituzional Analysis (in Powell e DiMaggio 1991).

Scott Richard 1995 *Institutions and Organizations,* Thousand Oaks, Cal.

Scott Robert 1967, The Selection of Clients by Social Welfare Agencies :the case of the Blind.

Social Problems, 14, n. 3 Winter pp. 248-257.

Selznick Philip: 1948 Foundations of the theory of Organizations, *American Sociological Review*, col.13, February.

1949Tva and the Grass Roots .A Study in the Sociology of Formal Organizations, Univ. of California Press.

1957 *Leadership in Administration. A Sociological Interpretation* Harper & Row NewYork.

Sudnow David 1964 Normal Crimes, *Social Problems*, 12, n. 3 Winter, pp. 255-275.

Tolbert Pamela, Zucker Lynne 1983, Institutional Sources of Change in the Formal Structure of Organizations: The Diffusion of Civil Service Reform, 1880-1935, *Administrative Science Quarterly*, 30, pp. 22-39.

Zald Mayer, Denton Patricia 1963 From Evangelism to General Service : the Transformation of YMCA, *Administrative Science Quarterly* , 8, n. 2 September, pp. 214-234.

Chapter 5

TRANSACTION COSTS ECONOMIC AND ORGANIZATIONAL POPULATIONS

The first part of the chapter discusses transaction costs theory and the new horizons that it has opened up for organizational analysis. It examines the consequences of extending the concept of organization to encompass, besides bureaucracy, also the market and networks. The second part of the chapter is devoted to so-called ecological theory, whose object of analysis is no longer individual organizations but entire populations of them.

1. TWO NEW PERSPECTIVES OF ANALYSIS

In the preceding chapters we saw that Weber's model of bureaucratic organization can have many variants; that organizations exist and function only if the balance between contributions and incentives induces individuals to participate; and that powerful external forces influence the action of organizations. However different these areas of inquiry may be, all of them represent organizations as well-defined entities, with institutional aims, and with hierarchy and bureaucracy as their typical command and functional structures. They also it take for granted that the units of analysis are individual organizations, for example a hospital, a school, a firm, or a newspaper.

This chapter examines two schools of thought which go beyond this view. The first is transaction costs economics (TCE), and the second is the analysis of organizational populations, or the 'ecological' approach. These schools study economic enterprises, but they can be applied to the analysis of other organizations as well. TCE advises us that the concept of organization is much broader than that of bureaucracy. One may speak of an organization not only in reference to informal or spontaneous groups, as said in the introduction (Laura's day), but also in reference to bodies and institutions not usually considered to be organizations, such as the market or networks of individual organizations. In other words, an organization is defined as any stable pattern of relations among actors, be these individuals or groups. Therefore, the concept:

Organization ≡ Bureaucracy[1]

is replaced by: Bureaucracy

Organization Hybrid or intermediate forms (networks) Market

This new conceptualization of organizations requires comment.

- Market and organization are not seen as opposites: the market can have some form of organization just as much as organizations can have some form of internal market.
- Organizations do not have stable and defined boundaries based on a single criterion. 'Boundary' becomes a relative notion which changes according to the criteria used to measure the intensity and nature of the relations among actors.
- Organizations, including the market, cannot be studied without taking account of their institutional context. From this perspective, TCE is an integral part of new institutional economics (NIE), which is the economic version of the new institutionalism discussed in the previous chapter.[2]

The ecological approach also goes beyond the assumption that only individual organizations existing at the time of the inquiry can be studied. Its subject of analysis is *organizational populations*, that is, all the organizations which operate, or have operated, in the same environmental niche for a certain period of time (for example, all the Chinese restaurants opened in a city in the past ten years, or all the provincial newspapers published in a given town over fifty years). Consequently subject to analysis are not only the organizations that have survived a selection process, but also those that have disappeared – and the reasons for whose failure must be investigated. We will also see that the ecological approach:

- offers conceptual tools with which to answer the question why contemporary society comprises such a wide variety of organizations;
- refers to the institutional context in order to understand the process by which organizations are generated, and therefore seeks to supplement the explanation of isomorphism processes furnished by new institutionalism.

2. THE CHANGING CONCEPTION OF THE FIRM: FROM PRODUCTION FUNCTION TO THE GOVERNANCE OF TRANSACTIONS

To convey the theoretical innovativeness of TCE, it is useful to start from the traditional conception of production enterprises. For a long time, practically until

1 The ° symbol signifies equivalence.

2 Two other strands of analysis pertaining to new institutional economics are the theory of incomplete contracts and the theory of the resource-based firm.

the 1970s, common experience and economic theory agreed that the institutional purpose of firms was to produce and sell goods, the aim being to achieve the maximum profit by making optimal use of the technologies available. In economic jargon, the firm was considered a *production function*. On this view, which reached its apogee during the Taylorist-Fordist period of mass production, establishing the boundaries of a firm was not a problem. In the common view, the physical confines of a business coincided with its economic, technical, financial and human boundaries. There were factories with walls, and everything behind them was the property and responsibility of the company: the purchase and use of plant, regulation of the workforce, storage of incoming and outgoing materials, and so on.

If we use the concept of *verticalization* to express the extension of the production phases carried out directly by the firm, we may say that traditional firms normally displayed marked verticalization. The highest theoretical degree of verticalization was when firms undertook the entire production cycle themselves: from the mines producing the raw materials, to the machines producing the packaging for the final products to be sold on the market. In truth, such extreme verticalization, or such long production chains, hardly ever existed. More common, even in the past, was the strategy of buying raw materials, or semi-finished products, from other firms and then producing finished products in the factory for sale either on the final consumer market or on an intermediate market consisting of firms 'downstream'. The greater the use of the components or production processes of other firms, the less the firm in question was verticalized. But even with a low level of verticalization, owing to inertia, firms were still seen as entities based on production processes undertaken in their own factories with machinery operated by their own employees. Technology, conceived as a physically indivisible whole, was deemed to be the decisive feature that established the boundaries of a firm.

During the 1970s, however, processes of deverticalization began to spread, because large firms found it economical to give other, generally smaller firms, contracts for specific jobs, or for even complex components of their own products. In their turn, these firms subcontracted part of the work assigned to them by the larger firms, with the result that they created a relatively stable network of suppliers and sub-suppliers. This was accompanied by the phenomenon, especially apparent in sectors like the clothing industry, of formally independent employees who worked at home. In this way firms saved a significant part of labour costs that they would otherwise have had to pay if these home workers were taken on as dependent employees.

The global spread of these phenomena became too great an anomaly with respect to the traditional model not to pose the theoretical problem of developing a new model that took them into account. And it is this that explains the birth and success of TCE, a school of thought whose best-known representative is Oliver Williamson (1930 – present).[3]

Williamson's analysis begins from the question: why is all production not undertaken by a single large firm? He replies by first pointing out that it is erroneous to consider a firm to be an entity whose essential function is to produce. Instead, it must be considered a 'governance structure' whose basic function is to stipulate and guarantee reliable and efficient contracts. When a firm's function is reformulated in this way, the framework of its strategic choices changes radically. In the classical model, an industrial firm could choose what and how much to produce, but it had no alternative but to produce. In the new model, the firm has a wider range of choices because it has the alternatives of producing in-house or purchasing externally (the *'to make or to buy'* choice).

To clarify this new definition, Williamson takes Adam Smith's famous example of the pins. A worker doing all the jobs necessary to make the pins by himself would take an enormous amount of time, and the pins would be prohibitively expensive. But the division of labour (Smith identifies eighteen distinct operations) solves the problem by increasing productivity tenfold. Williamson takes Smith's example to observe that today TCE does not ask how many pins to produce and at what price, but how to organize and govern the eighteen distinct operations described by Smith. In other words, which of those operations can be performed in-house and which should be performed by external producers and therefore purchased?

This new point of view has two consequences. The first is that the elementary analytical unit is no longer the good produced but the *transaction.* By this is meant any form of contract that the firm is able to stipulate: contracts with external suppliers of goods or services, work contracts with employees, contracts for specific or temporary jobs, hybrid contracts that tie workers to the business without them becoming an integral part of it, and so on.

The second consequence is that technology is no longer the primary feature that defines the boundaries of a firm. The idea that the physical indivisibility of a plant must correspond to a single owner or user no holds longer true. The same plant can serve two or more firms. In the same way, it may happen that two competing firms create a joint venture to design, build and use a given plant together.[4]

3 Two forerunners of the transaction costs school were John Commons and Ronald Coase. As early as 1934, Commons stressed the importance of judicial institutions in explaining the strategic choices of firms. In 1937, Coase wrote an article entitled *TheNature of the Firm,* which at the time went unnoticed but later gained such wide recognition as to win him the Nobel Prize in 1991. Williamson acknowledges his intellectual debt to Commons and, especially, to Coase.

4 This phenomenon is apparent not only in industry but also in transport. It is increasingly common for the same plane to be used for the flights of two or more airlines, in the sense that the company owning the plane leases some of the seats available to another company. Passengers who have bought tickets from two different companies thus find themselves flying on the same airplane.

3. TWO SOURCES OF UNCERTAINTY: BOUNDED RATIONALITY AND OPPORTUNISM

A range of possibilities for economic action therefore open up for firms. But on the basis of what criteria should the best choice be made? A full reply to this question requires developing a new economic theory, and this requires us, argues Williamson, to start from two assumptions about human beings: they have bounded rationality, as already theorized by Simon, and they are opportunistic. The assumption of bounded rationality entails that, although human beings seem to behave in intentionally rational manner, in actual fact they are much less rational than they seem owing to limitations of knowledge, farsightedness, technical ability, and the time available to act.

The assumption of opportunism entails that human beings may pursue their own interests with illicit means such as deception and fraud. One situation that favours opportunism is that of 'small numbers', where only a few individuals are involved in a transaction. In these cases, the suppliers of goods or services may take advantage of their monopoly to charge exorbitant prices.[5] It may also happen that a few people collude to deceive the other party by giving false information on the real market value of the goods subject to transaction. The best way to combat opportunism is to avoid small numbers situations, because as the number of individuals involved in a transaction increases, so does the competition among them, and the possibility of blocking information flows decreases. From this point of view, the pure market seems theoretically to be the ideal means with which to discourage opportunism (although as we shall see, there are other forms of defense, especially that of developing consolidated trust networks.)

If rationality were not bounded, and if human behaviour were always honest, Williamson observes, then stipulating contracts would not be a problem. Contracts would be able to foresee every eventuality, and with the greatest precision, and they would be fulfilled without the risk of fraud. But the fact that action takes place in conditions of bounded rationality and with the risk of opportunism generates widespread uncertainty and makes the stipulation of contracts problematic. Contracts can never be complete, either because it is impossible to forecast every situation that may arise until their expiry, or because the counterpart's performance may be less than the contractor expected when signing the contract. It is, therefore, necessary to develop the structures and procedures best able to economize on the scarce resources of bounded rationality, and to stipulate effective safeguarding clauses with which to counter the risk of opportunism.

From these premises, Williamson argues that economic theory must

5 Opportunism becomes crime when privileges are protected coercively by means of threats and force.

distinguish between two types of cost: production costs and transaction costs. Production costs concern the processes by which a given material is physically transformed from state A to state B: for example, the mining of raw materials, petrol refining, the smelting of metals, the transport of materials. These are the only costs considered by classical economics. Transaction costs, on the other hand, are those necessary to stipulate and manage a contract, and they may be paid both before and after it. Costs are paid before the contract in order to find a counterpart (a search that may at times be lengthy and costly), to conduct negotiations, and to stipulate the contract. Costs are paid after the contract in order to have it respected: typically legal costs in the event of disputes, but also the normal costs of ensuring that an action defined in the contract is carried out in the agreed time and manner ('safeguarding costs').

Transaction costs are involved in the purchase and sale of all goods – real estate, commodities, energy, services, work – and they are extremely variable (the transaction costs of immovable goods are normally higher than those of movable goods). On the assumption that production costs are equal and constant, Williamson considers them to be "the economic equivalent of friction in physical systems", a factor that can be reduced but never eliminated. Williamson constructs his theory on transaction costs: the need to economize on transaction costs is the crucial problem in the management of a firm.

4. THE BASIC DILEMMA: TO BUY OR TO MAKE?

The dilemma of a business – is it more convenient to buy or to make? – must therefore be addressed in relation to transaction costs. Williamson now introduces three variables:

- the technology used to produce the good or service requested;
- the frequency of transactions;
- the safeguards necessary for the contract to be fulfilled.

The technology can be generic or specialist. It is generic when it does not require particular know-how or investment, it has standard characteristics which make it easily available on the market, and its suppliers can be replaced without especial difficulty. In these cases, there is no need for special safeguarding clauses to protect the contract, and the normal legal institutions are enough to settle any disputes between the contractors. On the other hand, technology is specialized when it requires greater investment and meets particular and repeated needs. These are also the cases in which a firm has greatest need of safeguards against the risk of opportunist behaviour by the other party.

Williamson's thesis is that when a firm needs goods or services produced with generic technology and transactions are relatively infrequent, the best choice is to go to the market (*to buy*). This means not producing in-house, but buying goods or services from an external company offering them at competitive prices. In the opposite case, where technology is specific, transactions are continuous and there is a risk of disputes over fulfillment of the contract, the best choice is to produce in-house using technologies belonging to the firm and dependent employees (*to make*). The principle of market contracting is replaced by the principle of discipline accepted by the employees on the basis of a contract that stipulates a quantity of continuous work and is renegotiated only on its expiry. The firm establishes an internal governance hierarchy in order to ensure by direct control over the production process that all the work contracted with the employees is actually carried out.

Market and hierarchy are the two extreme choices available to a firm. But they are never stable and definitive choices, for they may be revised when incorrect behaviour provokes a failure in the market or the hierarchy. A failure of the market occurs when firm F continues to use the same supplier S until the latter occupies a privileged position with respect to other competitors. On the one hand, S will tend to specialize in order to cater to the needs of F; on the other, opportunistic behaviour is likely to develop. S may take advantage of its privileged position to alter the terms of the contract to its advantage, for example by raising the price, not respecting delivery times, or using confidential information. In this case, returning to the market to seek another supplier is not convenient to F, because S has accumulated specific know-how unavailable elsewhere. The best option for F is to purchase S with all its know-how and bring it under the direct control of its hierarchy. We may then say that F has chosen a strategy of vertical integration.

There is a hierarchy failure in the reverse situation, which is when the company decides to resort to the market because of difficulties caused by excessive vertical integration. Crises may have a number of causes: excessive conflict in the workforce; the onset of corporative behaviour that induces personnel to pursue particular aims (power, perks, etc.) not compatible with corporate interests; bureaucratic inertia which discourages innovation; or simply the difficulty of running an organizational machine that has grown too large and complex. In these cases, it is preferable to contract part of the production process out to external firms with which the contractor enters into normal commercial relations.

Such a drastic choice between hierarchy and market is rare, however. It is likely that more convenient to a firm will be a mix of hierarchy and market, or what is known as a 'quasi-market'. Typical intermediate forms are joint ventures (forms of temporary collaboration for specific purposes) and franchising (contracts between two formally independent firms where each allows the other to operate in its name and use its production and marketing methods in exchange for direct or indirect payment). Another form of hybrid contract is the collaboration established by a large (or parent) company with a network of smaller firms which, while remaining formally independent, accept internal controls by the parent company and become its permanent suppliers. Created in this case are *idiosyncratic* relations, that is to say bilateral dependence. On the one hand, the suppliers make long-term and specialized investments (almost) exclusively for the sake of the parent company; on the other, the parent company invests capital and knowledge to improve the chosen suppliers' performance.

In such diverse contractual situations, also diversified are the instruments available with which the firm can ensure that transactions are successfully concluded. In pure market conditions – where every transaction is a unique act, so that one can talk of 'instantaneous' contracts – the typical instrument of control is the price of goods purchased. In situations where production takes place internally to the firm (*to make* with regular employees), the typical instrument is hierarchical discipline (although it is increasingly common for firms to foster workforce involvement with material and symbolic incentives).

Finally, in the hybrid situations like networks between big firms and suppliers, the essential prerequisite is mutual trust. This must be nourished with specific initiatives like the prior selection of the most suitable suppliers, selective and continuing training programs, joint research and development projects, participation in investments by the parent company. Thus created is a broad network which is enduring because it is based on mutual obligations and interests. Consequently, trust becomes a more effective instrument with which to combat opportunism than the pure market.

5. INSTITUTIONS, MARKET AND TRANSACTIONS: MACRO AND MICRO DIMENSIONS OF THE ECONOMY

The conception of the firm as a governance structure rather than a production function has been the main theoretical development brought by transaction costs economics, and more generally by new institutional economics (NIE). The name of the latter denotes a school of thought that has profoundly innovated the foundations of classical economics and its view of the market as a universal and abstract institution, ruled by laws valid in every time and place because they are based solely on the balance between supply and demand. In the classical conception, all that matters is calculation of individual utilities, on the assumption that together these generate a self-regulating mechanism (whence derives the metaphor of the invisible hand guiding the market).

NIE questions that assumption because it believes that the market cannot be considered an abstract, self-sufficient mechanism extraneous to the social context. On the contrary, account must always be made of the specific historical institutions in which the market is embedded and which have conditioned its development. Some of these institutions are legislation on property rights, insurance and contracts; monetary and fiscal policy; and the more general group of incentives and constraints that induce firms to work in one way rather than another. Turvani comments on Williamson theory as follows:

> *"With this, institutional economics takes a step forward, placing the market inside an institutional environment, showing that the prosperity of nations cannot be disconnected from a suitable system of rules within which the market can operate" (1998, p. 22).*

The concept of a firm as a structure governing transactions has the important consequence of unifying previously distinct fields of research. One of the first of these unifying effects is apparent in relations between business economics and organizational sociology. As long as the firm was considered a production functions, the two disciplines went their separate ways: economics studied how firms could optimize profits with respect to investments and production, while sociology studied the bureaucratic organization, with its unexpected consequences and the relationships between the formal and informal. So it was that the two disciplines developed independent and parallel investigations into the same subject which only accidentally coincided.

Since the advent of NIE, and especially TCE, relations between economic analysis and organizational analysis have been radically recast, because the decision of a company to produce in-house, to purchase on the market, or to develop a select network of trusted suppliers, has a significance that is both economic and organizational. In the first case, the firm chooses to have numerous employees whose work is coordinated and hierarchically controlled. In the second case, it chooses to have few personnel but with expertise in conducting technical-commercial negotiations (the extreme case is the 'empty business', where there is only one owner-entrepreneur). In the third case, the firm takes the intermediate option and employs qualified personnel able to organize long-term work groups with colleagues from other firms in the network. Given this range of choices, business economists and organization scholars increasingly engage in joint research projects.

A second unifying effect is evident in relations between the macro and micro dimensions of analysis. The macro dimension concerns the institutional framework of transactions, while the micro dimension concerns individual transactions and the governance mechanisms that regulate them. To use a metaphor, while the macro level examines the rules of the game dictated by the institutions, the micro level examines the way the players (firms and individuals) choose how to play.

Connecting the two dimensions together means recognizing, on the one hand, that transactions are not guided by universal and abstract criteria but are embedded in an institutional context which defines opportunities and constraints; and on the other that specific choices are not deterministic because individuals have margins of freedom (and are therefore unpredictable) in their actions.

At the macro level, analysis is mainly concerned with the overall framework of legislative constraints and opportunities. Other conditions remaining equal, one may suppose that a firm operating in a context characterized by a robust system of industrial relations, with strong and recognized trade unions, centralized bargaining, and a government that actively mediates between the parties, will be strongly oriented towards *to make* options with institutionally negotiated labor costs. Vice versa, we may assume that a firm operating in a *laissez-faire* context with private work contracts and weak or non-existent trade unions, will tend towards *to buy* options with predominantly temporary employment relationships. Similar considerations apply to the presence or otherwise of antitrust legislation, to the rules regulating the relationship between firms and the banking system, to the constraints imposed by environmental protection law, and so on.

If it is to be complete, macro-level analysis must also consider the economic effects of non-economic institutions: social, religious, political, cultural, customary. Consider the economic impact of the female condition and the different criteria by which women's work outside the home is judged. There are countries with complete gender equality; others where female work is encouraged but only if it is paid less than male work; yet others where it is disapproved of or even prohibited. When a firm organizes production, hires personnel or sub-contracting, invests or otherwise in vocational training, it cannot ignore these cultural and social constraints.

On a more general level, only by considering the institutional framework is it possible to ask the question: what environmental conditions favour or discourage the growth of specific economic activities? No satisfactory reply can be given if we remain at the macro level alone. Macro analysis must be integrated with micro analysis, which entails observation of the real behaviour of firms and individuals. It is the task of micro analysis to open the 'black box' of what happens within firms and in relationships among them. Analyzed in this case is not only the formal structure and visible technology but also more intangible aspects such as the climate of human relations, the circulation of knowledge, the attitude towards innovation, the rewards system, and the presence of opportunism.

The further analysis moves towards organizational behaviour, the more necessary it is to bear in mind Williamson's remark that "the organizational man is less calculating than the economic man but his motivation is more complicated". Consequently, it is not enough to calculate equations of economic optimality in order to be able to forecast human behaviour. Thus introduced is the approach already indicated by Simon which analyses of the decision-making processes involved in transactions. And it also opens the way for more subtle analyses extending beyond Williamson's theory to comprise nano-economics (Arrow) and behavioral decision theory (Bazerman, 1994). This is inquiry into the mental processes that develop during decision-making. Its assumption is that individuals perceive the outside world differently from what one would expect on a simply logical basis, and it examines the importance of consolidated social knowledge in information processing, judgments, decisions and actions, as well as the factors that induce changes in that stock of knowledge.

As they delve into the micro dimension, approaches to a social and economic reality viewed as objective arrived at the subjective foundations of the mental processes that make sense of that reality. Just as in the study of sub-atomic particles the realization dawns that matter is no longer being investigated more but energy, so in the study of organizational behaviour the moment comes when the subject of analysis is no longer visible as external structures but mental processes.

6. IN THE WAKE OF TRANSACTION COSTS: PROBLEMS, APPLICATIONS AND VARIATIONS

The two main conceptualizations that have emerged thus far – the firm as a structure for the governance of transactions, and institutions as the reference framework within which to explain economic forms – have for many years fuelled debate in the economic, organizational and administrative sciences. Some of the issues addressed are directly connected with TCE, while others, though congenial to that school of thought, concern problems broader in scope. This section examines the problems, applications and variants of TCE with the most direct bearing on the analysis of organizations. It then turns to a much wider theme – the varieties of capitalism – showing that the economic version of new institutionalism and the sociological one discussed in the preceding chapter, even though they deal with the same phenomena, cannot merge into a single strand of analysis because they pursue different analytical purposes.

6.1 Productive sectors and the boundaries of firms

Among its many advantages, the concept of a firm as governance of transactions makes it possible to highlight significant differences among the various productive sectors. We have seen that both the corporate practice of purchasing goods and services externally, and the attention paid to the phenomenon by analysts, are relatively recent. However, there are production areas in which the practice has long been adopted in the form of sub-contracting. Two sectors in which this typically occurs are construction and shipbuilding. In both of these a number of professionals and experts in a variety of trades – architects, designers, joiners, smiths, tilers, carpenters, electricians, decorators – work together with circumscribed and dedicated actions to construct buildings and ships, individual products with thousands of components. Although these workers are in part employed by third parties, but they are mainly self-employed (artisans). They all supply their skills on the basis of temporary and *ad hoc* contracts drawn up with the contracting company. For the latter, the ability to create networks or quasi-organizations comprising hundreds of more or less temporary self-employed workers is fundamental for their economic success (on construction see Eccles 1981; on shipbuilding see Porter and Cho, 1987).

The construction and shipbuilding industries seemingly suggest, in line with Williamson's theory, that all sectors with highly differentiated processes for the production of composite goods find it particularly convenient to take *to buy* choices. There are exceptions, however, and the automobile industry is certainly the most important of them. A car, too, is the final outcome of the assembly of thousands of technologically heterogeneous components. Yet for nearly the whole of the twentieth century, automobile manufacturers epitomized the Fordist régime based on strong verticalization and *to make* choices (only tires and glass were purchased from external companies). The automobile industry warns us against deterministic explanations, such as those which consider only the technological characteristics of the sector, and invites us to recognize the importance of management convictions – and therefore a subjective and cultural factor – in explaining specific strategic choices.

Only in the 1980s did Western automobile manufacturers – following the example of the Japanese, who were the pioneers in the field – begin to shift to market choices (today more than two-thirds of the final cost of a car is made up of externally produced components). Prior to that decade, however, some research studies (Walker and Weber, 1984) showed that nearly always in the automobile industry the *to buy* choice did not spring, as Williamson claims, from the intention to reduce transaction costs but rather from the desire to reduce production costs. The reason was that components companies had begun to specialize in a narrow range of specific (core) competences, with the result that they could supply products which were cheaper and of better quality than the parent companies could produce in-house. The convenience of buying important parts of the final product fostered the 'tertiarization' of the production process (*outsourcing*) with considerable organizational consequences. Recent research on the subject (Bonazzi 2000) has shown that the economic convenience persists even if transaction costs increase as a result of the greater complexity of negotiations in the workplace. What matters is the algebraic sum of the two types of cost.[6] And this is an example of how the possibility of choosing between *to make* and *to buy* generates practical behaviour in firms that goes beyond the framework of theoretical expectations formulated by Williamson.

6 We shall return to this topic in the conclusions.

Robust analysis of these matters was conducted in the 1980s by Kanter [1989], whose study of eighty large American firms revealed three main tendencies:

- internal restructuring in order to create new synergies among the various components of the company. The latter becomes a confederation of semi-autonomous units which may compete against each other but at the same time are induced to develop cooperative strategies in pursuit of strategic goals;
- the opening of their borders to new alliances with suppliers, customers and other firms;
- the development of investment programmes with a view to forming joint ventures.

Decentralization, outsourcing, and the creation of service companies catering to both the parent company and others in competition with it: these are some of the most common forms in which the above tendencies are manifest. Firms do not lose their identities but reduce their autonomy by strengthening ties with a network of other firms.

The interpenetration among firms may thus become so close that it is difficult to distinguish the employees of one firm from those of another. If a firm is viewed as a structure of transactions governance, and if the transactions involve a large number of other firms to the point that a network is created with a continuous flow of goods, services and information, on the basis of what criterion can we establish where the contracting company 'ends' and the suppliers begin?

One criterion may reside in the concept of 'business group', so that one establishes whether all the firms involved in a given production programme belong to the same business group regardless of the ownership relations among them. If firm A gives a significant share of its turnover to firm B, and B solicits idiosyncratic investments from A, one may say that the two firms belong to the same business group. But even this concept seems inadequate, because suppliers – especially the leaders in the sector – increasingiy participate in the production programmes of several contractors, even if these compete against each other.

Furthermore, the problem of boundaries does not concern the relationship between a firm and the external environment alone. It may also arise within a firm itself, doing so as a result of competition which develops among its various units. These may not only reject goods or services supplied by units of the same group if they decide that it is more economical to purchase them externally; they may also be urged by central management to launch competing products on the market. In these cases, the firm can be defined as a broader business group with extensive autonomy among its various parts. Nevertheless, the problem of boundaries still remains.

In the 1970s, Pfeffer and Salancik (1977) proposed a micro-level solution to the problem of the boundaries of a firm (and more in general, of an organization). Because individuals may work for more than one firm, Pfeffer and Salancik suggested that the work activities undertaken for each firm can be taken as the boundary criterion. Thus, the unit of analysis is no longer the single individual but his/her behaviour, with the result that the boundary of the organization becomes moveable in that it depends on the momentary use of specific human resources. Pfeffer and Salancik's proposal makes implicit reference to a financial criterion: what is important is the economic balance of costs and profits, so that if the firm purchases a certain work activity, it is within its boundaries regardless of the legal status of who performs it. But what about work activities in joint ventures (typically the search for innovation) where two or more firms collaborate to achieve a particular result which they will then use in competition with each other? These are questions to which the modern debate has not yet given a satisfactory answer (Colombo 1998).

6.2 OUCHI: THE CLAN AS GOVERNANCE OF LONG-TERM TRANSACTIONS

An original variant of Williamson's model has been developed by William Ouchi, an American of Japanese origin, who refers to models of economic behaviour typical of Asiatic capitalism. Ouchi's theory is that market and hierarchy are not the only forms of transaction governance available to a firm. There is also a third possibility, what he calls 'the clan'. A clan is the most complex form of governance because for it to function mere reference to the price on the market, or to the price plus authority within the hierarchy, is not sufficient. The clan presupposes that the parties to the contract feel that they belong to an institution with a tradition, norms, and shared values.

Ouchi's thesis is that the clan is the only instrument that enables complex transactions to be governed, especially those that take place over a period of years, because it compels the contracting parties to respect obligations and undertakings that cannot be honoured immediately. The clan furnishes 'serial equity' between contractors as opposed to the 'instant equity' characteristic of the market, and in a certain sense also of the hierarchy, or bureaucracy. This is because belonging to the same clan is the basis for trust among the members, and because sanctions in the event of default are particularly severe in that they consist of expulsion from the clan, and therefore the loss of honour and the social death of the transgressor (*loss of face* is the maximum threat in Far Eastern culture).

Ouchi's theory prompts some considerations. The first is that the clan is a social aggregation which often predates the economic activity: belonging to the same race, country, social class, religious sect, or having shared a crucial experience (e.g. members of the same combat unit). Economic transactions are, therefore, facilitated by a typically non-economic factor, and this bears out the institutionalist approach's insistence that economic action should be studied as it is embedded in its social context. But the sense of belonging to a clan can also be instilled by an economic institution, typically a large business group. This is a traditional model widespread in the Far East and in Japan in particular, where joining a firm has an ethical value that goes way beyond the exclusively economic significance that it has in the West. (In Japan today this traditional significance is diminishing, but until the last decades of the twentieth century the *nenko* system, that is, lifelong employment in a company, was widespread).

The clan is also an appropriate model with which to study criminal economic organizations. As these are illegal, and therefore cannot use the safeguarding contracts provided by law, they set up complex apparatuses of control over their members: secrecy, initiation rites, inflexible rules on private behaviour, marks of dishonour, and death sentences for transgressors are the devices most frequently used to develop a strong sense of belonging to the organization.

Criminal organizations aside, the theory of the clan as particularly suited to governing complex economic transactions raises a disquieting challenge against the precepts that regulate Western economic-social institutions. The challenge arises from the fact that the clan, based as it is on criteria of inclusion/exclusion, conflicts with the universalistic criteria commonly cited as essential for the rule of law in the West. The conflict gives rise an ambivalent judgment. On the one hand, Ouchi sees the clan as the most efficient form of bureaucracy with which to manage complex economic transactions, and this superiority may be interpreted as indicative that there is no linear evolution from a traditional to a modern world; rather that forms and institutions from the past may easily acquire new meanings and new functions in contemporary society. On the other hand, it should not be forgotten, as Weber showed, that by virtue of its impartiality and effective neutrality, bureaucracy is best able to guarantee the universalistic administration of the *res pubblica*. Even if today numerous states are seeking new administrative structures with which to supersede the rigidity of classical bureaucracy, the universalistic criteria underpinning the rule of law cannot be called into question.

The clan as a form of economic governance, therefore, stands in potential conflict with those criteria because it assumes that the universality of rights is not a necessary prerequisite for economic success. The fact that economic efficiency can be removed from the universality of rights and obligations raises a worrying challenge against the optimistic assumption of Western political thought that a developed economy finds its best institutional form in the universalistic rule of law, and therefore in political democracy. Ouchi's analysis seems to suggest that that a high level of economic development can be achieved without the parallel development of political democracy: which is the situation, in fact, of quite a few Far Eastern countries.

6.3 MICRO AND MACRO APPLICATIONS OF THE MODEL: FROM THE DOMESTIC ECONOMY TO LOCAL DEVELOPMENT

Despite the theoretical questions that they raise, TCE and, more in general NIE, display an extraordinary flexibility of application. The range of choice between market and hierarchy and the institutions, as the frame of reference for specific forms of economic activity, proves a powerful conceptual instrument for use in micro and macro research.

TCE at micro level has been interestingly applied to domestic economics and household organization (Pollack, 1985). If we consider a household to be a special type of firm, TCE enables analysis of economic choices to be linked with study of organizational structure. *To make* or *to buy* are everyday choices that affect households: suffice it to consider eating at home, going to a restaurant, or intermediate forms like buying ready-made food to be consumed at home. At a more strategic level is the wife's choice between being a housewife (*to make*) or working outside the home, giving part of her earnings to a domestic helper (*to buy*).

Beyond these relatively simplistic examples, considering the household as a structure of transaction governance raises the interesting question of the link between economic and extra-economic criteria in the choices made by a household's members. Pollack examines the advantages and disadvantages that the household-cum-firm offers in the organization of an economic activity with respect to a firm which is institutionally such. He finds four advantages, all of them deriving from the fact that a family comes into being and develops for affective not economic reasons: the force of non-monetary incentives, the widespread and continuous circulation of information among the members, altruism, and loyalty. But these same affective factors can also bring the disadvantage that the household does not behave on purely efficient criteria: conflicts of a non-economic nature may have harmful consequences on cooperation and the domestic budget; the poor performance of some members of the family may be excessively tolerated; some members may take up work activities which the family does not need; finally, the small size of a household precludes economies of scale.

Equating the family with an economic business may seem a mere intellectual exercise. But it is not so if we remember that a significant amount of economic activities are undertaken by family firms: farms, shops, artisan and small firms, professional practices. In these cases, economic choices and levels of performance are heavily influenced by domestic factors: the choice of spouse, births, divorce, the decision of the children to continue studying or otherwise, these are all extra-economic matters that may determine the success or failure of a business. Although significant understanding of the environmental conditions favouring the creation of family firms has been accumulated, to date no research has been conducted on the relationship between economic and affective factors. An interesting approach in this regard would be, for example, exploration of how forms of economic collaboration survive when ties of affection break down (e.g. a divorced couple who remain business partners).

Another field of inquiry by TCE and NIE lies at an intermediate level between micro and macro: local development, and especially the development of environmental factors favouring the formation of entrepreneurship. This research is conducted mainly in regions with large concentrations of small firms. Some studies carried out in Italy highlight the 'virtuous circles' that arise between artisan traditions, non-traumatic urbanization processes and more specific institutional factors such as the presence of strong political sub-cultures (Trigilia, 1986). This analysis can also be considered study of the organization of the territory, where 'organization' denotes both intentional processes managed by specific political and economic agencies (local bodies, trade associations, consortiums) and the *ex-post* outcome of the sum of individual behaviours within a robust institutional framework.

A classic example of this type of research is Brusco's (1987) study on the Italian provinces of Modena and Reggio in which he set outs the so-called 'Emilian Model' (from the name of the region). These are two provinces with widespread and growing prosperity, and strong industrial development characterized by:

- a dense network of medium-sized and small firms specialized in niche products (machine tools, knitwear, ceramics)
- a dual production structure consisting of an initial layer of medium-sized companies with their own final markets and a second layer of a myriad of small and very small firms, including individual artisans, working mostly on commission for the relatively larger companies
- very low vertical integration, with relations between contractors and sub-suppliers regulated by pure market criteria. The sub-suppliers are not tied to fixed contractors but can freely change contractors when they consider the prices proposed are too low.

These characteristics give an extraordinary flexibility to production, and company crises can be absorbed without trauma. This is by virtue of two mechanisms. The first operates with particular frequency the knitwear sector. If a contracting company, writes Brusco, "gets the pattern-book wrong" and loses part of its final customers, it does not have to lay off employees; the sub-suppliers simply change contractor. "The work that is not commissioned from them by the company who got the patterns wrong will be commissioned from them by the business whose patterns were more successful than expected" (p. 268). The second mechanism for absorbing production shocks concerns all sectors and is linked to the low number of employees in even the relatively larger firms. Let us suppose that a company has to lay off 10 per cent of its workers. The social problem thus caused increases with the overall number of employees. If the company has a thousand workers, it will have to lay off one hundred, but if it has a hundred it will have to fire only ten. This is not a critical mass and can be absorbed relatively easily by neighboring firms. Moreover, numerous highly-skilled former employees may take advantage of the situation and set up on their own.

These purely market mechanisms operate in an institutional context characterized by:

- highly active trade associations;
- authoritative and moderate trade unions;
- banks willing to finance even micro-firms;
- local authorities efficient in protecting collective interests.

The trade associations of category have created centres providing firms with a variety services: for example, they prepare pay packets, keep accounts, pay taxes, prepare income declarations. This enables firms to devote more time and energy to their core competences and encourages new entrepreneurs to enter the market (we may say that the Emilian associations anticipated the now burgeoning phenomenon of outsourcing by some decades).

The trade unions (present only in the larger firms) have developed trust relations with management. They consequently know what the economic possibilities are and make reasonable demands. Management for its part, given that it operates in a climate where future labour costs are already known, finds it easier than elsewhere to plan production volumes and investments. The banks do not discriminate against firms on the basis of their size and thus foster the spread of innovation even in micro-firms. The local authorities play their part by developing infrastructures and creating vocational training consortia. Together, these institutions and practices have given rise to a particular type of regulated and diffused capitalism where market competition is driven by the associative and organizational capacities of individuals.

7. STINCHCOMBE'S APPROACH TO ORGANIZATIONAL POPULATIONS: LIABILITY OF NEWNESS AND THE 'IMPRINTING' OF THE SPECIES

Now discussed is the other school of thought mentioned at the beginning of the chapter: the ecological approach to organizations. This school originated in an article by the American sociologist Stinchcombe (1929 – present) published in the mid-1960s. The novelty of its approach is that the concern is not with individual organizations but the homogenous group or *species* of organizations that Stinchcombe terms 'organizational population'. This shift of level enables him to raise a number of entirely new questions, two of which are of particular relevance here:

- How does the structure of a given society affect the rate at which new organizations, and in particular new organizational species, are created? In other words, are there societies whose intrinsic qualities encourage or discourage the appearance of new organizations?
- Is there a connection between the historical period in which a given organizational species appeared and the social structure of the present-day organizations belonging to that species? In other words, do organizations today preserve typical characteristics of the period in which their species appeared?

If the first question is to be answered correctly, Stinchcombe argues, one must take account of the 'liability of newness', by which he means that the percentage of failures is normally much higher among new organizations – especially in previously untested organizational species – than in old and tested ones. Founding new organizations, above all inventing new organizational species, is a risky undertaking which alters balances, constituted interests and consolidated patterns of behaviour. Newness can only be successful if the benefits brought by the new organizational species are clearly superior to those offered by the old order.

The question must, therefore, be rephrased to ask which human societies offer the best conditions in which the liability of newness can be overcome. Stinchcombe's answer is that they are the most modernized ones, those in which a dense network of organizations has already developed: "A population's level of organizational experience is the major determining factor in its capacity to form new organizations" (p. 152). 'Organizations that generate other organizations' are particularly important, and above all the large industrial empires that constantly create new units, be they economic or non-economic (foundations, schools, etc.). But the argument holds for any type of organization.

Stinchcombe's approach makes two breaks with the traditional view of the relationship between societies and organizations in two ways. It does so first by maintaining that the organizations of a new species find it more difficult to establish themselves than do those belonging to old species. Emphasising the liability of newness is to reverse the conventional wisdom that it is normally new phenomena that are at an advantage. This belief is fallacious, Stinchcombe claims, because it arises from the fact that only ever observed is what manages to survive. The novelties that fail are not visible and are generally ignored. But they must be considered if the overall level of innovativeness in a given society is to be correctly evaluated. Hence the birth and death rates of organizations yield crucial information with which to understand the relationship between societies and organizations.

Stinchcombe's second break with tradition is his contention that, if economic and social growth is the most fertile ground for the rise of any type of organization – and therefore also political, ethnic, religious and cultural ones – then pluralism, tolerance and associative life are more common in more developed societies than others: "the greater the number and variety of formal organizations in a community group", writes Stinchcombe, "the higher the probability of the existence of social solidarity" (p. 145). He argues against the romantic theory that the greatest group solidarity is to be found in archaic societies, those that Durkheim defines as being of mechanical solidarity, and which Tönnies described as natural communities (*Gemeinschaft*) as opposed to modern and urbanized societies (*Gesellschaft*) founded on the division of labour. It is not the case that there is greater solidarity in archaic societies, Stinchcombe affirms, not just because of their material poverty but also because a lack of culture and communications hinders human relations. Instead, the more advanced is economic and cultural development, the more ethnic and social pluralism increases and is expressed in everyday life marked by levels of associationism and solidarity unknown in archaic societies.

Stinchcombe then turns to the second question: whether organizations preserve distinctive features of the historical period in which their species was born. He examines the history of industrial development and argues that there are 'spurts', that is, brief and intense periods in which particular species of firms arise rather than others. These species have characteristics that distinguish them from those that have appeared in other historical periods. Using data from American censuses, Stinchcombe demonstrates that sectors which came into being before the industrial revolution, like agriculture, commerce, hotels, building and publishing, still today consist predominantly of small, family-run firms. The light industries created in the eighteenth and nineteenth centuries, like textiles, lumber and glass, are sectors in which firms (even recent ones) are of small-to-medium size and have little internal bureaucracy. Finally, the heavy industries established in the nineteenth century, for instance steel and railroads, and then those created in the nineteenth and twentieth centuries such as chemicals and automobiles, comprise firms that require mass technology and a large size if they are to be competitive. The conclusion is that the older a given sector of activity, the smaller the average size *still today*, and the greater the likelihood that family firms will predominate in that sector.

It, therefore, seems that an 'imprinting' takes place at the level of the organizational species which is handed down over the years. *Regardless of the year in which it was born*, every business belonging to a given sector displays features that reflect the historical period in which the sector to which it belongs came into being. (Should we wish to update Stinchcombe's analysis, we might add that the archetypal sector of the beginning of the twenty-first century, information technologies, exhibits a return to small size, reduced internal bureaucracy, and large-scale outsourcing: characteristics that will presumably persists in the IT firms of the future.)

On this basis, Stinchcombe develops a model which adapts the Darwinian explanation of natural evolution to that of society. The model is based on two assumptions. The first is that the economic and technical conditions of a given period select the organizational species best able to achieve some aims and not others. The second assumption is that those species cannot exist before the appropriate technology and social structure have appeared.

Stinchcombe uses this model to explain both the appearance of new organizational species and their survival. Just as natural selection regulates the relationship between natural resources in an environmental niche and the populations belonging to various biological species, so the connection between the technical-social opportunities that arise at a given historical moment and the appearance of given organizational species determines both the overall variety of those species and their inertial continuation in time. As long as there is a balance between population and resources, the niches can survive indefinitely, even when new opportunities prompt the advent of new organizational species with their own niches.

Stinchcombe draws on industrial history to provide a number of examples of how new organizational species appear as new technical and social means become available: printing houses due to invention of the printing press, textile factories due to mechanical looms, railways due to steel production, automobile producers due to petrol refining (and today the proliferation of software houses due to the invention of the personal computer). But Stinchcombe's argument goes beyond firms. His thesis is that any type of organization, for instance political parties, universities, or voluntary associations, can be studied by returning to the historical period in which their species arose. An example from Italy is provided by the political parties born in the nineteenth century from the 'opinion clubs' and which have preserved their original elitist imprinting (typically the Liberals and Republicans) throughout their history. The Socialist and Catholic parties born in the nineteenth and twentieth centuries with the rise of the social question and universal suffrage have maintained their imprinting of mass organization and are today in difficulties because they cannot abandon that form. Finally, the parties that have arisen in recent years display a media-driven imprinting that will presumably distinguish them for as long as they last.

8. ECOLOGY OF ORGANIZATIONAL POPULATIONS: SELECTION AS A FACTOR IN ISOMORPHISM AND VARIETY OF THE SPECIES

Stinchcombe was the forerunner of a school of thought that arose in the late 1970s and gave itself the name of 'ecology of organizations'.[7] The school adopts an approach at the level of the macro-social which:

- starts from the assumption that the lives of organizations are precarious: those organizations that currently exist are only the survivors of a relentless selection process, so that analysis must also take account of those organizations that have disappeared;[8]
- studies the long-term transformations brought about by reciprocal influence between the evolution of organizational populations and changes in the surrounding social environment;
- identifies selection and social competition as the factors responsible for both isomorphism processes and the proliferation of organizational forms and species.

Michael Hannan and John Freeman (1977), the two best-known representatives of the school, observe that the most common explanation of organizational change is that it results from the strategic adaptation of individual organizations to changes, challenges or opportunities arising in the environment. This is also the explanation offered by new institutionalism when it stresses the pressure for isomorphism exerted by institutions. But Hannan and Freeman claim that change may have other explanations as well: in particular, it may be the overall effect of the creation of new organizational forms that gradually replace old ones. In this case, the change is not the sum of the transformations deliberately undertaken by individual organizations in order to survive; rather, it is provoked by large demographic shifts in organizational populations. With the appearance of new technical and social phenomena which alter the environment of a given organizational population, some units fail because structural inertia makes them unable to change. Others, however, are able to adapt, and yet others come into being to exploit the new opportunities. In these cases, therefore, change is the result of a selection process, and what counts is large numbers more than the intentionality of individuals.

But on the basis of what criteria can we explain successes and failures in the selection process? Hannan and Freeman take up the neo-Darwinian explanation put forward by Stinchcombe: every organizational population occupies an environmental niche that provides the resources that it needs. There thus arises a relation of reciprocal dependence whereby a niche shapes a given population

---

[7] Ecology is not used in the usual sense of environmental protection, but as discourse on the environment (from the Greek *oikos*).

[8] The precariousness of the lives of organizations has already been emphasised by Barnard (see Chapter 2).

in its quality and size and the niche is shaped by the collective action of that population. But the resources offered by the niche are limited, and this induces the units making up the population to develop competition among themselves to select those fittest for survival. The others are destined to disappear.

The result of competition is a parallel process of *isomorphism* and organizational *pluralism*. There is isomorphism because the competition to secure the resources available selects the fittest individuals: which means that they possess fundamentally similar qualities and consequently form an increasingly homogeneous population. And there is pluralism because individuals unfit to compete in one niche can compete successfully in another. The overall result is a group of populations that differ from each other but are internally homogeneous.

But the selection process is blind, in the sense that it is not intrinsically end-directed, it is not linear, and it has random outcomes. On the one hand, changes in individual organizations are not *per se* guarantees of their success. Stinchcombe's rule of the liability of newness applies, because there are only a small number of changes that enable organizations to cope with alterations in the environment. On the other hand, structural inertia is not always a negative factor. This is especially the case of large organizations, where structural inertia is the greatest. Thanks to their power, these organizations are able to control the environment and to a certain extent condition newness. Their structural inertia, therefore, rather than condemning them to disappear, enables new niches to be found in which to insert new units interstitially. A case in point is IBM, the electronics giant that conditions the market but not to the extent of preventing the appearance of a number of new businesses as volatile as they are innovative.

Apart from firms, the ecological model offers an explanation of isomorphism alternative to that provided by new institutionalism. Moreover, the explanation flanks the complementary one of organizational plurality in any social situation marked by a high level of competition. Examples are provided by sport and the mass media. The proliferation of sports disciplines and categories can be explained as resulting from the creation of increasingly specialized niches in order to display athletic prowess in the best possible light. At the same time, the increasingly rigorous selection of athletes leads to a leveling at the top (isomorphism) of their performance. In the case of the mass media, one witnesses a proliferation of programme genres and specialized television channels (dedicated to music, thrillers, quizzes, soap operas, news). But the abundance of the programmes available is accompanied by the increased homogeneity of their content, so that the final impression is one of simultaneous differentiation and repetition.

The theoretical strength of Hannah and Freeman's is that it offers an explanation of isomorphism and social segmentation which is entirely new with respect to new institutionalism. Those processes are explained, not as the effect of the conscious imitation of successful models, but as the result of a blind selection process in a highly competitive society like the United States.

However, in later research (1984, 1986), Hannah and Freeman abandoned the idea of presenting a model entirely alternative to that of new institutionalism and admitted that the two models can be integrated. Although selection remains a decisive factor in change processes, the fact that it occurs in human society requires one to acknowledge that the spread and intentional imitation of culture radically alters the dynamics of selection on a purely biological level. Hannah and Freeman have therefore shifted their attention to the processes by which organizational populations are formed, and how their boundaries are determined and discontinuity created within society. Thus, although they pursue a different line of inquiry, they have converged on issues central to transaction costs economics.

Having admitted that not only blind and random forces are at work, Hannah and Freeman discuss the factors that induce the formation of an organizational population. In doing so, they review the theories of the various organizational schools and acknowledge that each of them has a useful contribution to make: technological factors, transaction costs, closures of social networks, collective action and, above all, institutional processes are all factors to be considered when defining the boundaries of an organizational population.

Hence, Hannah and Freeman highlight perspective of importance for organizational analysis. Rather than opting for a theoretical model that excludes other models, such analysis requires a broader view which encompasses the various contributions available and links them together. This is also the rationale for this chapter's emphasis on the continuity between the economic and sociological versions of new institutionalism and its joint presentation of two apparently such distinct schools of thought as the theory of transaction costs and the ecological school.

DISCUSSION

Many of the themes dealt with in this chapter, from the plurality of capitalism to evolution as a factor in isomorphism, lend themselves to theoretical discussion but not to practical fieldwork. Other themes fit very well with the analytical simulations set out in previous chapters.

In the first place, the 'to make- to buy' choice, with its various intermediate solutions, can be the basis of interesting analysis of business strategies. Imagine interviewing an executive from a firm that has always operated in a stable network of contracts, typically a building firm. How much (in commercial value) of a building constructed is the direct work of his company and how much is the work of other firms to which he contracted jobs? How did he build up his network of contracting firms? How does he check on the quality the work contracted out? On what basis did relations of trust develop? Are they purely commercial relations or are they also based on friendship or family connections? Have any of his employees set up on their own and then received work from him? Have there been crises of trust that made him stop using one or some of them? Has he ever worked on contract for another firm?

Now imagine interviewing the executive of a company which has recently 'discovered the market' – in the sense that it contracts out work to third parties. Try to compare his opinions with those of the first businessman. What differences can you find in their business methods? How does he explain his decisions? Does he use rational arguments or is idiosyncrasy and imitation of others more important? Do you think he works well or does he make mistakes? What do you think he could learn from the first businessman?

Then imagine applying the 'to make-to buy' model to a hybrid situation, where a family runs the firm. The chapter has considered the hypothesis that the separation of a couple may have repercussions on their firm. But there are an infinite number of other questions on the links between affective relations and business interests. Were the couple already working in the sector before the got married, did one convince the other, or how did they decide to set up the firm? Did one of the two give up a previous job so that they could together and therefore adapted to a job that s/he did not know. Was the fact that one of them already had a going concern a stimulus to build a private life together? How do they divide the work? What do they want their children to do? Does their network of suppliers consist partly of relatives or did it grow independently of family connections?

Finally, we can theorize on clans: groups of people, not necessarily related, who because they are close friends or belong to the same social group, establish business relations. Can we say that their 'blood pact' is an important factor in developing relations of commercial trust and enduring obligations? Can that pact give them advantages over the competition?

REFERENCES

Albert Michel

1991 *Capitalisme contre capitalisme*, Editions du Seuil, Paris Aoky Masahiko e coll.

1990 *The Firm as a nexus of Treaties*, Sage Londra Arrow Kenneth.

1983 *Collected Papers* , Harvard University Press, Cambridge, MA, Bazerman M.H. *Judgment in Managerial Decision Making*, Wiley, New York.

Bonazzi Giuseppe.

2000 Il mercato in fabbrica. Effetti e problemi delle terziarizzazioni in Fiat Auto, *Studi Organizzativi* n. 3.

Brusco Sebastiano.

1989 *Piccole imprese e distretti industriali*, Rosenberg Torino.

Coase Ronald H.

1937 The Nature of the Firm, *Economica* n.4 (ripublished in Williamson O. e Winter S. *The Nature of the Firm: Origin, Evolution, Development*, Oxford Univ. Press, N.Y. 1991).

Colombo Massimo G. (ed.).

1998: *The Changing boundaries of the Firm. Explaining evolving inter-firm relations*, Routledge, De Jong H.

1995 European Capitalism : Between Freedom and Social Justice, *Review of Industrial Organization*, n. 10

Eccles Robert G.

1980 The quasi-firms in the Construction Industry, *Journal of Economic Behavior and Organizations*, n.2.

Hannan Michael, Freeman John :

1977 The population ecology of Organizations, *American Journal of Sociology* , n.82 pp 929-964.

1984 Structural Inertia and Organizational Change , *American Sociological Review*, 49, pp. 149-164.

1986 Where do Organizational Forms come from? *Sociological Forum* 1986 , marzo vol. 1, n.1.

Kanter Mos Rosabeth :

1989 *When Giants Learn to Dance: Mastering the Challenges of Strategy, Management and Careers in the 1990s*, Simon and Schuster, New York.

1991 The Future of Bureaucracy and Jerarchy , in *Social Theory for a Changing Society*, a cura di P. Bourdieu e J:Coleman , Westview Press, New York.

Orrù Marco, Woolsey Biggart Nicole, Hamilton Gary.

1991 Organizational Isomorphism in East Asia in W. Powell e P. DiMaggio *The New Institutionalism in Organizational Analysis* , Univ. of Chicago Press.

Ouchi William

1980 Markets, Burocracies and Clans , *Admnistrative Science Quarterly* n. 25, marzo.

Perulli Paolo.

1995 Stato, regioni, economie di rete, *Stato e Mercato*, n. 44, agosto.

Pfeffer Jeffrey e Salancik Gerald.

1977 *The External Control of Organizations. A Resource Dependence Perspective*, Harper & Row, New York.

Pollack Robert A. : 1985 A transaction Cost Approach to Families and Households, *Journal of Economic Literature*, giugno pp. 581-605.

Porter M. Cho D.

1987 Il cambiamento di leadership in un settore globale: il caso delle costruzioni navali in *Competizione globale*, a cura di M. Porter , Petrini Torino.

Regini Marino.

1995 La varietà italiana di capitalismo. Istituzioni sociali e struttura produttiva negli anni ottanta, *Stato e Mercato*, n. 43.

Sabel Charles.

1991: Moebius Strip Organizations and Open Labor Markets: Some Consequences of the Reintegration of Conception and Execution in a Volatile Economy, in *Social Theory for a Changing Society*, a cura di P. Bourdieu e J:Coleman, Westview Press, New York.

Soskice David.

1993 *Product Market and Innovation Strategies of Companies and Their Implications for*

Enterprise Tenure: A Comparative Institutional Approach to Cross-country Differences, Wissenschaftszentrum, Berlino.

Stinchcombe Arthur : 1985 Social Structure and Organizations, in *Handbook of Organizations* James March ed. Rand McNally Chicago, pp. 142-193.

Streeck Wolfgang.

1991 *Social Institutions and Economic Performance* , Sage Londra.

Trigilia Carlo.

1986 *Grandi partiti e piccole imprese,* Il Mulino Bologna.

Walker Gordon, Weber David.

1984 A Transaction Cost Approach to Make-or-Buy Decisions , *Administrative Science Quarterly*, n. 29.

Williamson Oliver.

1975 *Markets and Hierarchies :Analysis and Antitrust Implications*, Free Press N.Y.

1985 *The Economic Institutions of Capitalism*, Free Press, N.Y.

1986 *Economic Organization*, Wheatsheaf Books, Brighton.

1996 *The Mechanisms of Governance*, Oxford Universty Press, N.Y.

Chapter 6

'Soft' Approaches : Culture, Sensemaking and Structure Processes

The chapter explains the significance and success of 'soft approaches' to organizations. It emphasises the extreme variety of theories ranging from a culturalist 'pole' represented by Schein to a cognitivist one represented by Weick. It then discusses the intermediate positions taken up by other authors, notably Martin, Kunda and Barley, who develop reflexive, post-modern analyses centred on the concept of the structuration of organizations.

1. THE RATIONALE OF 'SOFT' APPROACHES

This chapter examines so-called 'soft' approaches to organizations, or in other words, approaches that give priority to cultural, symbolic and reflexive aspects, and also to the sense-making processes realized when people interact with organizations. These approaches first came to the fore in the second half of the 1970s, and their rationale lay in two concomitant and partly connected factors.

The first factor was the tendency of large firms to switch from mainly bureaucratic-disciplinary instruments of control to more refined normative ones based on the internalization by employees of the values embraced and the goals pursued by the firms for which they worked. This shift confronted researchers with new scenarios: their object of research was no longer the ruses and strategies with which people react to a visible system of incentives and sanctions (see the analyses of Roy and Crozier discussed in Chapter Two), but rather the efficacy of a set of much more subtle pressures intended to increase employee involvement, but which were also able to induce employees to form a complex love/hate relationship with firms that, although increasingly concerned with their professional growth, demanded their total commitment as well.

The second factor was the growing dissatisfaction in those years with 'hard' approaches focused on structural aspects of organizations connected with numerical magnitudes like hierarchical levels, areas of competence and control, or the frequency of communications. These approaches of contingentist inspiration (see Chapter One) were based on the assumption that there is a connection between the degree of environmental turbulence and the optimum structure of the organization. A series of critical studies (amongst others: Child 1972; Silverman 1975; Burrel and Morgan 1979) showed that, despite sophisticated methodological apparatus and an impressive accumulation of information on these structural aspects, knowledge about the linkages between organizational structure and the external environment was uncertain, contradictory and of little significance.

The challenges raised against the contingency school were prompted by two principal considerations:

- the strategic choices of firms could not be explained by their structural features; instead, they largely depended on the strategic action of decision-makers. Contrary to the implicit determinism of the contingency school, the emphasis was placed on margins of discretion relative to such subjective factors as managerial convictions and attitudes, leadership styles, and the ability to forge alliances.
- firms operating in the same sector, of similar size and with comparable organizational structures, exhibited very different internal climates, motivations to participate, and levels of performance. These differences were particularly marked when comparisons were made between Western firms and the Japanese ones then penetrating international markets by virtue of their greater efficiency and aggressiveness.

Account should also be taken of the growing popularity in the 1970s of qualitative research methods, most notably case study, participant observation, ethnography and the reconstruction of significant events in organization life-histories. The importance accorded to soft factors in explanation of a range of organizational behaviours and the preference given to qualitative methods were choices both closely congenial and mutually reinforcing. But it should also be pointed out that soft approaches did not characterize one single school of thought. Rather, they were shared by a number of schools, like symbolic interactionism, cognitivism, phenomenology and ethnomethodology. Some schools had already existed for some time on the margins of the sociological debate, and then found that organizational studies were a fruitful area of application which provided an opportunity to square accounts with more canonical and traditional currents of thought.

It would be beyond our present purposes to explore the theoretical differences among these various schools. However, we may identify the object/subject axis as the conceptual continuum along which to arrange the approaches examined in this chapter. At one extreme lie *objectivist* approaches, so called because they start from the assumption that organizations possess a culture, understood as a stock of knowledge and beliefs accumulated over time, study of which provides the key to understanding of both how organizations work and how the people who belong to them behave. For this reason, these approaches have also been called *culturalist*. At the other end of the continuum we find *subjectivist* (or interpretative) approaches, so called because they start from the assumption that external reality is only a social construction resulting from the sense-making activity performed by people amid the flux of their experience.

A number of intermediate positions lie between these two extremes: those of authors who, as they examine organizational cultures, take account of the ways in which actors interpret and give meaning to those cultures; and the positions of those authors who, although they acknowledge the objectivity of social structures, emphasise that they are constantly structured by the people who interact with them.

The first part of this chapter will examine contributions by proponents of the culturalist approach. After Schein, who put forward the most objectivist version of culturalism, discussion will move to Martin and Kunda, authors of studies on organizational cultures in which significant emphasis is given to more subjectivist self-reflection. Then examined is the thought of Weick, one of the main exponents of cognitivism, or radical subjectivism, and finally the intermediate positions taken up by Giddens and Barley. A study by the latter author is examined in detail because it conducts particularly interesting comparison between different structuring processes in two similar organizations.

2. EDGARD SCHEIN AND THE CONCEPT OF ORGANIZATIONAL CULTURE

Schein's (1985) fundamental thesis is that studying an organization is equivalent to studying its culture. He defines an organizational culture as follows: the coherent set of basic assumptions that a given group has invented, discovered or developed in learning to cope with its problems of external adaptation and internal integration, and which have worked well enough to be considered valid, and therefore to be taught to new members as the correct way to perceive, think and feel in relation to those problems (ibid., p. 35).

This is a complex definition which requires itemized commentary. It has three main components. The first is the concept of culture as a set of 'basic assumptions'. By this Schein means that knowledge of an organizational culture is acquired through analysis which proceeds at different levels of profundity. Lying at the most superficial level are the *artifacts*, or the immediately observable products, of a given organization: its architecture, décor, technology, but also the ways in which its members behave, the slang they use, their dress, mimicry, symbols and rituals.

By definition all artifacts are visible, but this does not mean that they are easy to construe. Indeed, it is the ability to construe artifacts that is the acid test for any organizational analysis. For example, what is the purpose of a particular style of architecture? Is it to foster sociability among the organization's members or is it to maintain hierarchical barriers? Are the clothes worn by members freely chosen or do they manifest membership of the organization through uniforms and symbols of rank? Are there rituals (prize-givings, anniversary celebrations, but sometimes also, more or less symbolic punishments); and if so for what purpose? Do the organization's members use a specialist jargon which outsiders find difficult or impossible to understand? And if jargon is used, does it reflect only the existence of a particular technical expertise or is its purpose to defend and symbolically separate a particular social group from others? Schein stresses that careful observation of artifacts is the first step in organizational analysis: preliminary impressions are collected, working hypotheses are formulated, and the terrain is prepared for a second and more profound level of analysis.

Lying at the second level are what Schein calls the organization's 'explicit values'. This is the sphere of manifest and accepted discourses often created and circulated by the leadership in order to strengthen the sense of belonging and solidarity, to identify dangers and external enemies, to clarify and legitimate the organization's decisions, and to create consensus among its members. The researcher's task is to analyse these discourses, both written and oral (conversations, interviews), and to examine their evolution over time and the extent to which they correspond to artifacts.

But research does not stop at the level of explicit declarations. It must descend to a third and more profound level, to what Schein calls the level of basic assumptions. These are the organization's deep-seated and unexpressed convictions, taken so much for granted that they do not attract attention, and of which the organization's members themselves may often be unaware. But it is precisely this level that is most important for understanding the organization's soul, the deep-lying motives for the actions of its members, and the way in which they have been selected and shaped. Bringing out an organization's basic assumptions is the most difficult task, but at stake is the value itself of the research, its ability to go beyond banal description of things that are already known.

Schein shows how to uncover these assumptions. They concern the universal aspects of human experience: mankind's relationship with nature, the perception of time, the nature of humanity, human activities, and interpersonal relations. Mankind's relationship with nature may be one of dominance and exploitation or it may be one of respect and harmony. There is a cyclical conception of time as constantly returning upon itself (the conception typical or rural and archaic societies) and a linear conception of time as one-directional. The conception of time may also be connected with the idea of progress. There are then pessimistic conceptions of human nature as tainted by original sin, and optimistic ones which view mankind as indefinitely capable of improvement.

There are finally democratic or authoritarian conceptions of human relationships: group-based or individualist, competitive or solidarist, masculinist or gender paritarian. This set of assumptions furnishes answers to important questions such as the following. What is the right way to frame human relationships, to distribute power and love? Is life cooperative or competitive? What is work and what is play? Should the social order be maintained by imposing hierarchy and control or by constructing relationships based on trust, the delegation of responsibility and equality?

Basic assumptions can be combined in various ways to produce articulated and complex belief systems. Depending on the particular combination in place, the ways in which people work, communicate and assess their own performance and that of others change profoundly. However, belief systems must always satisfy the fundamental requirement of internal coherence, and this applies to both the manner in which assumptions are combined and their relationship with the levels of explicit values and artifacts. Inconsistencies and contradictions give rise to distrust, tension, scepticism and cynicism, provoking crises that may lead to an organization's decline and demise. However, inner coherence does not entail that there can be only one single belief system within an organization. There may be several of them, partly different in nature, which reflect the organization's various parts. In a complex organization, for example, it is likely that the corporation of engineers and technicians will have developed a belief system that partly differs from that of the marketing personnel, just as employees in outlying branches will have assumptions that differ somewhat from those of staff working at headquarters.

3. SCHEIN: THE FORMATION OF AN ORGANIZATION CULTURE

But how are an organization's basic assumptions formed? This question takes us to the second part of Schein's definition of organizational culture. His reply is that a culture is always formed within a group made up of persons who have been together long enough for them to have shared significant problems, addressed them, observed the effects of the solutions tried out, and then transmitted these solutions to newcomers. The more the group is homogeneous and stable, with long and intense experience, the stronger and more articulated its culture will be. Conversely, if the group is composed of persons with little shared experience and who have never coped jointly with difficult problems, its culture will be weak, precarious and poorly differentiated. In short, to develop a shared culture a group must have a shared history.

All this amounts to saying that a culture is not made up of abstract ideas. Rather, it consists of responses to concrete problems, which must be solved by inventing or discovering solutions to be subsequently learned by new members of the group. The validity of responses does not lie solely in their efficacy in solving practical problems; it also depends on the extent to which they reduce anxiety. Anxiety arises in unknown or hostile environments, where there is no perceivable order or inner coherence. This explains the ritualistic and symbolic aspects always present in an organizational culture: the propitiatory dances by a primitive tribe before the hunt, but also the recurrent ritual ceremonies in a large modern company caught in the vortex of competition.

Schein then distinguishes between two broad categories of problems: those that regard the group's adaptation to the external environment, and those that regard its internal integration. A minimum of consensus on these problems is necessary lest the group disintegrate. But problems may change as the organization deals with them successfully and moves on to another phase in its life cycle. Schein provides the example of a recently founded company which initially sets itself the goal of "winning in the market against all other competitors" but subsequently finds it convenient to "develop its own market niche" or even adapts to "becoming an undemanding partner in a oligopolistic sector" in order to survive.

Problems of integration instead concern the ability of the group to function as a group within the organization. Here too consensus is necessary, and in this case on the criteria for including and excluding members, distributing power, developing friendship, trust and affect, and establishing rewards and punishments. Consensus is required most of all on the group's ideology, or the system of discourses which attribute meaning and reduce the anxiety provoked by inexplicable or traumatic events.

All these problems have specific features which reflect the organization's history and the environment in which it operates. In order to deal with them, the organization develops assumptions which, according to the definition given by Schein, must work well enough to be considered valid. These assumptions form the *culture* of the organization; a culture which is in constant formation because learning how to relate to the environment and handle internal affairs is always in progress. Thus created is a tension between the need to conserve the stock of assumptions formed from previous experiences and the need to test these assumptions and adapt them to contrary new phenomena. This tension between conservation and innovation is displayed by every organizational culture. It is the leadership's task to handle it with far-sightedness and acumen: a good leader knows that the organizational culture cannot be either allowed to fossilize or transformed too hastily.

But a culture is more than a heritage shared by people already belonging to an organization; it must be transmitted to new members if the group is to survive. Transmission is relatively straightforward when the new members are young and still unformed. But it becomes a complex undertaking when the new members – especially those introduced at high levels of the organization – bring with them ideas and values already acquired elsewhere. In this case, the entry of newcomers may provoke changes in the organization's culture. This poses the problem of how to study the processes of reciprocal adaptation between the organization's already-existing culture and the changes occasioned by new members. Schein has no *a priori* answer to this problem, because it involves dynamics that must be studied empirically case by case.

It is not easy to study culture, Schein warns, given that it pervades every aspect of human relationships. As mentioned earlier, it is not enough to ask the founders or leaders of an organization about its values and goals, because this restricts the inquiry to only what is manifest. Analysis must be integrated with an approach which focuses on the following three aspects:

- the socialization of new members, or how the organizational culture is transmitted, internalized and adapted;
- responses to critical events in the organization's history: these responses constitute a stock of memories that form the organization's collective identity;
- the anomalies or unexpected features observed as research proceeds. An organizational culture can be brought into sharper focus if its inconsistencies, flaws and latent tensions are examined.

Finally, all these elements relate to the manner in which leadership is exercised. For Schein, leadership and culture are two aspects of the same phenomenon: studying the leadership of an organization is to study its culture, and vice versa.

4. JOANNE MARTIN AND THE PLURALITY OF ORGANIZATIONAL CULTURES

There is a strength and a weakness in Schein's theory. Its strength is methodological, for it offers a useful tool with which to analyse organizational cultures. Schein's work provides field researchers with valuable suggestions on research design, on what they should observe, and on how they may deepen their knowledge by moving from the more visible features of organizations to their more latent ones. Its weakness is theoretical, because it propounds a substantially holistic and homogeneous view of organizational cultures as wholes with coherently connected parts. Although Schein accepts that organizations may comprise subcultural features tied to particular segments of their internal populations, he pays little attention to the matter. As a consequence, in his theory these aspects more closely resemble local variants of the predominant culture than different and counterposed systems.

Joanne Martin is an author (also American) who adjusts the absolutist thrust of Schein's model. This she does not reject but relativizes, in the sense that she considers it to be one possible reading of organizational dynamics which does not exclude other readings. The originality of Martin's (1992) position is that it develops a discourse which she herself calls postmodern and comprises three different perspectives of analysis. Her contention is that by continually shuttling among these perspectives it is possible to gain reflexive knowledge on organizations which takes constant account of the fact that these perspectives generate mutually incompatible discourses. No one of these discourses is truer than the other two, and it is precisely this incompatibility that enables us to grasp the intrinsic ambiguity of organizations and their cultures.

The three perspectives from which organizational cultures can be studied are the following:

- *integrative*, according to which culture is the source of harmony and consensus;
- *differentiating*, according to which different and sometimes conflicting subcultures exist in an organization;
- *fragmentary*, according to which well-defined cultures do not exist in an organization, but rather a multiplicity of fluctuating and ambiguous points of view.

In order to understand how these three perspectives can coexist, one must bear two points in mind. The first is that they do not reflect objectively existing situations. They are interpretations subjectively imposed on the collection and analysis of material. It is true that there are aspects of organizations apparently more congenial to one perspective than to the other two. But this can be said of each of the perspectives; hence none of them is more correct than the others. The second point is that shifting among the three perspectives – precisely because they are mutually exclusive – furnishes the researcher with deeper understanding of the organizations studied. Martin writes:

If any cultural contest is studied in enough depth, some things will be consistent, clear, and generate organization-wide consensus. Simultaneously, other aspects of the culture will coalesce within subcultural boundaries and still other elements of the culture will be fragmented, in a state of constant flux, and infused with confusion, doubt, and paradox. (p.4)

Awareness that it is possible to pass from one perspective to another is the premise for a meta-theory which enables examination of the rationale and limitations of each perspective. But the meta-theory, too, must be scrutinized to bring out the simplifications and biases introduced by the personality of the researcher (Martin talks of *deconstruction*, a postmodern term for a reflexive process which reveals what has been omitted from a given discourse).

In support of her arguments, Martin cites the result of research conducted by herself in a large electronics company, pseudonymously called OZCO (but which everything suggests is IBM). The method used was in-depth interviews and group discussions with an unspecified number of employees. Everything was recorded and transcribed so that detailed examination could be made of the discourses collected. Among the many topics covered, Martin concentrated on the following three in particular:

- equality of treatment and career opportunities for employees;
- the management's attitude to innovation;
- the company's concern for the physical and mental well-being of its employees.

On inspection of the materials collected, Martin found elements to support each of the three perspectives outlined above. There thus emerged three distinct accounts which Martin discussed in the light of a like number of strands in the literature congenial to each of the three perspectives.

From the integrative perspective, reassuring judgement is passed on the corporate climate and collaboration between management and employees. The latter share in the company's profits, they have job security, they receive props according to need, and they enjoy lateral transfers from one department to another, which increase their career opportunities. Egalitarianism is safeguarded in everyday practices as well: the employees share parking spaces and company canteens with the managers, everyone dresses informally, and employees have easy access to managers, who frequently wander through the offices. Innovation is encouraged in order to create organizational structures that integrate production and market more closely and meet customer requirements. Finally, it emerges from the interviews that the company is closely concerned with its employees' welfare: it provides assistance for young married couples, subsidises school fees, offers flexible working hours, gives a second chance when mistakes are made, and avoids individual sanctions as far as possible.

These various features enable an integrative account of the corporate order to be developed. This account is related to a specific strand of the organizational literature in which, besides Schein, Martin' includes Ouchi and other authors on management. This literature conceives change as a process which invests the entire organization through successive phases of creation, maintenance, collapse, and then re-foundation of a cultural unit. The integrative approach acknowledges the existence of ambiguities and conflict, but only as temporary crises to be overcome in new orders.

Martin next examines the evidence for a differentiating view of organizational culture. On this view, a firm is a set of diverse occupational communities each with its own sub-culture. All the values emphasised by the integrative perspective are now called into question. There is no genuine egalitarianism at OZCO. The engineers have privileges, incentives are used to pressurise employees, decisions are authoritarian and top-down, the managers' friendliness is merely a device with which to control the employees, career opportunities via lateral transfers are at the management's discretion, very few women occupy senior positions in the company. Innovation is not pursued homogeneously but is often obstructed by internal barriers. Finally, the management's purported concern for the employees' well-being is deemed to be a merely paternalistic expedient.

Martin judges these criticisms to be the expression of sub-cultures belonging to well-defined social groups: design engineers, marketing personnel, production technicians. These occupational categories interweave with ethnic differences to produce a motley corporate population. According to the literature which emphasises the importance of sub-cultures in enterprises, organizational change is localized, incremental and brought about by localist pressures applied by various sections of the organization. Conflict, moreover, is almost never viewed as a pathology but rather as a positive change-inducing factor.

There is finally the fragmentary perspective, the one that Martin declares she finds most persuasive. Gainsaid from this perspective is the existence not only of a homogeneous corporate culture but also of numerous sub-cultures, for the organization's most distinctive features are confusion and ambiguity. From the accounts gathered at OZCO it appears that the use of incentives, career opportunities, the introduction of innovations, personnel policies and even routine practices are regulated haphazardly and unpredictably.

This view of the company is congruent with a body of literature which emphasises the randomness of decision-making processes, organized anarchies, the constant and unpredictable nature of change. Individuals are depicted as possessing multiple personalities which emerge according to circumstances. This is why, during a single conversation, the same subjects may shift among discourses which support the integration perspective, some which come close to the differentiation perspective, and others which bear out the fragmentation perspective. Because the three perspectives are incompatible, the researcher must resist the temptation of seeking impossible syntheses of them. S/he should instead keep all three of them in mind, in the knowledge that evidence can be found for the validity of each:

At any point in time, a few fundamental aspects of an organization's culture will be congruent with an Integration perspective – that is, some cultural manifestations will be interpreted in similar ways throughout the organization, so they appear clear and mutally consistent. At the same time, in accord with the Differentiation perspective, other issues will surface as inconsistencies and will generate clear sub-cultural differences. Simultaneously, in congruence with the Fragmentation viewpoint, still other issues will be seen as ambiguous, generating unclear relationships among manifestations and only ephemeral issue-specific coalitions that fail to coalesce in either organization-wide or subcultural consensus. Furthermore, individuals viewing the same cultural context will perceive, remember, and interpret things in different ways. (pp.168-9).

In order to adopt this multi-faceted approach, it is necessary to discard the objectivist assumption that one perspective is more correct than the other two. Each of them is nothing but an interpretative schema which focuses on some aspects of the culture rather than others. It does so, not because of oversight by the researcher, but because of limitations intrinsic to the perspectives themselves. A cultural setting can be fully understood only if we view it from all three perspectives at once. Excluding one of them is to restrict what we are seeking to understand. All that we are able to know about organizations, concludes Martin, is discursive representations of them. If we adopt a typically postmodern perspective, it becomes possible to comprehend the interpretative game that constantly shifts from one discourse to another, mindful that these are nothing but discourses, and that knowledge – as Derrida, the leading representative of postmodern thought, has put it – proceeds solely by discourses which constantly 'defer' to other discourses.

5. GIDEON KUNDA: CORPORATE CULTURE AS AN INSTRUMENT OF CONTROL

Also the Israeli sociologist Gideon Kunda has conducted a postmodern study of corporate culture; and he too has chosen to examine a large American electronics company, this one pseudonymously known as 'Tech' (although Kunda confides in private that the company was Digital). But the intent of his research, the method used, and the definition of postmodernity differ considerably from those of Joanne Martin.

The aim of Kunda's study (1992) was not to examine which and how many perspectives can be applied to a corporate culture. Rather, it set out to study in what such culture consists, how it is transmitted and instilled in the workforce, and how the latter reacts. Consequently, Kunda did more than record interviews and discussions; he carried out a year-long ethnography in the course of which he collected documents, took part in work meetings, and garnered confidences and confessions from employees, most of them engineers and managers. The postmodernism of his research consists not in the declared co-presence of several readings of the same corporate reality, but in the subtlety with which it investigated the relationships between corporate pressures and the personalities of individuals, and then in the self-analysis with which the final chapter questions the author and his results.

Kunda apparently uses a method similar to the one advocated by Schein. He begins by observing the most manifest aspects of the work environment and the company's organization, and then descends to increasingly implicit and latent levels. However, the outcome of his analysis is not an uncovering of the deep-lying beliefs that inspire the company's culture; instead revealed is the ambiguity of the employees' attitudes towards Tech: the mix of dedication and irony, enthusiasm and sarcasm, callousness and compassion expressed in their actions and discourses. These aspects co-penetrate so intimately that Kunda talks of 'multiple selves'. This is the postmodern motif of his analysis, but as mentioned, it is a postmodernism different from Joanne Martin's. Whilst Martin relates a flow of contrasting discourses to three distinct perspectives of analysis, Kunda instead endeavours to understand why those discourses are produced by the same people, and whether their contradictoriness does not express a hard-won existential balance.

The rationale of Kunda's research can be understood better if we remind ourselves of the arguments put forward by Barnard, an author whom Kunda frequently cites. For Barnard, the central problem of both managerial practice and organizational analysis is the relationship between organizations and people. No matter how exigent and demanding an organization (read 'a firm') may be, it will never go so far as to demand the total erasure of its members' personalities. Although employees are urged to develop an organization personality, they will always maintain an irreducible quiddity, which constitutes the core of their private selves and can never be entirely identical with their organization selves. According to Bernard, it is recognition of this irreducibility that underpins both organizational theory and management science.

Barnard formulated this thesis – which is both a theoretical position and an ethical choice – at a time when social order and productive performance were still achieved through a mixture of coercion and bureaucratic controls. This point should be borne in mind because it explains Barnard's stress on moral and cultural incentives as factors that foster cohesion and cooperation between individuals and organizations. Since Barnard's time of writing, however, businesses have adopted more sophisticated forms of control, ones based on the internalization by employees of corporate values, codes of conduct, and goals. This is known as 'third-level' control (Perrow 1986), as distinct from coercive (first-level) and hierarchical-bureaucratic control (second-level) – or 'concertive' control (Barker 1993), a term which indicates that employees have internalized corporate codes so well that they have become their most diligent enforcers, as regards both themselves and their colleagues.

Cultural control by the firm does not stop at the threshold of its members' private selves, as Barnard recommended. It endeavours to shape them utterly, in the conviction that only total and passionate commitment to the firm's values and goals can give rise to discipline and self-control. This is to go further than Barnard, therefore; or rather it is to reinterpret him so that the relationship between employees and organization can be shifted to a basis more favourable for the latter. This is the situation that Kunda found at Tech, when he writes about the "abolition of the boundaries between the individual self and the organization" and the fact that "once this stage has been reached, the interests of the company and those of individuals come to coincide" (p. 115). It was the radical nature of this undertaking that stimulated Kunda's intellectual curiosity:

> How effective ,we must ask, are the corporate attempts to influence employees? What is the experience of the people against whom such heavy claims are made? What kind of people are produced in this process? (p.14)

In order to answer these questions, Kunda divides the exposition of his research into three parts. The first is devoted to the distinctive features of the Tech culture; the second describes the rituals by which that culture is instilled in the company's employees; the third examines how the employees assimilate the culture, and the human costs that this entails.

6. THE IDEOLOGY AND COMMUNICATIVE RITUALS OF THE CORPORATE CULTURE

The concept of 'ideology' is useful for analysis of corporate culture. Ideology, writes Kunda, quoting the anthropologist Geertz, is "an authoritarian system of meanings" which power-holders present to public opinion as a map with which they may interpret reality and behave as a consequence. An ideology can be viewed as a sub-set of a broader culture which comprises all its features. These features are articulated to provide a schematic image of the social order and to exercise authority. Ideology is thus distinguished from other aspects of a culture, like good sense or tradition, which are implicit, taken for granted, and often less systematic.

The distinction is important because what Kunda examines at Tech is exactly the presence of an ideology of the corporate culture. This ideology proclaims that Tech has a strong culture, enunciates its principles, and emphasises that if employees want to contribute to the company's success, and hence be successful themselves, they must assimilate them. An office run by a young manager of appropriately sleek and thrustful demeanour is charged with propagandizing Tech's corporate philosophy, drafting new texts, launching awareness campaigns, and organizing seminars at which employees are invited to discuss the strengths and weaknesses of their work.

There follow some of the principles set out by an in-house document on what Tech conceives to be its corporate culture:

> *We are one big family,* with the comment that "inter-cultural differences are encouraged, failure is to some extent tolerated, people are encouraged to express their feelings, all doors are open, informality and communication are fostered".

People are creative, they work hard, they are able to manage themselves and to learn, where, on the 'sink or swim' principle, members are warned that they must always take the initiative, respect the differences of others, and find ways to have fun while working.

Truth and quality result from a plurality of points of view, from free enterprise, where all must participate to win: this requires the ability to ask key areas for what one needs, to sell one's ideas to gain the necessary support, to take risks and to tolerate mistakes (provided they are not serious).

Individual freedom, entrepreneurship, and especially *doing the right thing* are constantly cited as Tech's fundamental values. As a consequence, "he/she who proposes, does and is judged on his/her results". Tech expects all its members (this applies in particular to managers and engineers) to devise the best ways to do their work, to decide by themselves the initiatives they deem best for the company, and to accept responsibility for them. The work is openly acknowledged to be stressful, but if it can be made demanding and creative, it can also be fun. Later, the document offers advice and practical guidelines. One of them runs as follows:

> The Tech world will overload you if you let it. Only you can say no. An absence of a no connotes a yes. Making aggressive commitments and meeting them is a success. Making foolishly aggressive commitments and missing is failure even if the actual result is the same as the aggressive commitment. (p.74)

However, the document offers the reassurance that failure is (almost) never definitive. Failure only means being unable to achieve a particular goal; it can, therefore, be put right. Indeed, one must learn from one's failures so that they are never repeated. These reassurances should be read in the light of one of the cornerstones of Tech's policy: that employees never quit the company. However, this is not to imply that the company does not sanction employees who fail to meet objectives. They are transferred for a period of time, marginalized, deprived of their previous responsibility and authority, and even if they continue to receive the same salary (or better for precisely this reason), psychologically humiliated.

Another rule warns that "controls appear to be lax. But do not delude yourself that they can be ignored, you will be caught". Employees must also get used to the fact that every two years the organization and their work will undergo radical and unexpected change. They must, therefore, be flexible and ready to take on work outside traditional career paths.

Finally, the Culture Office had compiled a glossary of the terms most frequently used at Tech: somewhat daunting expressions like humiliated, burnout, do-it-yourself career, lose, sink or swim, personal reputation, fund cutting. All of these express unpleasant experiences that the company does not seek to exorcise but instead subjects to reflection so that employees can learn the Tech rules of the game even better.

These values, rules and recommendations are constantly communicated. Meetings and workshops of varying degrees of formality constitute the rituals by which the corporate culture is inculcated. Long discussions are held and may become heated. The skill of those in charge of these meetings, Kunda observes, consists in defusing the tension with jokes, quips and self-mockery. As a result, the serious message is transmitted but is played down, again reminding those present that work at Tech is both a demanding challenge and fun.

7. THE EMPLOYEES' REACTION THE SPECTRE OF BURNOUT AND ITS 'CULTURE'

How do Tech's employees react to the initiatives and pressures just described? To answer this question, Kunda draws on Goffman's concepts of role embracement and role distancing. Goffman writes:

> The individual is best seen as a stance-taking entity, a something that takes up a position somewhere between identification with an organization and opposition to it, and is ready at the slightest pressure to regain its balance by shifting its involvement in either direction (p. 161)

It is the constant interweaving between role embracement and distancing that forms the sense of self. Goffman again writes:

> The self is not an entity half concealed behind events but a changeable formula for managing oneself during them. Just as the

> current situation prescribes the official guide behind which we will conceal ourselves, so it will provide for where and how we will show through. The culture itself prescribes what sort of entity we must believe ourselves to be in order to have something to show through in its manner (p.573, quoted on p. 264, note 3 chap. 6).

Goffman warns us that understanding socialization processes require more than analysis of the integrative mechanisms that induce role conformity. Consideration should also be made of the mechanisms that prompt people to distance themselves from prescribed roles, because it is in the shifting balance between adherence and distance that our overall personalities are created. Kunda starts from this premise to interpret the reactions of the Tech employees to the pressures applied to them by the company. Role embracement means submitting to the definition of one's self given by Tech. But the employees regard total adherence as undignified, as signalling that they are losers. The paradox is that Tech itself wants its members to be able to decide by themselves, to use their own creativity in the management of uncertainty.

Kunda describes three modes of role distancing. The first is cynicism intended to debunk the corporate ideology by insisting that it is at odds with reality. For example, the maxim 'do the right thing' really means 'do what your manager wants'. The second mode is cool and detached analysis of Tech, whereby members, normally the subjects of social research become scholars of their own organization and its culture. The third mode is an appeal to good sense, described as a body of practical knowledge much more useful than "all that stuff about culture".

Role distancing is also manifest in emotional reactions which Kunda calls rejection, depersonalization or play-acting. Rejection takes the form of a declaration that the only reasons for working at Tech are instrumental, that there is no love, no real involvement. Depersonalization is the response of those who appeal to their professionalism, viewed as a carapace which protects the authentic self against possibly harmful emotions. But, Kunda points out, "when someone cannot cope the others notice". Finally play-acting takes place when people see emotional reactions as a simple strategic device with which to achieve particular goals. But the authenticity of these manifestations is doubtful: they are merely games which require perfect self control.

It is precisely this control that is most difficult to achieve. All Tech employees are haunted by the spectre of burnout: the exhaustion caused by an excessive workload, the stress of being under constant scrutiny by the system, and the pressures applied by colleagues. The typical symptoms of burnout are a loss of self-control, verbal aggression against colleagues or superiors, outbursts of anger against Tech and its infernal rules.

Burnout is so common at Tech that a culture has grown up around it. The longest-serving employees are able to recognize its early symptoms in their colleagues, and wagers are made on who will be the next to succumb. Victims of burnout are reassured by management that it can happen to anyone, and they are then temporarily assigned to less stressful tasks. Their colleagues steer clear of them, but are careful not to take too much advantage of their difficulties, knowing that sooner or later they too may be afflicted. The victims are ambivalent towards their burnout. On the one hand they regard it as a stigma, as an illness which they could have avoided had they recognized its symptoms sufficiently early; one the other, they view a burnout overcome as the scar left by a wound received in combat, so that one may hear it said of someone: "He's worked so hard for Tech that he's even had a burnout".

8. THE AMBIVALENCE OF THE CORPORATE CULTURE

What conclusions can be drawn from this research? Kunda insists on the ambivalence of working at Tech, an ambivalence which is the more profound, the more senior the role occupied. As members move up the corporate ladder and increase in importance, they are subjected to ever closer normative control, with the risk that they may lose their personal independence. The 'culture engineers' seek to turn them into ideal members driven "by profound beliefs and intense emotions, by authentic feelings of loyalty, commitment and the pleasure of work". Yet the result of these efforts is only "members who have internalized ambiguity, who have placed play acting at the centre of their sense of self" (p. 253). The self thus undergoes a constant process of construction, an incessant balancing of appearance and reality:

- the central experience of membership is not only that which ideology seeks to instill, but also the experience of struggle with it. In this sense, members have internalized the 'problem of control' that lies at the heart of organization, and the private selves of members have become part of the 'contested terrain' (p. 221).

Thus the private self has not been entirely colonized. It still persists in interstices where members may take refuge with irony, cynicism and self-analysis. This induces Kunda to deny that Tech is a 'total organization', as Goffman defines those in which constant and absolute control eliminates all possibility of defence (prisons, concentration camps, mental hospitals). Nor should one forget that the salaries and fringe benefits at Tech are anything but negligible, and that "working at Tech is considered by many to be a desirable situation". Its members, Kunda stresses, enjoy all the freedoms and gratifications that capitalist society has to offer. One therefore understands those members who feel that the company exerts an attraction that is difficult to resist.

The human cost is confinement in a gilded cage, or better in a gilded labyrinth where people, like Alice in Wonderland, must not only run as fast as possible to keep up with their rivals but also find the way out by themselves, and above all to play-act, because the boundaries between reality and fiction grow increasingly blurred. Despite the persistent erosion of the boundaries of the private sphere, the company is unable entirely to capture its members' souls, although it systematically undermines their foundations.

Kunda's conclusions are worrying though not apocalyptic, therefore. He concludes by raising a more far-reaching problem, that of the impact of corporate cultures like Tech's on society as a whole. What force, he asks, can be exerted by a moral order based solely on the search for material and individual well-being, and where the internalization by individuals of the company's goals insulates them against any critical appraisal? Kunda's question poses the disquieting problem that excessively powerful companies may be detrimental to democracy. This problem was touched upon earlier when Ouchi's description of the clan as a structure of firm's governance was discussed. Both in Ouchi's model and at Tech, an excess of cultural conformity may lead to the atrophy of dissent, and to conflict with the universal guarantees on which the rule of law is founded.

Finally to be stressed is that Kunda's research belongs to the strand of sociological analysis that focuses on the relationships between organizations and people.

The foregoing discussion can be considered a continuation of Chapter Two of this book, which began with the theories of Barnard and Simon and continued with discussion of Roy's and Crozier's field studies. The linking of Kunda with these latter two works testifies to the immense variety of forms that the relationship between people and organizations may assume in workplaces. They describe incommensurable worlds.

Roy describes the ruses and manoeuvres resorted to by workers and managers in an old factory where covert conflict was the principal collective experience; Crozier investigates the micro-strategies of minor bureaucrats in a public office blocked by the lack of a market and business opportunities. In both cases one may speak of a 'corporate culture' made up of rituals, reciprocal expectations, and more or less implicit codes of behaviour. However, neither in Roy's factory nor in Crozier's bureaucracy did the management use culture as an overt instrument of power and control. Yet this is what happens at Tech; and as a consequence it is precisely from the culturalist perspective that Kunda warns us that a developed capitalism, with its immense financial, technological, knowledge and managerial resources, may gain much more ubiquitous and subtle control over people than at any time in the past. The intent of this control is so ambitious that it challenges Barnard's postulate on the irreducibility of human beings to the all-encompassing logic of organizations. Hence, Kunda's entire research can be read as an analysis of the phenomena that spring from the clash between the corporate endeavour to colonize minds and the ambiguous human response that finds its only means of resistance in irony and self-analysis. Who wins, Barnard or Tech? It is difficult to answer with certainty. The appeal of Kunda's study lies precisely in the deliberate ambiguity of its conclusions.

8. ON THE SUBJECTIVITY SIDE: KARL WEICK AND COGNITIVE PROCESSES

As mentioned at the beginning of this chapter, of the three approaches examined thus far Schein's is the most objectivist because it assumes organizational culture to be something given in external reality and which the researcher need only uncover and interpret. This objectivity is tied to Schein's conception of culture as a collective stock of assumptions developed in the course of time by a social group as it copes with internal and external problems. For Schein, therefore, culture is *cumulative, consensual* and *pragmatic*, in the sense that it springs spontaneously from the experience of an entire group and is likewise spontaneously transmitted to new generations. Absent from Schein's account is the idea that culture may be an ideological outcome deliberately constructed by a power group, which uses it as an instrument of normative control. Schein, therefore, does not envisage the need to examine the various ways in which people react to this control, even less to develop critical reflection on those dynamics.

Such reflection is instead present in Martin's and Kunda's studies. In Martin's it takes the postmodern form of a meta-discourse constructed on the interweaving of three different discourses; in Kunda's, the form of an investigation into the mind-sets of the people subject to Tech's cultural pressures. This reflexivity distances Martin and Kunda from Schein's objectivism, bringing them closer to more subjectivist positions mindful of the cognitive processes with which sense is made of a given social reality.

To understand what is meant by cognitive processes and 'sensemaking', we must examine the theory's most radical version, of which Karl Weick is the best-known exponent. Weick is rather difficult to understand because of the novelty of his theoretical apparatus. But precisely for this reason he is one of the most important and most widely cited authors in contemporary organizational theory. The novelty of his thought may initially be disconcerting; and the effect is compounded by his penchant for paradoxical statements apparently intended to disorient readers most closely wedded to ingenuous realism. But as soon as one grasps the innovative thrust of Weick's thought, it is evident why it has enjoyed such fortune in the scientific and managerial communities.

Weick's subject of study is the cognitive processes by which people make sense of their flows of experience. Like any other external reality, culture acquires sense only through these processes. But what is a cognitive process? To answer, we must begin with Weick's assumption that nothing exists outside the flow of experience, and that the categories of internal/external, within/without, are purely logical in nature: they serve to slice up reality so that sense can be made of it.

Weick, therefore, adopts a position of radical subjectivism. But this should not be taken as a denial that the external world exists, as if it were only a dream. Weick's thesis is that the external world does not possess intrinsic sense, for it always and only has the sense that we attribute to it: it is only possible to know the external world and to interact with it through our sense-making processes. Delivered to our minds is a chaotic and formless flow of experience, to which we give order and form as the cognitive process unfolds. In this process we make deductions which are arranged into 'cause maps', or meaningful and logically ordered constructs. These maps – also called 'cognitive-normative' – predispose our future behaviour and are in their turn modified by the uninterrupted flow of new experience.

This theoretical stance has two consequences. The first is that analysis of sensemaking processes is of central importance; the second is that sensemaking processes and organizing processes are totally equivalent. For Weick, making sense of a flow of experience and organizing the reality that surrounds us are nothing but two sides of the same coin. There is no difference between the processes with which a person, say a manager, organizes his/her business – allocating tasks among his/her staff, negotiating relationships with other businesses, deciding on investments – and the processes with which the same manager makes sense of his/her relationships with the staff, competitors, representatives of banks or other businesses. Sensemaking and organizing are not metaphors for each other: they are exactly *the same thing*, and this holds for both the most powerful manager on earth and the humblest man in the street.

Weick gives the example of a flow of sounds perceived in indistiguishable form. By relying on the mental maps already acquired from previous experiences, we begin to make sense of the flow: we identify words, we separate them from each other, we add punctuation, and so on, until the flow of sounds has been transformed into a meaningful sentence. For Weick this sentence is an enacted environment. The same applies to any other flow of experience: a melody or a theatrical performance, or a more or less fortuitous meeting with other people.

The process is simultaneously cognitive and ontological, and it concerns both individuals and organizations. "The organization paints its own scenario, observes it with binoculars and tries to find a path in the landscape" (1993, p.

193) is one of the many images used by Weick to suggest the absence of boundaries between cognition and ontology, between seeing and creating what is seen.

At the core of Weick's thought, therefore, is the equivalence between making sense of a flow of experience and organizing. From this equivalence a derive are a number of important consequences. The first is that Weick is much more interested in the dynamics of the organizing process than in the statics of the organization generated by that process. Organizing is more important than organization; the verbs that express action are more replete with meaning than the nouns that denote things or structures. The second consequence is that organizing aspects or moments of everyday life (household chores, shopping, a dinner with friends) is not in principle any different from running an organization as a profit-making enterprise, or any other form of administration. The differences are purely factual and concern the degree of complexity and formality of the procedures to be followed.

This helps clarify Weick's assertion that everything that we are accustomed to conceiving as a reality external to us – structures, norms, hierarchies, flow charts, etc. – only exist within the minds of the persons who experience them. An organization should not be viewed as an entity endowed *a priori* with formal structures externally to people; it should instead be seen as "a body of thought by thinking thinkers". Weick adds a little later that the organizational flow charts so widely trumpeted are nothing but symbols, labels or snapshots in the flow of experience. The manager who controls meaningful labels to his/her employees "is able to segment and indicate portions of their experience in consequential manner, so that the employees assume those segments more seriously and treat them in organizationally more appropriate forms" (put more simply: the manager is able to assign roles and tasks and expects consistent behaviour by the employees).

10. PROPERTIES AND OCCASIONS FOR SENSEMAKING

Further, four points should be borne in mind with regard to Weick's thought. The first is that although reality is produced from making sense of flows of experience, this does not mean that reality can be indefinitely shaped. An environment retroacts on those who have enacted it; it compels them to take account of its constraints and behave accordingly. People enact the environment in which they then act. This environment conditions them by the very fact that they have enacted it on the basis of their cognitive maps. But the flows of experience can be reinterpreted and organized differently from the past. It is part of our life-experience to change the meanings that we attach to the episodes making up our life histories: we may come to dislike activities, people and places that we previously liked; conversely we may discover attractive features in things or people that previously left us indifferent.

The feedback from the environment on the persons who have enacted it has direct application in formal organizations. Weick gives the example of a small firm that has struggled to find its market niche, finds it, navigates in it, and grows larger. As it expands, it acquires power and shapes the external environment. But this does not mean that the firm is exempt from obligations towards the environment that it itself has created. Weick writes: "As an organization grows in size it increasingly invents its own selection system, and finally literally imposes the environment that imposes itself upon it" (in Zan, p. 269). The market, which is frequently perceived as an objective entity which impends on the actors that operate within it, is in reality nothing but the outcome of a continuous series of strategic choices made by those actors: alliances investments, policies. But the cumulative effect of those choices may be such that those that have made them are crushed.

The concept of 'enacted environment' is used by Weick to conduct penetrating analysis of technology (1995). It would be simplistic to think of technology as solely a set of inanimate machines. Technology also embodies the ability of persons to run those machines, to interact with them and to understand their potential. By way of example, consider a computer: its technology is not only the hardware, nor is it the combination of the hardware and software. Technology is also the human capacity to get the computer to perform operations unthought of by its designers, and therefore to create an environment previously accessible to a handful of initiates but which rapidly comes to dominate the market as an indispensable standard capability.

The second point to bear in mind concerns the crucial role of language in the processes of organizing and sensemaking. It is crucial at both the metaphorical and substantive levels. At the metaphorical one, an organization can be viewed as "a consensually validated grammar for the reduction of ambiguity through meaningful interdependent behaviours" (It. trans. 1993, p. 14). In the same way that grammar is the structure of a language, and language is the device that enables human beings to communicate – that is, give a shared sense to things and actions – so too is the action of organizing . We are surrounded by an ambiguous and incomprehensible world: only by developing a common language of acts, procedures and rites to which we give unequivocal sense can we put together a series of interdependent actions in meaningful sequences which generate meaningful outcomes. The organization as the final (but never definitive) result of organizing serves to reduce the range of ambiguities and ambivalences. "It is an invention of people which is overlaid on flows of experience and which imposes momentary order on those flows" (It. trans. 1993, p. 26).

There is then the substantive importance of language in sensemaking. If it is true that people know what they are thinking when they see what they are saying, this means that words are present in every phase of the cognitive process. "Words constrain the speech that is produced, the categories imposed to see what has been said, and the labels with which the conclusions of the process are fixed" (It. trans. 1997, p. 115). Without words it is possible neither to define reality nor to communicate. Words generate sense, but at the same time they do not suffice to represent reality exhaustively. They attach discrete labels to a content that is continuous. They approximate the territory but they never map it perfectly, because there is always a mismatch between words and their referents. This is why sensemaking never ceases. It springs from the effort to grasp reality with words, but this is an endless endeavour because words are unable ever to represent reality completely. Words define reality in ways that can always be gainsaid by other words.

The third point to bear in mind concerns an apparent contradiction in Weick. He claims that sensemaking is a process with neither a beginning nor an end. Elsewhere, however, he talks about occasions that provoke sensemaking. But if sensemaking is provoked, this means that it is not a continuous process. How can this contradiction be resolved? The answer lies in the ramifications of Weick's thought. It is true that sensemaking is a continuous process, but it is also true that it is subject to constant fits and starts, with consequent changes in the raw materials of which the person makes sense. Sensemaking processes are like waves which overrun each other. For example, falling in love is an occasion for sensemaking. But this is not to say that the person who falls in love has never previously engaged in sensemaking. His previous life may have been monotonous and devoid of emotions, and precisely its tedium occasioned sensemaking in order to answer the question: what sense does my life have, what do I do with my days? On falling in love, this person enacts a radically different environment. His days are now full, rich with emotions and encounters, and his sensemaking rotates around the question: what is the sense of this affair, how long can it last, should I drop everything and go where the heart leads?

Weick describes the occasions that generate sensemaking as 'shocks'. A shock occurs whenever an event interrupts an ongoing sequence of events (actions, projects, trains of thought). A shock can be both positive and negative, in the sense that it may announce a desirable situation as well as an undesirable one. In all cases, the interruption of the ongoing flow, or the discrepancy between the expected course of events and the unexpected event, triggers sensemaking. The shock prompts people to see things in a different manner: what happened?, Why did it happen? What does it all mean? are the questions with which they begin to make sense of the interruption (one of the properties of sensemaking is that it is always interwoven with emotions).

But it should also be stressed that there is no guarantee that sensemaking will be successful. It may fail, and the consequences of its failure may prove to be fatal. The interruption of a flow of experience provokes a state of anxiety or alarm which activates the sensemaking process. But anxiety has the characteristic of monopolizing much of a person's ability to process information, so that there is less information available for sensemaking. This gives rise to a vicious circle: the prolonged loss of information makes sensemaking more difficult; this difficulty heightens the state of anxiety; greater anxiety causes the loss of more information; sensemaking diminishes even further; and so on. In states of anxiety, responses are cruder, and better-known procedures are hastily implemented, not those best suited to dealing with the emergency. In extreme cases, the sensemaking process collapses, with possible fatal consequences: as in the case of the prairie fire examined by Weick (1993) when fourteen young fire-fighters perished because they had lost the sense of what was happening, and therefore the ability to organize a rational response to the danger.

Finally, a fourth point to be borne in mind concerns the problem of power. One of the objections most frequently raised against Weick's theory by those habituated to thinking in terms of traditional realism can be expressed as follows: if each of us enacts his or her own environment, on what basis can a collective experience of reality be possible? How can the spread of shared ideas and emotions be explained? Weick's reply is that certain persons endowed with particular power are able to enact environments which they then propose as a reading of reality to others. For example, a manager who reviews the history of the firm, remembering the heroic moments of the past and then naming the enemies to be defeated today, provides his employees with an 'enacted environment' which they are solicited to accept and make their own. The possibility of a shared reading of reality is, therefore, based on the existence of power centres with sufficient authority to furnish people with as many specific cognitive maps as there are environments enacted in accordance with those maps. This subjectivist base of shared experiences is an antidote to the danger that an excessively conformist view of consensus will be assumed. Because each of us has his or own personal flow of experience (and is able to distinguish its private aspects from its public ones), it follows that acceptance of an externally enacted environment will never be total, but will always and only concern a portion of that experience. The fact that people agree on their sensemakings does not make them indistinguishable. They keep their irreducible specificity by endlessly making sense of their life experiences.

11. FROM GIDDENS TO BARLEY: THE PROCESSES OF ORGANIZATIONAL STRUCTURING

Of the various subjectivist theories discussed, Weick's cognitivism has been most influential on organizational and managerial thought. It has been so because of the provocative challenge that it raises against traditional theories, and especially because of the intriguing areas of inquiry that analysis of sensemaking in organizations opens up. Other currents of thought, like symbolic interactionism, phenomenology and ethnomethodology, have radically undermined the ingenuous realism which holds that an already-formed world exists 'out there' independently of ourselves. However, though cited and appreciated, the often hermetic radicalness of these theories has confined them to the margins of sociological debate.

Greater fortune has been enjoyed by positions lying midway along the object/subject continuum and reflecting in various ways the 'structuration theory' developed by Giddens, a leading British sociologist. Giddens' thesis is that we must reject the hegemony of both the subject and the object. This twofold rejection is possible if we take as our subject of study, not the experience of individual actors nor the existence of 'social totalities' (i.e. given structures which exist prior to subjects), but "a set of social practices ordered in space and time" or institutionalized patterns of behaviour observable in everyday life.

This singling out of social practices as the subject of research springs from a profound rethinking of the concept of social structure. The latter should no longer be conceived as a set of stable connections which constrain human action, but rather as "a set of resources and rules generative of human behaviours". In other words, the social structure should be viewed as a device which both enables the recursive (i.e. repeated in time) organization of human behaviour and at the same time results from that behaviour. The social structure has a dual character, therefore: on the one hand it makes human action possible; on the other, it does not exist independently of that action, but is involved in its constant production and reproduction. Thus it is possible to resolve the traditional antithesis between static and dynamic in social analysis.

Spoken language provides an apt metaphor for this dualism. If we consider language to be a structure, we see that it "is a condition for speech acts to be generated and dialogue to take place, but it is also an unintentional consequence of the production of discourse and the performance of dialogue" (1979, p. 178). Language consists of words, a grammar, a syntax and a quantity of idiomatic expressions which enable people to communicate. Language is, therefore, a structure in the sense that it is a set of communicative resources and rules which permit the generation of meaningful discourse. But it is also a structure that constantly modifies itself through the recursive use that speakers make of it.

This duality prompts Giddens to identify structuring processes as the central concern of social analysis. By 'structuring' he means the conditions which govern the continuity or change of structures in space and time, and therefore the reproduction of social systems. Examining the processes by which social systems are structured consequently requires study of the ways in which these systems are constantly produced and reproduced through interaction:

Every act that contributes to the reproduction of a structure is also an act of production, a new initiative, and as such it may give rise to change by altering that structure in the same moment as reproducing it, in the same way as the meaning of words changes during and through their use (1979, p. 179).

Structuring theory opens up new and fascinating areas for research into everyday interactions in the most disparate of social settings. It is a perspective that lends itself well to organizational analysis which uses ethnographic methods to explore the ways in which recurrent patterns of action are applied and simultaneously modified by the people's actions themselves. A lively strand of inquiry has developed on this basis. One of the most important studies has been conducted by the American Stephen Barley, the author of acute research on work practices in scientific laboratories, the role of technicians, and the formation of occupational communities.[1]

Here, I shall examine Barley's study (1986) of the different organizational consequences of introducing radiology scanning technology in two hospital diagnostic wards. Barley begins with discussion of the long yet inconclusive debate in the social sciences on the organizational changes brought about by technological innovations. It is true that the latter induce new ways of working; it is equally true that the knowledge of those consequences accumulated in more than twenty years of research is contradictory and confused. The reason for this failure, Barley maintains, is that the authors of these studies start from two erroneous premises: they consider an organizational structure to be a set of autonomous and formal relations which constrain everyday action; and they conceive technology to be a material cause which imposes imperatives on that structure. From these premises he derives the presumption that there are regular connections between technology and structure which remain the same whatever the context. It is precisely this presumption that so many years of research have failed to confirm.

Barley's contention is that to escape from the impasse, we must abandon the idea that structure is an external reality which exists previously to human action.

1 Interestingly, Barley wrote an essay on occupational communities (1988) jointly with Kunda, which is indicative of the convergence between their theories along the object/subject axis. Among authors of ethnographic-interactionist inspiration particular mention should be made of Manning (1977) and Van Mannen (1978), the authors of important studies on the American police.

We must follow, he says, the suggestion put forward by Weick, Giddens and other interactionist authors that structure is a property which emerges from a course of action. This recasting of the notion has three important consequences for the manner in which research into the relationships between technology and structure is conducted:

- because the structure is not a static phenomenon but develops in the course of time, research must reflect this development; it must, that is to say, be of duration sufficient to grasp the changes which occur over a significantly long time-span.
- because the social context is important, it is pointless to conduct research which lumps different settings and histories together; research should instead focus on individual cases and their particular contexts;
- because technology has a direct impact on human actions, its implications for structuring processes cannot be understood unless one explores the way in which technology itself is incorporated into the everyday lives of an organization's members.

Research carried out on these principles refuses to accept that there is a causal nexus between technology and organizational structure. The advent of new technologies should instead be seen as an occasion which generates structuring processes whereby a given organizational setting is progressively altered. Because each of these processes involves unique factors and circumstances, one may presume that identical technologies used in similar contexts will produce different structures. These processes are, therefore, non-deterministic, and they have different outcomes according to the factors at work.

The aim of Barley's research was to observe these processes in their everyday development. To this end he used the notion of 'script' suggested by Goffman. Scripts are outlines of recurrent interactions which broadly define the actors' roles. As in an improvised stage play, a script does not rigidly prescribe a sequence of behaviour. Instead it provides a rough sketch which can be modified according to circumstances and the personalities of the actors. Barley hypothesised that the structuring processes induced by the advent of new technologies pass through various phases in which the repetition of scripts change them from initially vague outlines to increasingly specific definitions. This progressive structuring is brought about by interactions between changes of external origin, institutional constraints on action, and the effects of human action on the structure.

The organization is not a pre-established and formal framework within which the script is structured; it is the entire structuring process in its various phases. A dynamic and interactive phenomenon, it changes over time because it is shaped by the practices of people who, day after day, concur more or less deliberately in its progressive definition. An organization is, therefore, by definition an open structure which may change as soon as new human, technical, cognitive, social, financial or political factors come into play.

12. THE SAME TECHNOLOGY, DIFFERENT ORGANIZATIONAL STRUCTURINGS: THE CONCEPT OF SCRIPT

The foregoing considerations prompted Barley's research hypothesis with regard to the two diagnostic centres that he studied. Technologists and radiologists worked in both units, which he called Urban and Suburban. The technologists were responsible for operating the equipment and for the technical quality of the radiographs, while the radiologists attended to clinical interpretation of the scans. One might, therefore, presume that the units followed the command script, in that the radiologists were of higher professional status than the Technologists and told them what to do. Except that from the outset different scripts developed in the two units.

Because nobody at the Suburban hospital knew how to operate the new equipment, a radiologist and two technologists with the requisite knowledge had to be hired. This led to an initial stage of informal negotiation over the margins of discretion available to the two technologists. During this phase the command script gave way to three other scripts consisting of the following recursive patterns:

- The technologists began working without seeking prior approval from the radiologist. The latter merely enquired as to the reasons for their actions. When told, he gave his approval.
- The technologists asked questions, the radiologist answered, the technologists commented on the diagnosis and the radiologist confirmed their interpretation.
- The radiologist explained to the technologists why he had recommended one procedure rather than another, and the technologists began to expect such explanations as their due.

After some weeks had passed, a second phase in the structuring of the Suburban unit began. Barley calls this phase 'usurping autonomy'. Those radiologists in the unit unacquainted with the new scanning technology were given rapid instruction by their expert colleague, and then had to interpret the scans on their own. Three further scripts emerged, which Barley calls 'clandestine teaching', 'role reversals' and 'blaming the technologists':

- The inexpert radiologists began asking the technologists how to interpret the *x*-rays correctly. Because they were embarrassed at seeming ignorant to their inferiors, they avoided overly explicit questions. The technologists played along, pretending that the radiologists knew what they were talking about, and increasing their displays of deference.
- The fiction could not last for long, however, and the role reversal script emerged with increasing frequency. This, however, made the radiologists embarrassed and the technologists anxious.
- The radiologists began to mistake equipment malfunctions for errors by the technologists, and to reject the explanations made by the latter.

These three scripts caused relationships in the unit to deteriorate. The technologists were contemptuous of the inexpert radiologists, and the radiologists were hostile towards the technologists. In order to reduce the tension, the technologists began to perform the routine tasks on their own, while the radiologists sought to save face by no longer supervising the scanning operations. In this way, Barley comments, the structuring process gave rise to an unexpected organizational model: that of the broad independence of the technologists and substantial separation between the two categories of workers.

Barley observed a very different structuring process at the Urban unit. Here it was the radiologists who knew their jobs, while it was the technologists – only just hired – who were inexperienced. The radiologists, therefore, had to teach the technologists how to use the equipment. But because they were unfamiliar with teaching techniques, they merely gave detailed instructions on how to operate the machinery, without explaining why. The direction giving script thus became almost the only form of verbal communication between the radiologists and the technologists. Little by little, however, the countermands script took over, when the radiologists realized that orders given previously were unsatisfactory. The counter-orders were almost always due to personal preferences and rivalries among the radiologists, who frequently argued over who the best technologists were and countermanded each other's orders. Because the technologists were not present at these discussions, they found the counter-orders capricious and unreasonable.

After the first three weeks, two further scripts appeared which exacerbated the dependence of the technologists. Barley calls them 'usurping the control' and 'direction seeking:

- Sometimes the radiologists took over the equipment and halted the technologists' work without explanation. The technologists felt frustrated but did not have the courage to react. This induced them to develop the second script:

- asking the radiologists what they should do even if they already knew. Perversely, their questions confirmed the radiologists' belief that the technologists did not know how to do their job. As a consequence, they increased their control.

When about four weeks had passed, the radiologists realized that they had to encourage the technologists to become more independent. They consequently decided to spend more time in their offices. But this decision only increased the confusion of the technologists, who now felt obliged to seek out the radiologists in their offices. This increased dependence provoked the sarcasm of the radiologists. A few days later the radiologists changed their minds and resumed their practice of spending much of their time in the laboratory so that they could directly supervise the technologists' work.

This situation continued for many more weeks until the more expert radiologists were transferred to another department. This transfer changed the interaction patterns in the unit, because those radiologists who remained had little experience of the scanning equipment. They did not hide their ignorance, however, and openly asked the technologists for help. Thus a new script arose, what Barley calls 'technical consultation', which reversed the situation of the first few weeks. This reversal did not undermine the authority of the radiologists, however: unlike their counterparts at the Suburban unit they only asked for technical information, not for interpretations of the scans. The technologists began offering advice on how to proceed, and the radiologists complimented them on their knowledge. There thus finally emerged a script of mutual consultation based on complementary knowledge: the technologists became more independent and the radiologists relaxed their supervision of the technologists' work.

This concludes the account of the organizational structuring processes in the two diagnostic units. Its purpose has been to demonstrate that an organization is not made up solely of formal structures and technology; it instead lives, and it is shaped from day to day by the manner in which people interact, by their knowledge resources, and by the uses they make of them. Yet Barley's study is not merely a narrative. During his long ethnographic observations, carried out on alternate days at the Urban and Suburban units, Barley systematically logged the frequency with which he observed recurrent patterns of behaviour: what he calls 'scripts'. He identified a total of fourteen such scripts, and then calculated their frequency and degrees of statistical significance. He was thus able to bear out with mathematical criteria his conclusions on the differences between the two processes of organizational structuring.

Its merits aside, Barley's method should be signalled for its originality. It teaches us that ethnographic analysis need not be solely qualitative but may avail itself of a variety of methods. A study restricted to few cases does not rule out the use of quantitative criteria, if events recurring with a certain frequency are used as the units of analysis. The scripts identified by Barley enabled him to combine statistical analysis with interpretative description. But to single out these scripts, he needed the theoretical apparatus of structuring processes in which the scripts were treated as so many elementary organizational units. Thus the differing frequencies and combinations of scripts became criteria with which to assert the existence of different types of organization.

DISCUSSION

This chapter suggests numerous ideas for research. All of them relate to the fact that the studies discussed above employ qualitative ethnographic methods available to anyone with an interest indirect observation, and an aptitude for it. Schein, Martin and Kunda show how research can be conducted by entering a new environment, or even by observing an already familiar environment with new eyes.

Let us return to Laura, the student whom we left behind in the introduction to this book. And let us try to read with her the 'culture' of the university at which she is enrolled, using the tools suggested by these authors. Is her university a campus or is it embedded in the urban fabric? Look at the green spaces and car park around the main building (if they exist), and then at the entrance lobby, the porters' lodge, the staircases, the corridors, the lifts, the number and size of the lecture rooms, the layout of their furniture, the student common rooms, the service rooms, and so on. What can one deduce about the kind of university that the designers had in mind? Did they envisage a university for the masses or one for the elite, democratic or authoritarian, somewhere to spend the whole day or just to attend lectures and then hurry away. Then look at the cleanliness of the building, the announcements on the notice boards, the soft drinks dispensers, the toilets and the graffiti on the walls. What do they tell you about the suitability of the building for its everyday functions? Is it well cared for, do the students cooperate or do they not care?

And what can be said about the work of the lecturers by looking at their rooms: the books on the shelves, the piles of photocopies, the computers, the pictures and photographs on the walls, the objects on the desks. Are they normally used for work or merely to receive students? Then observe the library and its regulations, its opening hours, the reading room, the reference collections and the photocopiers. To what extent does the library meet the students' needs and how does it combine ease of access with security? Likewise inspect the administrative offices, the premises used by student clubs and associations, the cafeteria, the sports facilities, and the network of shops that have sprung up around the university.

And then consider the everyday behaviour of people: students, teachers, tutors, porters, librarians, administrative staff. Are there students working part-time in the university's various services. If so, on what criteria were they given the work? What are the relationships among these various categories of people? Do lecturers and students only meet at lectures, receptions and examinations or do they mix socially as well? On what criteria do the students judge the lecturers and the lecturers judge the students? Are there some rules accepted by everybody and others which everyone seeks to evade?

More generally, is it possible to identify the common culture envisaged by Schein, or are the different sub-cultures theorized by Martin more evident? Or do the official norms imposed by some member of the academic staff provoke the ambiguous mixture of acceptance and resistance, of cynicism and commitment, displayed by the people who Kunda investigated?

All these observations can be interpreted from the points of view of Weick, Giddens and Barley alike. Try to describe a lesson from the sensemaking perspective: the initial announcements by the lecturer, his/her explanations, the students' questions; the initial bewilderment caused by an unusual or abstruse theory, and then the students' progressive endeavour to make sense of it through questions or comments after the lecture. Try also to see whether the lecturer manages to communicate his/her sensemaking to the students, not only of the topic being taught, but of their gathering for the lecture, of group learning and learning through dialogue. Can it be said that the lecturer exerts power? Can the power that Weick discerns in shared sensemaking be also described as charisma in the sense given to the term by Weber?

Finally to be observed are structuring processes, fascinating to study but with the drawback that precisely because they are processes they require a long period of observation. However, if there is time, the method used by Barley is certainly fruitful. Try to follow the lectures of certain teachers for an entire semester: can you identify recurrent scripts in the relationships between students and lecturer, record their frequency and distinguish phases in the cycle of lectures? What differences can you find between one class and another in the nature and frequency of scripts on the basis of the number and type of class members, the lecturer's personality, the characteristics of the course topic, or technical or timetable constraints? Do episodes occur (progress tests, talks by external speakers, requests by students, unexpected tensions) which modify the scripts? More in general, are you able to reconstruct a process of organizational structuring of one or more classes or courses in which the various actors concerned have actively participated and defined day by day?

REFERENCES

Barley Stephen

1986 Technology as an Occasion for Structuring :Evidence from Observations of CT Scanners and the Social Order of Radiology Departments, *Administrative Science Quarterly* 31, pp. 78-108.

1994 In the backrooms of Science. The work of Technicians in Science Labs, *Work and Occupations*, 21, pp 85-126

1996 Technicians in the Workplace: Ethnographic Evidence from Bringing Work into Organization Studies , *Administrative Science Quarterly*, 41, pp. 404-441

Barker James

1993 Tightening the iron cage: concertive control in self-managing teams, *Adminisirative Science Quarterly*, 38, pp. 408-37

Barley Stephen e Kunda Gideon

1992 Design and Devotion: Surges in Rational and Normative Ideologies of Control in Managerial Discourse, *Administrative Science Quarterly*, 37, pp.363-399

Bonazzi Giuseppe

1999, *Dire fare pensare. Decisioni e creazione di senso nelle organizzazioni* , Franco Angeli Milano

Giddens Anthony

1976 *New Rules of Sociological Method. A Positive Critique of Interpretative Sociology*, Huthinson, London

1984 *The Constitution of Society Polity Press*, Cambridge

Goffman Erwing

1961 *Asylums*, Anchor ,Garden City New York

1974 *Frame Analysis*, Harper and Row, New York

Kunda Gideon 1992

Engineering Culture. Control and Commitment in a Hig-Tech Corporation, Temple University

Martin Joanne

1992 *Cultures in Organizations*, Oxford University Press, New York, Oxford

Schein Edgar 1985 *Organizational Culture and Leadership* , Jossey Bass

Perrow Charles

1986 *Complex Organizations. A critical Essay* (third edition), Random House, New York

Weick Karl

- 1969 *The Social Psychology of Organizing* (1a ediz.) Random House, New York,

- 1977 "Enactment Processes in Organizations", in Staw B.M. and Salancik G.R. (a cura di) *New Directions in Organizational Behavior*, St.Clair Press, Chicago

1993 The Collapse of Sensemaking in Organizations: The Mann Gulch Disaster, *Administrative Science Quarterly*, 38, pp. 628-652

-1995 *Sensemaking in Organizations*, Sage Publications.

Chapter 7

Conclusions

1. WHAT MODEL FOR THE TWENTY-FIRST CENTURY? MINIMAL ORGANIZATIONS AND BOUNDARY-LESS CAREERS

In a postscript to the Italian translation of *Engineering Culture* (2000), Kunda warns his readers that Tech, the subject of his ethnographic research in the 1980s, is no longer an independent company. At the beginning of the 1990s, amid accelerating crisis, the board sacked the company's charismatic founder. But his departure did nothing to improve the situation. Indeed, after further vicissitudes, staff cutbacks and threats of bankruptcy, Tech was taken over by another company. The latter decided to keep Tech's technical know-how but to liquidate its corporate culture, judging it to be a futile impediment to competitiveness and creativity.

Kunda observes that the history of American management has always been characterized by the rapid turnover of fashions. And so it has been for the fad of corporate culture. Kunda writes:

> ...instead of descriptions of cold-hearted discussion of efficiency-driven work force reductions resting on popular key terms to describe organizational structures like the earlier mentioned downsizing and outsourcing—transferring in-house organizational functions to outside contractors; instead of a discussion of the organization's contribution to its employees in terms of career planning and enhancement, intra-organizational mobility and the creation of a sense of belonging and inclusion, one would find terms such as employability—a popular term in the field of human resource management according to which workers, in return for their heavy investment in work can expect to receive experiences and learn skills that would help them find new jobs when their services are no longer required; and instead of a discussion of the deep psychological significance of membership

> in a community of work, the reader will find terms that characterize workers relation to their employers such as free agency—a very popular view that describes in idyllic terms workers who see themselves not as employees belonging to an organizational community but as independent agents in an open and flexible labour market, devoid of loyalty to employers, and selling their services for fixed periods of time to the highest bidder. (p. 291-2, Italian edition, 2000).

Thus in the space of ten years capitalism has turned the page, and America is once again in the vanguard of change. But it is not sufficient to register yet another manifestation of that 'creative destruction' which Schumpeter saw as the soul of capitalism. In a book like this one devoted to the study of organizations, Kunda's remarks raise two questions. The first is the distinction between corporate culture as a managerial fashion and corporate culture as an object of analysis. It is a matter of fact that sociological interest in corporate culture arose in concomitance with managerial interest in corporate culture as a 'third-level' instrument of control over the workforce. However, the fact that the culture fashion subsequently flourished in companies and business schools does not mean that it is less possible to research the culture of organizations. The corporate world described by Kunda in the passage just quoted has its culture, though it is different from the one in vogue during the 1980s. The corporate "culture of culture", which presupposed job security and identification with the company's fortunes, has given way to the culture of ephemeral employment, job mobility, employability, and the free agency of workers operating in the market as entrepreneurs of their own selves. And this culture can be studied ethnographically in exactly the same way as the corporate culture of the previous age.

The second question concerns the organizational changes brought about by the passage from the period of the corporate culture to that of fixed-term employment and rampant flexibility. What model of organization can be foreseen for the twenty-first century, and what problems will it pose for sociological research? A stimulating approach to the question is taken in an essay by Miles and Snow (1996) published in a book significantly entitled *The Boundaryless Career*. Miles and Snow argue that:

- every type of organization establishes core competences, the necessary professions, the structure and governance of careers;
- the typical organization in the twenty-first century will be minimal, made up of a few self-entrepreneurs able to perform a multiplicity of tasks and roles.

Miles and Snow identify four great waves in the history of industry. The first, which will not be dwelt upon here, was initial industrialization. This was followed by a second wave which lasted for more than a century from the mid-1800s to around 1970. This was the classical period which culminated in Fordism, when firms were driven by the principles of:

(*a*) producing everything themselves;

(*b*) improving themselves through progressive size growth;

(*c*) managing the production process by means of rules and administrative procedures. Corresponding to these principles were careers in which employees:

(*a*)worked for only one employer; (*b*) moved up the company hierarchy; (*c*) deployed technical skills specific to the company; (*d*) left it to the employer to decide career advancements.

One may add that this was also the wave whose final phase saw corporate culture being used to control work performance. This phase entered crisis when firms began to abandon the principle of producing only 'in-house' and adopted, as we saw when discussing transaction costs economics, 'to buy' strategies. Firms consequently forsook the centralized gigantism of the previous phase. They assumed leaner forms and articulated themselves into conglomerates made up of autonomous profit centres. There thus began, in the last decades of the twentieth century, the third wave of industrial history, the one conventionally called post-Fordist. Firms were now driven by the principles of:

(*a*) producing only what they were best able to produce and outsourcing the rest;

(*b*) improving through the development of a network of suppliers, customers and partners;

(*c*) managing the production process by means of market mechanisms. Corresponding to these principles were careers in which:

(*a*) people worked for numerous companies, increasing their specialization;

(*b*) moved among different projects to acquire ever new experience;

(*c*) deployed skills not only technical but also commercial, collaborative and governance capable;

(*d*) defined their career advancements together with the employer.

However, Miles and Snow maintain, this wave is destined to be short-lived. Already on the horizon is a fourth wave which, they believe, will characterize firms in the twenty-first century. Whereas during the second wave firms constructed and used hierarchies, and in the third wave flattened them and broke them up, Miles and Snow predict that in the fourth wave firms will tend to eliminate every form of hierarchy. Firms, especially those specialized in professional services, will tend to have a minimal organization whose only task is to accommodate and facilitate the work of small groups of professionals-entrepreneurs. The latter will not depend on a hierarchical superior; rather, they will coordinate their work independently, creating mini-firms driven by the following principles:

(*a*) being able to do everything everywhere and at any time;

(*b*) improvement through a mix of competition and collaboration;

(*c*) self-management through the constant creation of knowledge and the allocation of responsibilities (whence extremely heavy workloads with peaks of 12 to 15 hours a day). Corresponding to these principles will be careers characterized by:

   (*a*) professional work on one's own account;

   (*b*) enhancement of one's own professional capabilities;

   (*c*) exclusive reliance one one's own capacities for collaboration and self-governance.

Miles and Snow describe minimal organizations as spherical and cellular. They call them spherical both to contrast them with the traditional hierarchical pyramid and to highlight their ability to "rapidly deliver resources in all directions at the exact point in which they are required" (p. 105). In these organizations everyone does everything, having developed the maximum capacity to connect rapidly with a multiplicity of partners along the entire value creation chain. But minimal organizations are also called cellular to evoke the metaphor of the cell, a living organism endowed with every capacity to act on its own, but which in collaboration with other cells is able to perform more complex functions. A cellular organization is made up of autonomous elementary units which interact with other units to achieve more complex objectives. Knowledge and information are shared by all the cells, so that the DNA of one cell contains the genetic make-up of the entire organism.

The overall organization is a conglomerate of 8-10 cells, each formed by 12-15 professionals who may elect their project manager as a *primus inter pares*. The cells may freely join together in internal alliances, but they may also form alliances with external subjects, mainly customers and suppliers. In these organizations, where the administrative and service staff is reduced to the essential minimum, each professional is also a business procurer and an entrepreneur, for s/he alone constructs his/her career.

2. TRENDS AND PROBLEMS FOR FUTURE RESEARCH

Miles and Snow offer provocative insights. Although it is unlikely that the model of the minimal organization will be the only one to impose itself in the twenty-first century, it will assuredly be one of the most typical and widespread. It has already been adopted in the entertainment industry for some years (Jones, 1996; De Filippi and Arthur, 1998), and it is acknowledgedly congenial to the new economy, from project design to information services (Jones et al., 1997). The new scenario not only raises unprecedented problems of organizational inquiry but also requires sensibilities and discourses profoundly different from those of the past.

This book concludes with examination of four issues raised by the new way of organizing and conceiving organizations. We shall see that subjectivist approaches (from sensemaking to structuration theory) are particularly suited to grasping the new reality, but we shall also see that there is important scope for the neo-institutionalist approach as well.

2.1. *The subjectivist foundation of making sense of organizations*

In traditional organizations, making sense of people's action (in particular their work) has an objectivist origin because it is based on the premise that powerful external structures exist prior to human action and condition it. In the minimal organizations outlined in the previous section, making sense of people's action has a subjectivist origin because it is based on the premise that weak organizational structures are shaped by human action and reflect its intentionality. The distinction is crucial because the objectivist mode of sensemaking can only have an *ameliorative* effect on the quality of work and human relationships. The subjectivist mode has instead a *generative* effect, because it is not possible to conceive of viable organizations except through the sense that people confer on them, and through the sense that they acquire from that conferral.

To understand the distinction we must look at the history of organizational thought. The objectivist mode of sensemaking arose in the early decades of the twentieth century as a reaction against the Taylorism dominant in large organizations. It found expression first in Human Relations, then in the denunciation by the French sociology of work of industrial mechanization and the human problems that it provoked (Friedmann, 1949), and finally in the motivationist school from Maslow to Herzberg to Likert. These various theories shared the assumption that human beings are crushed by ruthless and 'objective' organizations which determine the content of work, careers and social relationships. This was not solely a question of exploitation and of authoritarian – or in the best of cases, paternalistic – management. It also concerned the meaninglessness of work which consisted in mere passive obedience to the dictates of the production regime. In the face of the relentless productive structure, the problem of psychologists and sociologists of work was to find ways to attenuate the harshness and inhumanity of organizations, making work not only less toilsome and repetitive but also to some extent meaningful to those who perform it.

However, there was an objective shortcoming to these proposals: they envisaged the binding technology of a still Fordist production regime. This shortcoming undermined proposals for reform, because only a tiny number of workers could realistically benefit from a job redesign which made their work more intelligent and gave them opportunities for personal growth. As a consequence, discussion on the humanization of work concerned not so much giving it greater meaningfulness as improving the economic and environmental conditions in which people worked.

It was the motivationist school that laid the theoretical basis for abandoning the objectivist approach to making sense of work in productive organizations. Particular mention should be made of the work of Argyris (1978; 1982), who has merit of being the first to emphasise the importance of continuous learning. His concept of 'double-loop' learning how to learn, and therefore the theorization of the 'learning organization' that arose from it, led to recognition that the meaning of organizations does not spring from a harsh and immutable external reality but is constantly attributed, enriched and modified by people. The concept of the learning organization announced that the time was ripe for discarding the traditional objectivist premise and switching to a subjectivist one: namely that giving meaning to organizations and to one's work is not a costly concession wrung from the other party but a fundamental requirement for an organization's success.

However, the shift from one premise to the other cannot be explained solely in terms of the history of ideas. The fortune of the passage, the ease with which it found acceptance in the world of management (among the 'practitioners'), can only be explained in the light of a certain epochal changes taking place in both the production system and organizational action in general. One of these changes was the spread of the minimal organizations and the boundary-less careers discussed earlier. These organizations should be borne in mind so that what is meant by giving meaning to the action of people crucial to the workings of organizations becomes clear. Minimal organizations could not exist if it were not for the constant sensemaking performed by their members. Nothing is objectified as a reality independent of the actors concerned, everything is constantly redefined, including the effects of previous actions which, on the one h nd, constrain subsequent action and the other lend themselves to ever new retrospective and problematic interpretations.

Commenting on the kind of organization, Weick (1996) talks of the disappearance of external guide for sequences of work experience. The experience of work is detached from specific organizations and links with less predictable processes of organizing. Consequently, careers are no longer variables dependent on organizations. Instead, it is the organization, understood as organizing, that is the outcome of the career. Career success is defined by the amount of learning, by the meaningfulness of the continuities constructed, by the ability to handle organizing processes, by the comfort that derives from constantly returning to learning roles, by tolerance for fragmentary experiences, by the capacity to make retrospective sense of previous experiences, and by the capacity to improvise when unexpected situations arise.

2.2. *Professional identity, occupational communities and labour markets*

In the classical Taylor-Fordist age, when most of the production process took place 'in-house', work was largely deskilled and control was eminently bureaucratic. Firms obtained the manpower that they needed from the external labour market. Because very few skills were required to perform job tasks, vocational training was minimal and career prospects limited. In the absence of corporate policy to encourage employees to work permanently for the organization, the decision whether to stay or whether to seek work elsewhere depended essentially on the dynamics of the external labour market.

There then came the late-Fordist period, when network development, technological progress and increased competition persuaded firms that they needed employees with specific technical skills, and they should, therefore, foster the attachment of these employees to the firm. Vocational training schemes were introduced, and internal labour markets were developed so that employees could have opportunities for career advancement within the firm, or in the network of firms connected with it. We have seen that this was also the period in which corporate cultures were used to create internalized control and ideological-emotional identification with the fortunes of the business. Belonging to a firm, perhaps for one's entire working life, became a factor in professional and social identity.

The most recent period has seen the advent of the minimal organizations outlined in the previous section. What type of labour market develops in a network of organizations characterized by extremely high mobility combined with extremely high skill content? On what basis can a social and professional identity grow, when firms are no longer heavy structures with their own power of attraction, but only the formalized projections of work by professionals, or of the offices that accommodate it? And where does one live the paradox that competition in the market requires constant innovations which can only be achieved through cooperation (Saxenian 1994)?

An answer can be given to these questions if we adapt the concepts already coined in the 1980s of 'occupational community' (Van Maanen and Barley 1984) and 'occupational labour market' (OML, Marsden 1986) to the new situation.

Occupational communities consist of groups of people engaged in the same kind of work, from which they draw a shared identity, codes of conduct and values. It is consequently no longer firms – now too volatile and minimal – that furnish identity to their employees. Instead, it is the professionals themselves who find their identity in membership of communities that operate crosswise in firms. Because the necessary skills require long training and constant updating, occupational communities are highly selective. Their key criterion is reputation based on shared or similar work experiences. Fierce competition, especially on innovative projects, does not prevent a constant and pervasive flow of communications (it is standard practice to advise other members of job vacancies not of interest to oneself).

Occupational communities establish rules of behaviour, and sanctions for those members in breach of them, so that in certain respects, they resemble the medieval guilds and the nineteenth-century crafts leagues (Bauman p. 7. But the procedures for expulsion in the case of misconduct are much simpler: the miscreant need only be excluded from the information network on the web to have no more work: cf. Miles and Snow, p. 110).

2.3. *Isomorphic pressures on occupational communities and firms*

Occupational communities thus function as self-regulated labour markets on the goods and services supply side. Firms in need of specialist capabilities increasingly less developed internal markets (too rigid and costly) and increasingly more recruit workers from within occupational communities on the basis of reputation and previous experience (people with whom they have already had contracts in the past).

However, this strategy raises the problem of the uncertainty of delivery intrinsic to every contract. On examining occupational labour markets, Marsden (1986) maintains that the best way to deal with this uncertainty is to standardize skills, training and the professional classification. Agencies created by occupational communities themselves (consortia, schools, authorities, etc.) promote initiatives for this purpose. Instead of regulatory mechanisms managed directly by firms (as in internal markets), within and around occupational communities there arise institutional pressures to obtain standardized performance. As consultants migrate from company to company, it is part of their professionalism to minimize the time taken to learn and acclimatize themselves to the organizations to which they furnish their services. This is reminiscent of the theatre companies and sports teams that work together for brief periods. The general effect is a strengthening of the isomorphic processes described by the neo-institutional school (see Chapter 3).

But isomorphism also operates on the demand side: that is, with regard to the large firms for which external professionals work on a temporary basis. Here the isomorphism does not only spring from the competition in a global market which induces firms throughout the world to standardize their production processes and products. It stems from the increasingly common practice of outsourcing (tertiarization). We saw in Chapter 3 that outsourcing consists in the contracting out to other enterprises of certain services or phases of the production process, so that the outsourcer can specialize in a restricted range of core competences and thus withstand competition more effectively. But where do the activities that can be outsourced finish, and where do the essential ones that constitute the firm's core competences begin? There is no straightforward answer to the question: the boundary between the two types of activity shifts with time, so that the area of core competences shrinks while that of transferable ones expands. What some years previously seemed essential, some years later is transferred without problems. In the car industry, for example, auxiliary services like catering, security, cleaning, and routine administration are outsourced, but also services more directly to do with the production process like logistics and maintenance, or even specific phases of the production process itself. Finally, there is nothing to prevent firms from outsourcing the most delicate phases of new product design to external professionals, provided the new products carry the commissioning firm's brand name

It is the extreme forms of outsourcing that foster isomorphism, due to the fact that external professionals do not work for a single firm, but for several, which may be in competition with each other. Consequently, although these professionals are involved in projects specific to each firm, they use the only know-how available on the market, so that firms end up by designing largely similar products.

2.4. *Future research: logo, globalization and world commodity chains*

The following question now naturally arises: if products increasingly resemble each other, on what basis does competition come about? A reply by now widely accepted is that competition is increasingly shifting from the real quality of products to the symbolic quality of the brand image. This is one of the main contentions of the anti-globalization protest movement (Klein, 2000), which claims that this shift is part of a more general divarication between the symbolic and material aspects of production. The former are developing excessively in the wealthier countries, while the latter are increasingly transferred to the poor countries, where labour is cheap, trade unions non-existent, and environmental protection unknown.

Proliferating in those countries are the so-called 'industrial export zones', often resembling large-scale concentration camps and closed to outside visitors. Here thousands of men, women and children toil in squalid workshops for up to twelve hours a day, receiving subsistence wages as they produce anonymous goods to which the large purchasing firms affix their trademarks. There is little new to study and a great deal to denounce in these workshops, which in terms of the organization and conditions of work recall the primordial phases of industrialization.

This is the ugly side of the globalization process. But the novel feature is that the exporting to the poor countries of the most vexatious and archaic conditions of human exploitation is part of a global capitalist process by which the firms that buy the products at rock-bottom prices are the selfsame firms that, in the rich countries, develop sophisticated initiatives to design them and enhance their value.

A powerful conceptual tool with which to study these phenomena is that of the 'world commodity chain' (Hopkins and Wallerstein, 1986; Gereffi, 1992). The term denotes a set of inter-organizational networks aggregated around a given good or commodity and which connect together domestic economies, firms and nation-states within the world economy. The analytical advantage of this concept is that it goes above and beyond the individual phases of the production process to view their concatenation at the world level, from the raw materials to the finished article. It is thus possible to reconstruct at both micro and macro levels that amount of value added in every passage of a commodity from one country to the next, in relation to the state institutions, labour control and the links between producers and sellers.

At this point I shall stop. I have completed my task of describing the main organizational theories, and I have brought the reader to a boundary beyond which organizational analysis becomes a component of other forms of interdisciplinary inquiry. This is subject matter for other studies.

REFERENCES

Argyris Chris

1978 *Organizational Learning: A Theory of Action Perspective*, Addison Wesley, Reading, Mass

1982 *Reasoning, Learning and Action*, Jossey-Bass, San Francisco

Arthur Michael B. e Rousseau Denise

1996The Boundaryless Career. A New Employment Principle for a New Organizational Era, Oxford University Press

Bauman Arne

2000 *Qualification in the German and British Media Production Industries: How do Firms obtain Sdkills and how do workers obtain Employment in an Environment of Discontinuous Producion and Freelance Employment?* Department of Political and Social Sciencs European University Institute, San Domenico di Fiesole, Firenze (mimeo)

DeFillippi, Robert e Arthur Michael

1998 Paradox in Project-.Based Enterprise: The case of Film Making, *California Management Review* . vol. 40, n.2, pp 125-139

Friedmann George

1946 *Problémes humains du machinisme industriel*, Gallimard, Paris (trad. ital. *Problemi umani del mucchinismo industriale* Einaudi, Torino; ried. 1971)

Gereffi Gary e Korzeniewicz Miguel

1992 *Commodity Chains and Global Capitalism*, Greenwood Press, Westport. Conn.

Hopkins Terence e Wallerstein Immanuel

1992 Commodity Chains in the Capitalist World-Economy Prior to 1800, in Gereffi e Korzeniewicz

Jones Candace

1996 Careers in Project Networks: The Case of the Film Industry, in Arthur e Rousseau

Jones Candace, Hesterly William , Borgatti Stephen

1997 A General Theory of Network Governance :Exchange Conditions and Social Mechanisms *Academy of Management Review*, vol. 22, n. 4, pp. 911-945

Klein, Naomi

2000 *No logo*

Marsden David

1986 *The End of the Ecomic Man? Custom and Competition in Labour Markets* Weatsheaf, Brighton

Miles Raymond. e Snow Charles

1996 Twenty-first. Century Careers , in Arthur e Rousseau

Saxenian Annalee

1994 *Regional Advantage: Culture and Competition in Silicon Valley and Route 128*, Harvard Univ. Press, Cambridge, Pass.

Van Maanen John e Barley Stephen

1984 Occupational Communities:Culture and Control in Organizations, *Research in Organizational Behavior* pp. 297-365

Weick Karl

1996 Enactment and the Boundaryless Career: Organizing as We Work, in Arthur e Rousseau

Attention: Students

We request you, for your frank assessment, regarding some of the aspects of the book, given as under:

07 408 HOW TO STUDY AN ORGANISATION
Prof. Giuseppe Bonazzi *First Edition 2006*

Please fill up the given spaces in neat capital letters. Add additional sheet(s) if the space provided is not sufficient, and if so required.

(i) What topic(s) of your syllabus that are important from your examination point of view are not covered in the book ?

....

....

....

....

(ii) What are the chapters and/or topics, wherein the treatment of the subject-matter is not systematic or organised or updated?

....

....

....

....

....

(iii) Have you come across misprints/mistakes/factual inaccuracies in the book? Please specify the chapters, topics and the page numbers.

....

....

....

....

....

(iv) Name top three books on the same subject (in order of your preference - 1, 2, 3) that you have found/heard better than the present book? Please specify in terms of quality (in all aspects).

1 ....

....

2 ....

....

3 ....

....

(v) Further suggestions and comments for the improvement of the book:

....

....

....

....

....

Other Details:

(i) Who recommended you the book? (Please tick in the box near the option relevant to you.)

☐ Teacher ☐ Friends ☐ Bookseller

(ii) Name of the recommending teacher, his designation and address:

....

....

....

(iii) Name and address of the bookseller you purchased the book from:

....

....

....

(iv) Name and address of your institution (Please mention the University or Board, as the case may be)

....

....

....

(v) Your name and complete postal address:

....

....

....

(vi) Write your preferences of our publications (1, 2, 3) you would like to have

....

....

The best assessment will be awarded half-yearly. The award will be in the form of our publications, as decided by the Editorial Board, amounting to Rs. 300 (total).

Please mail the filled up coupon at your earliest to:

Editorial Department
S. CHAND & COMPANY LTD.,
Post Box No. 5733, Ram Nagar,
New Delhi 110 055